Byron's Political and Cultural Influence in Nineteenth-Century Europe

Thomas Phillips' portrait
of Byron (1814) from the
Roe–Byron Collection

Byron's Political and Cultural Influence in Nineteenth-Century Europe
A Symposium

EDITED BY

PAUL GRAHAM TRUEBLOOD

"European nineteenth-century culture is as unthinkable without Byron
as its history would be without Napoleon."

Northrop Frye, *Fables of Identity:*
Studies in Poetic Mythology

HUMANITIES PRESS

Atlantic Highlands, New Jersey

© Paul Graham Trueblood 1981

First Published in the United States of America 1981 by
HUMANITIES PRESS INC.
171 First Avenue, Atlantic Highlands, New Jersey 07716.

Photoset in Great Britain by
REDWOOD BURN LIMITED
Trowbridge & Esher
and printed in Hong Kong

Library of Congress Cataloging in Publication Data

Main entry under title:

Byron's political and cultural influence
in nineteenth-century Europe.

Includes index.
1. Byron, George Gordon Noël Byron, Baron, 1788–1824—
Political and Social views. 2. Byron, George Gordon
Noël Byron, Baron, 1788–1824—Influence. Politics and
literature—Europe. 4. Europe—Politics and government—1789–1900. 5. Europe—Civilization—19th
century. I. Trueblood, Paul Graham.
PR4392.P64B9 1981 821'.8 80–21384
ISBN 0–391–02164–8

To
Dennis Walwin Jones, M.C.
and
Elma Dangerfield, O.B.E.
founders of the restored Byron Society

Contents

Preface

An increasing interest in the life and work of Lord Byron has marked the third quarter of the twentieth century. Two of the greatest contributions to modern Byron scholarship appeared in 1957: Professor Leslie A. Marchand's magnificent three-volume biography of Byron and the monumental *Variorum Don Juan* edited by Professor Truman Guy Steffan and Professor Willis W. Pratt. An ever-increasing number of important scholarly contributions to the understanding of Byron both as man and poet have been accumulating since the mid-century, including, among others, excellent critical studies by Rutherford, Escarpit, Marchand, Ridenour, Marshall, Joseph, Gleckner, Elledge, McGann, Cooke, Jump and Blackstone, and brilliant biographical studies by Doris Langley Moore, Elizabeth Longford and others.

Furthermore, what is certain to be the major contribution to Byron scholarship in the twentieth century is now appearing: *Byron's Letters and Journals*, edited by Professor Marchand, and *Byron's Complete Poetical Works*, edited by Professor McGann. These definitive multi-volume works supersede the turn-of-the-century Coleridge–Prothero edition.

Indicative of the genuine, though belated, recognition and appreciation of Byron was the dedication in Westminster Abbey, at the instigation of The Poetry Society of Great Britain, of a white marble floor memorial to Lord Byron in 1969. Mr William Plomer, President of The Poetry Society, unveiled the memorial and the late C. Day Lewis, England's Poet Laureate, placed a wreath on the stone, while Dr Abbott, Dean of the Abbey, pronounced a benediction. Thus, a century and a half after his death, Lord Byron's name was entered among those of his peers in the Poets' Corner of Westminster Abbey.

Another evidence of the resurgence of interest in Byron has been the recent revival of The Byron Society, originally founded as "The Byron Club" in London on 22 January 1876, at the Temple Club, 37 Arundel Street, which premises, known in Byron's day as the Crown and Anchor, served as the meeting place for the Greek Committee that invited Byron in 1823 to be its representative in Greece. The Society received further impetus in 1888, the centennial of the poet's birth, at the instigation of King George I of Greece who desired to preserve the memory of the great Romantic poet who died in the Greek War of Independence.

The Byron Society flourished during the early decades of the twentieth century, numbering Sir Winston Churchill among its members, until it ceased activities at the outbreak of World War II. The Byron Society was re-founded in 1971 by the late Dennis Walwin Jones, M.C. and Elma Dangerfield, O.B.E., to whom this symposium is dedicated, and it has since grown into The International Byron Society headquartered in London with branches in twenty-seven countries. The Society, which has as objectives the promotion of interest and research in the life and work of Byron, publishes a journal devoted to Byron biographical, critical and editorial scholarship; holds annual international seminars; and arranges tours to countries with which Byron was associated. Five Byron Seminars have taken place in five countries of Europe and the sixth was held in America in 1979.

The First Byron Seminar was held at Trinity College (Byron's college), Cambridge, in 1974, in co-operation with The British Council, in commemoration of the 150th anniversary of Byron's death. The theme was "Byron's Influence on European Thought", chaired by the late Professor Terence Spencer, Birmingham University, with Byronists from all over the world participating. It was my privilege to open the programme with a paper on "Byron's Championship of Political Freedom on the Continent from 1812 to 1824".

The inception of the present book may be traced to my experience in the Cambridge Seminar. It seemed to me appropriate to launch an investigation of the far-ranging and pervasive influence of Byron, both culturally and politically, in Europe throughout the nineteenth century. Inquiry revealed that a thorough and comprehensive investigation of the subject had not been notably undertaken.

To this end I solicited the assistance of Byronists throughout

Europe, inviting a distinguished collaborator from each of ten countries to participate in the symposium. A brief personal account about each participant appears in the Notes on the Contributors. The historical introduction by Douglas Dakin, Emeritus Professor of History at the University of London and the leading British authority on diplomatic history of nineteenth-century Europe, lends added stature to the enterprise.

The scope of the symposium is limited to those European countries in which Byron's influence appears to have been the most overt and extensive. His relation to The Lowlands and Scandinavia must await a further extension of this investigation. The countries in the order of their national treatment in the symposium are England, France, Germany, Greece, Italy, Poland, Portugal, Russia, Spain and Switzerland.

The purpose of the symposium is to explore and assess the nature, extent and effectiveness of Byron's influence, both cultural and political, on the climate of thought and social action in nineteenth-century Europe, especially in relation to the general struggle of the peoples for political freedom and national independence. I have encouraged each participant to develop as he thought appropriate the role of Byron in relationship to the cultural and political life of his own country; and I am pleased with the variety of approach and achievement that has emerged in relation to the general topic of the symposium: *Byron's Political and Cultural Influence in Nineteenth-Century Europe.*

Each participant was free to decide for himself how extensive a reference apparatus his own contribution required and to some extent what form the references might appropriately take. I want to acknowledge for some of the contributors, including myself, the prior publication of excerpts from articles that have appeared in *The Byron Journal* (London), and in my own case, from my *Lord Byron* (Twayne Publishers, Division of G. K. Hall, Boston, 1977).

I want to express my appreciation to the American Council of Learned Societies and the Modern Language Association of America for substantial travel grants which made possible my participation in international Byron symposiums and consequent consultation with my European colleagues in this enterprise. I am grateful to the Emeritus Enrichment Program of Willamette University for a grant which has helped defray the considerable costs of my editorial responsibilities in connection with this volume, and to my esteemed colleague, Emeritus Dean and Professor of Modern

European History Robert D. Gregg, College of Liberal Arts, Willamette University, for his authoritative knowledge and expert advice.

I am deeply indebted and grateful to Professor Andrew Rutherford of the University of Aberdeen, Great Britain's leading Byron scholar, for the inspiration and challenge of his superb achievements in Byron studies, especially for his *Byron: A Critical Study*, one of the most brilliant, perceptive and sustained critical analyses of Byron that has ever been written.

I am particularly grateful to Dr Cedric Hentschel for his enthusiastic encouragement and generous and perceptive advice during the prolonged editorial procedures, as well as for his many, well-remembered "acts of kindness". And, finally, I want to thank my wife, Helen Churchill Trueblood, for her patience and the "infinite variety" of her invaluable assistance.

PAUL GRAHAM TRUEBLOOD

WILLAMETTE UNIVERSITY
October 1979

Acknowledgements

The author and publishers wish to thank the following for the use of copyright material:

Professor Robert Escarpit for the chapter based on his essay, "Byron, figure politique", in *Romantisme*, Revue de la Société des Études Romantiques, 1974

Professor Giorgio Melchiori for the use of material from his Byron Foundation Lecture, "Byron and Italy", University of Nottingham, 1958, and his essay, "The Influence of Byron's Death on Italy", in *The Byron Journal*, no. 5, 1977

Juliusz Zulawski for the use of material from his essay, "Byron's Influence in Poland", in *The Byron Journal*, no. 2, 1974

Professor Ernest Giddey for the use of material from his essay, "The Influence of Byron's Death on French-Speaking Switzerland", in *The Byron Journal*, no. 5, 1977

Twayne Publishers, a division of G. K. Hall & Co., Boston, for quotations from *Lord Byron* (Twayne's English Authors Series), 1969, and 2nd edn., 1977.

Notes on the Contributors

Douglas Dakin, Emeritus Professor of History, University of London, M.A. Cambridge, Ph.D. London, is the leading British authority on the diplomatic history of nineteenth-century Europe as well as the greatest living British expert on Greek affairs. He holds an honorary doctorate from the University of Thessaloniki and is a corresponding member of the Academy of Athens. Among his publications are *Turgot and the Ancien Régime in France* and several works on Modern Greece, including *The Greek Struggle for Independence, 1821–1833* and *The Unification of Greece, 1770–1923.* He is currently editor of the first series of *Documents on British Foreign Policy, 1919–1951.*

Nina Diakonova was graduated from the University of Leningrad in 1937, became Assistant Professor in 1944 and Professor of English Literature in 1966 at the University of Leningrad. Her publications include (in English): *Three Centuries of English Poetry,* 1967; (in Russian): *The London Romantics,* 1970, *Keats and his Contemporaries,* 1973, *Byron in Exile,* 1974, *Byron's Lyrical Poetry,* 1975, "The Prose of Lermontov and Byron", in *Russkaya Literatura,* 1969, no. 4, as well as a number of other books and papers in both languages.

Robert Escarpit, President of the Université de Bordeaux III since 1975. He has been Professor of Comparative Literature at the Faculté des Lettres de Bordeaux since 1951 and at the Université de Bordeaux III since 1969. He has published eight novels and five books of essays since 1958. As the leading Byronist of France, he has written *Lord Byron, Un Tempérament Littéraire* and *Byron,* as well as books on Kipling and Hemingway and has contributed a daily humorous column to *Le Monde* since 1949.

Ernest Giddey is Professor of English Literature and Vice-Rector of the University of Lausanne, Chairman of the Swiss Byron Committee and Joint President of the International Byron Society. He has written several monographs about Byron and other foreign writers living in Switzerland in the eighteenth and nineteenth centuries, including Sterne, Gibbon, Beckford, and Rogers. He contributed a remarkable essay, *Les Trahisons du Byronisme*, to *Études de Lettres* (series III, vol. 3, Faculté des Lettres, l'Université de Lausanne, 1970). The present essay is based on a paper Professor Giddey read to the Third Byron Seminar at Missolonghi in 1976.

Cedric Hentschel, M.A., Ph.D., studied modern languages at University College, London. After lecturing there and in the English Departments of the Universities of Innsbruck, Breslau and Uppsala, he served with the British Council in the Netherlands, Israel, Mexico, Finland, Jamaica and Germany where he was Regional Director in Munich from 1966 to 1974. Trained as a Germanist, wide travel and personal inclination have fostered his abiding interest in Comparative Literature. Among his publications are *The Byronic Teuton*, "Alexander von Humboldt's Synthesis of Literature and Science" and books and articles on Byron, Powys, Disraeli, Lassalle and Stehr. He has translated two volumes of German and Austrian short stories and is currently editing some letters of John Cowper Powys.

Giorgio Melchiori, Professor of English at the University of Rome, is a pupil of Professor Mario Praz, Italy's most distinguished Byronist and author of *The Romantic Agony*. He delivered the Byron Foundation Lecture at the University of Nottingham in 1958 on "Byron and Italy", and he has read papers on the influence of Byron on Italian thought and culture at the First Byron Seminar at Cambridge in 1974 and the Third Byron Seminar at Missolonghi in 1976. Though a Shakespeare specialist and general editor of a bilingual edition of the complete plays, he has been lecturing on Byron and Italy since 1960.

F. de Mello Moser, Professor of English Literature, University of Lisbon, M.A. 1959, Ph.D. 1970, Lisbon, Associate Professor 1971, Full Professor since 1973, is a specialist in English Medieval and Renaissance Drama, Cultural History and Romanticism. He is

President of the Portuguese Byron Committee and Director, 1977/ 78, of the International Byron Society. He participated in the First Byron Seminar, Cambridge, 1974, and organised the Fourth Byron Seminar at Lisbon, 1977, editing the symposium volume, "Byron/Portugal 77", which includes his "Three Approaches to Byron", 1977. Among his printed works are "*Shakespeare, o Poeta*", 1965; "Shakespeare in Portugal", 1977; "*Tomás More e o Teatro*", 1968; "Had Lord Byron read Utopia?", 1976 and "Three Approaches to Byron", 1977.

E. G. Protopsaltis, Professor Emeritus of Political Science, the University of Athens, Ph.D. Athens, post-doctoral study in Paris, is the leading Greek authority on the Greek War of Independence. He served as Director of the National Archives for many years and later became Professor in the Pandios School of Political Science of the University of Athens. Among his many published studies are the following: *The Filiki Eteria*, Athens, 1964; *The Revolutionary Movements of the Greeks during the Second Russo-Turkish War*, Athens, 1959; *The Historical Archives of Alexandros Mavrocordatos*, vols. I–V, Athens (continuing); *The Correspondence of the Guard of Missolonghi (1825–1826)*, Athens, 1963; *Philhellenism apparent in European Co-operation*, Athens, 1976.

Estaban Pujals, Professor of English Literature, University of Madrid, Licenciado en Letras (Universidad de Barcelona), Doctor en Letras (Universidad de Madrid), Ph.D. in English (University of London), is the leading Byronist of Spain and President of the Spanish National Committee of the International Byron Society. Professor Pujals participated in the First Byron Seminar at Cambridge in 1974 and the Fourth Byron Seminar at Lisbon in 1977. Among his published books are the following: *Espronceda y Lord Byron*, 1951, 1972; *Dylan Thomas: Poemas*, translated into Spanish, with an introduction, 1955, 1976; *Drama, pensamiento y poesía en la literatura inglesa*, 1965; *El romanticismo inglés*, 1969; *La poesía inglesa del siglo XX*, 1973; *Literatura inglesa actual*, 1975; *Espana en la poesía del siglo XX*, 1977.

William Ruddick is a lecturer in English literature at the University of Manchester. He has written on Lord Byron's historical tragedies and on Byron's relations with Thomas Moore. He contributed the essay, "Don Juan in Search of Freedom: Byron's

Emergence as a Satirist", to *Byron: A Symposium*, edited by Professor John D. Jump, 1975. Ruddick is currently engaged on a study of the poetry of George Crabbe.

Paul G. Trueblood, B.A. Willamette University, M.A., Ph.D. Duke University, attained his doctorate on Byron under the direction of the eminent Shelley biographer, Professor Newman Ivey White. He is author of *The Flowering of Byron's Genius* (1945), a pioneering study of *Don Juan*, Byron's masterpiece, and Twayne's English Authors Series *Lord Byron* (1969; 2nd edn., 1977). As a specialist in English Romanticism, Professor Trueblood has taught at the Universities of Idaho, Washington, Oregon, British Columbia, and Willamette University where he was Chairman of the English Department for fifteen years, becoming Professor Emeritus in 1971. Professor Trueblood is a founding member and member of the board of directors of the American Committee of The Byron Society and has participated in International Byron Seminars at Cambridge, Missolonghi and Delaware, as well as having contributed essays on Byron to *The Byron Journal*, London. In 1975 he addressed The Byron Society in the House of Lords on the 163rd anniversary of Byron's maiden speech in Parliament, speaking on "The Political Influence in Britain of Byron's Parliamentary Speeches".

Vadim Vacuro was educated at the University of Leningrad (Ph.D.). Since 1962 he has been on the staff of the Institute for Russian Literature (Puškinsky Dom) of the Academy of Sciences, USSR. His publications include (in Russian): *A New Pushkin Autograph* (together with M. Gillelson), 1968; "Thomas Moore's Irish Melodies in the Work of Lermontov", *Russkaya Literatura*, 1965, no. 3; *Across Intellectual Barriers* (together with M. Gillelson), 1972, and many other works and studies. Dr Vacuro is an eminent specialist in Russian literature.

Juliusz Zulawski, son of the famous Polish philosopher, poet, novelist and playwright, Jerzy Zulawski, is himself author of numerous novels, short stories, plays, essays and poetry published since 1933, including a four-volume selection of Byron's works, with prefaces and notes (Zulawski's own translation). Zulawski has also published (in Polish translation) selected works of Shelley, Keats, Browning, Longfellow and Whitman, and critical biographies of Byron (1964) and Whitman (1971). From 1972 he has been President of the Polish PEN Club, and he is corresponding member for Poland of the Byron Society. He was recipient of the prestigious Jurzykowski Foundation Award in New York in 1971, and he lectured widely throughout America in 1977 under the auspices of the Kosciuszko Foundation.

1 The Historical Background

Revolution and Counter-Revolution 1789–1848

DOUGLAS DAKIN

In 1789 events in France precipitated movements that were to have profound effects on Europe, Asia and South America. Those events had been heralded by a period of ideological development, the so-called Enlightenment or the Age of Reason. Most of the ideas of that age have been misconstrued by those who have inherited them. By selecting what seemed to be admirable, by taking passages of writings out of context and by failing to grasp fundamental assumptions, those heirs have fashioned ideologies which are vastly different from those of the Enlightenment. Indeed what made Rousseau so important an influence on later generations was the misinterpretation of his works. In his day, his political writings were little read, but after 1789 distorted and eclectic versions became the stock in trade of journalists and orators. Less misconstrued and more widely read than the writings of the *philosophes* and *économistes* were the writings containing conventional thought, which could claim to be just as rational and just as enlightened as the new ideas.

The most striking feature of these new ideas in circulation before 1789, despite their underlying assumption that a natural order must ultimately replace an order fashioned by the dead hand of history, is that at first they were enlisted to serve and adorn essentially utilitarian aims. Almost everywhere in France (and in certain other parts of Europe) the literate classes, meeting in local academies, literary societies and salons, discussed theories of taxation, industrial restrictions, new inventions, farming methods,

1

feudal dues, the grain trade and so forth. Despite their metaphysics, they showed no urge to promote violent upheaval but
merely to introduce prosaic reforms. They envisaged a new age to
be brought about by peaceful means. Mably, one of the most outspoken critics of feudal privilege, like the more extreme thinkers,
Meslier, Linguet, Rétif de la Bretonne and the Abbé Morelly harboured no design to destroy by violent political action the mono-
poly of power and wealth vested in the land-owning and
office-holding classes. What all the critics of the *ancien régime* envisaged was a comprehensive programme of reforms imposed by the
administration. They assumed that reason was bound to triumph
in the end, but, as the masses were incapable of speedy enlightenment, immediate hopes had to be placed in an enlightened monarchy and bureaucracy. All the same, the thinking of the
Enlightenment was fundamentally revolutionary and, given
certain circumstances, capable of developing a revolutionary
creed. It was revolutionary because it established new criteria and
because it denounced many practices of the *ancien régime*.

   The hopes of reform from above were fostered by the attempts of
the European monarchs to establish enlightened despotisms.
Facing a steady rise in prices, often burdened with the debts of their
forebears and needing to expand their armies and bureaucracies,
these rulers, having become receptive of the new ideas, were compelled to increase the yield of taxation by improving the methods of
collection, by reducing the scale of tax exemption and by increasing the amount of taxable wealth, the last object implying the promotion of the prosperity of their subjects. The monarchs of Europe,
however, were neither fully enlightened nor possessed of truly despotic power. In Prussia, Frederick the Great's mercantilist policy
(a policy pursued with differences in other states) impeded economic development and his grants of privileges to the nobility and
the creation of the *Beamtenstand* (a corporate body of civil servants)
were but a repetition of that time-honoured process by which monarchs sought to become more absolute by granting power away. In
Russia, Catherine the Great, ruling an unwieldy territory, failed to
establish an adequate bureaucracy, and made but little impression
on her vast continental empire. In the Habsburg lands, Joseph II's
achievements were likewise limited and his fervent activities were
little more than a show of his good intentions: in all his territories
he was frustrated by the Church, the nobility and provincial
separatism.

This lack of despotic power was also evident in France, where the attempt to introduce reforms under the pressure of increasing State insolvency encountered continual opposition. The French monarchy, although served by an apparently well-developed and centralised bureaucracy, found itself confronted by a privileged nobility, provincial separatism, municipal administrations, an all-powerful Church and corporations of lawyers in Paris and the provinces. It was a prisoner of its past: its ostensible power had grown by the paradoxical process of granting away rights – by creating a whole range of prescriptive powers. Under Louis XVI, a weak and vacillating ruler, reforming ministers were left helpless in the face of the combined hostility of the nobility and the Church. When in 1776 Turgot, the Controller General of Finance, attempted to abolish forced labour on the roads and the trade guilds in the towns, his enemies contrived his dismissal and the revocation of his reforms. In much the same way Necker (who concealed the bad state of the finances) fell from power in face of opposition from the court nobility and the *Parlement* of Paris, the most powerful of the thirteen *parlements* in France. Primarily courts of Appeal, these *parlements* had acquired, as a result of their right to register the royal edicts and ordinances, a considerable political power. Their members had come to enjoy the status of nobility and hereditary office. No longer "lions under the throne", they claimed, as the custodians of the fundamental laws, the right to annul or revise the royal legislation and to control taxation. Their conflicts with the Crown gave rise to much constitutional debate, and it may well be that these were a greater stimulus to the discussion of political ideas than were the writings of the *philosophes*. Although the causes they upheld were essentially illiberal, the theories they advanced were a greater danger to the monarchy than the literature of the Enlightenment. In opposing the *parlements* (on occasion he sent them into exile), the King laid himself open to the charge of despotism and to loss of popularity.

In August 1786 the Controller General Calonne, faced with an increased annual deficit, submitted to the King a plan involving tax and other reforms, the formation of district and provincial assemblies, and the convention of an Assembly of Notables to be nominated by Louis himself. He fondly hoped to confront the hostile *Parlement* with a show of public opinion, but when in February 1787 he presented his plans to the assembled Notables he encountered fierce opposition, and in April, following court intrigues, he was dismissed. His successor, Loménie de Brienne, having persuaded the King to disperse the Notables, later prevailed upon him to hold a *lit de justice* to enforce the registration of certain financial measures. The magistrates condemned this procedure as unconstitutional. Louis remained firm and exiled them to Troyes. Thereafter these magistrates continued the struggle by way of public pronouncements and in May 1788 drew up a declaration of fundamental laws. Five days later Louis enforced the registration of six edicts prepared by the Chancellor Lamoignon. These transferred the right of registering the royal edicts to a new plenary court composed of docile lawyers and other persons, established forty-seven grand bailiwicks to deal with appeals from the lesser courts, curbed the extent of private jurisdictions, and introduced reforms in criminal procedure. The magistrates represented this *coup d'état* as an attack on personal liberty and their opposition was supported by the clergy and the lay nobility. There were serious disturbances in several provinces. The King relinquished, suspended the judicial reforms, and announced for 1 May 1789 a long advocated meeting of the Estates General which had not met since 1614. Brienne resigned and Louis recalled Necker as Director General of Finances.

The revolts against Turgot, Calonne and Brienne amounted to the manifestations of a counter-revolutionary movement directed against attempts by the monarchy to impose revolutionary changes. Men so different as Robespierre and Chateaubriand later said that the nobility began the French Revolution, but they would have been more explicit if they had said that the nobles led a counter-revolution which eventually gave rise to the political revolution of May–June 1789. There was indeed no such thing as "the French Revolution" except as an abstraction, or rather as a series of abstractions, made by politicians and thinkers in France and other parts of Europe, each one according to his fancy, some approving, some denouncing what they imagined had come to pass. During the period of turmoil which began before 1789 there was, not a single revolution, but a whole series of revolutionary and counter-revolutionary movements. This ebb and flow was to continue for five decades or more. Throughout there emerged a restatement, a distortion and a development of the ideas of the Enlightenment, some so transformed as to appear entirely new. At the same time, there was a reiteration of older ideas, often so refurbished as to appear original. Into this effusion of ideas the growing corpus of knowledge in the natural and social sciences was introduced, as were the mental reactions to economic developments, social changes and political events. Many writers who were heirs to both the old and the new, attempted to make new syntheses, only to render the world of ideas more bewildering than ever. It is because of this complexity that it is difficult to give writers, politicians and parties ideological labels. The so-called Romantics are particularly difficult to categorise. Romanticism had no exclusive ideology, no steadfast political affiliation and no firm artistic and literary precepts. Romantics went their various ways by intuition in defiance of ideologies, social conventions and religious traditions, but they never escaped completely from the trammels of society and the political environment. Indeed they pervaded and released great energy into a world from which they had no wish to escape. They permeated the world of art and literature and the political world in many of its aspects. Themselves full of contradictions, they served and adorned apparently contradictory causes. They welcomed and even helped to prepare the revolutionary demand for individual liberty but rejected liberal egalitarianism; they resented the discipline of organised society but lauded Napoleon and strong men who imposed law and order; some were rebels at home but patriots abroad; some were nationalists, believing that history had fashioned the nations with individual characteristics, but others hankered after medieval universalism, pre-revolutionary society and a revival of medieval Christianity, perhaps not as these had been but as they imagined them to have been. Some were aligned politically with liberals; others, however, were the allies of conservatism or even counter-revolution.

After the fall of Brienne the struggle in France became essentially a conflict between the privileged and non-privileged orders. In a declaration of 25 September the magistrates demanded that the Estates General should take the form of 1614, the implication being that the three estates should have equal numbers of representatives and should vote separately. This declaration conflicted with the hopes of the potential leaders of the Third Estate who during the twelve or more years of crisis had become more politically minded and greatly encouraged by sympathisers among the aristocracy. These sympathisers, who were particularly active in the political clubs and in the growing number of freemason lodges, came to constitute a "patriot" party. In November 1788 they formed a committee of thirty which, having links with the provinces, circulated political literature for the edification of those who would represent the Third Estate in the forthcoming Estates General. One important idea to emerge was the need for a new constitution to rescue the Crown from the Court aristocracy and magistrates and to give the monarchy a national basis. Underlying this idea was the conception of political equality – in other words a new conception of freedom which found its most succinct exposition in the Abbé Sieyès's *Essay on Privileges* and his widely circulated pamphlet, *What Is The Third Estate?*. When, however, the representatives of the Third Estate arrived at Versailles, they discovered that they were expected to sit as a separate order. Prolonged discussions ensued. On 17 June 1789, however, they declared themselves a National Assembly and were joined by a number of clergy and nobles. On 20 June, finding themselves barred from the main assembly hall, they repaired to a tennis court and there took an oath not to disband until they had established a constitution: they had no intention of creating social upheaval, but, having defied the privileged classes, they had been forced to defy the King, who failed to seize the opportunity to broaden the basis of his power.

Under pressure from the Court and his advisers, Louis, having posted strong military forces in and around Versailles, on 23 June announced a programme of reforms and ordered the estates to resume their labours in separate rooms. The Third Estate, joined by yet more clergy and nobles, remained defiant. In Paris there were serious disorders and, as the royal troops were unreliable, the King posted three new regiments, mainly Swiss and Germans. On 11 July he dismissed Necker and formed a reactionary ministry under Breteuil. Three days later came the storming of the Bastille not, as often said, by the workers from the Faubourg St Antoine, but by guards on orders from the municipal authorities, who feared that the arms alleged to be stored in the Bastille would be used against Paris. Throughout the world this event, which quickly passed into the mythology of the Revolution, was regarded as the dawn of liberty. It was indeed important: it led to the withdrawal of the troops surrounding Paris and to the recall of Necker; it marked a defeat for the counter-revolution; and, since it led to the formation of the Paris commune, it brought an urban democracy into the political arena: outside Paris it led to widespread municipal revolts and therefore to decentralisation; and it transformed the wide-spread *jacqueries* in the countryside into revolts which destroyed the greater part of the feudal régime. Here indeed was a second revolution – the revolt of the lower classes against feudal proprietors. This *fait accompli* the National Assembly legitimised, not without certain reservations, in their legislation of 4 to 11 August. On 26 August that same body drew up the long-advocated *Declaration of Rights* which, cast in a sober and practical form, established the personal and political rights of the individual and the principle that all political power derived from the nation and not the King.

Thereafter, owing to a constant fear of counter-revolution, a growing shortage of food in Paris, the rise of popular agitators, and cleavages in the political leadership, the revolution continued on its wayward course. After its transfer to Paris, following the march of the women to Versailles, the National Assembly became a constituent body. Essentially a chamber directly representing not more than 50,000 men of substance and intellectuals, it drew upon, modified or developed the ideas of the Enlightenment and adopted many of the extensive reforms planned during the closing years of the *ancien régime*. Despite the political upheavals which were to follow, its achievements were remarkably durable: its division of France into 83 departments and some 44,000 communes later served the centralising policies of the Jacobins and Napoleon and remained the basic structure of French administration. Similarly, its legal and fiscal systems, though subsequently modified, were to serve the Empire, the Restored Monarchy and the Third Republic.

The Assembly's attempt to deal with the annual deficit was, however, less successful and it was to lead eventually to the loss of the control of the revolution by moderate men. In the winter of 1789 the Assembly nationalised the lands of the Church and on the strength of this enormous wealth issued treasury bonds (*assignats*) which, in the course of time, became worthless. There were even more serious repercussions; for the Assembly had necessarily to attempt to adjust the relation between Church and State. Like the Enlightened Despots, the men of the Assembly were disposed to bring the Church under State control. In August 1790 they promulgated the "Civil Constitution of the Clergy". This made the bishoprics coincide with the departments, provided for the election of bishops and parish priests and transformed clerics into salaried officials. In November (in face of growing opposition) the Assembly required all clergy to accept the constitution on oath. Most bishops and about half of the lower clergy declined – a situation which led the Papacy to condemn the revolution and all its works. Hitherto popular movements had worked mainly to the advantage of the revolution: from now on the forces of counter-revolution could count on support among the masses. An even more immediate consequence of the papal condemnation was that Louis began to think more seriously of escaping from France and of organising counter-revolution from outside. Up to that time he had given vacillating support to the revolution, which was, in a sense, his own revolution and not so vastly different from that attempted by Joseph II and Leopold. On the night of 20 June 1791 he began his ill-planned flight to Montmédy which ended in his capture at Varennes, his ignominious return to Paris, and eventually his trial and execution.

These events, combined with the outbreak of the Revolutionary Wars, gave the French Revolution a new European context. Hitherto the ideas of the French Revolution, not all of which were uniquely French, had found admirers in the European courts and intellectual circles where similar modes of thinking had been long established. With the coming of the Revolutionary Wars, French ideas, always in a process of development, assumed a more proselytising character, as indeed did the ideas of the counter-revolution. Further changes came with the advent of Napoleon, a complex product of revolution and counter-revolution. Even more than the earlier revolutionary armies, Napoleon's legions exported the achievements of revolutionary France, finding willing collaborators, but at the same time arousing enmity and counter-revolution in all its forms. Insomuch as Napoleon promoted the cause of nationalism – perhaps the least contested cause that gained strength in the revolutionary period – he prepared his own destruction, for it was the nationalist opposition in Spain, Russia, Prussia, and above all in England that, combined with his own shortcomings, led to his downfall.

At first the French Revolution was regarded in English official circles as a kind of *Fronde* which would lessen the chances of France, an imperialist enemy, of launching a war to achieve those ends left unfulfilled in 1783 at the end of the American War. In intellectual and certain political circles, however, events in France were hailed as the dawn of liberty, a step toward universal peace, and encouragement to reform. The Revolution societies, revived in 1788 to celebrate the Glorious English Revolution, found themselves celebrating the Revolution in France. But it was not long before more discerning onlookers began to appear. As early as 1790 Edmund

Burke denounced the French Revolution as a danger to society. Loyalist and anti-leveller organisations grew up and threatened the radical reformers, and upper class members drifted away from the London Corresponding Society and various other reform bodies. But although Burke was to gain adherents both in England and on the continent, it was the outbreak of war in the Spring of 1792, the establishment of a new insurrectionary commune in Paris, the September massacres, the King's trial and execution in January 1793 and the declaration of war on England the following month that aroused great hostility among the English to what they considered the very antithesis of ordered liberty. For its policy of stamping out subversive movements, the British Government had overwhelming support. Pitt's repressive measures were carried in Parliament by large majorities. But although these measures checked, they did not eradicate British radicalism, which was organised on a nationwide basis. In 1798 agitation became persistent and more widespread. This development brought further repressive measures – the Newspaper Publication Act, the suppression of the Corresponding Society and other similar bodies, and laws against workmen's combinations. By that time danger of the French Revolution as distinct from the dangers of French imperialism had receded; and the revival of agitation in effect was the harbinger of the industrial–political conflicts of the nineteenth century.

On the continent the first effects of the French Revolution were similar to those that had occurred in England, and, as in England, it was not long before Burke's *Reflections* gained a hearing. Like the privileged classes in France, the European nobility felt that their power, their wealth and their way of life were in jeopardy – a feeling which became more pronounced after the burning of the *châteaux*, the destruction of the French feudal order. On the continent, however, there was no deep-seated radical tradition. In Germany, where there were more than 300 independent political authorities, and in the Habsburg hereditary possessions, the small-scale industries and handicrafts remained much the same as at the time of the Reformation. Italy, once the home of the prosperous trading Empires of Genoa and Venice, had failed to profit from those Empires, which had long been in decline. Italian agriculture was backward nearly everywhere and the peasantry was saddled with onerous feudal dues and obligations. There was indeed less serfdom than in central and eastern Germany, or in the Habsburg lands (here many serfs remained in spite of the abolition of serfdom by enlightened rulers), but the Italian peasantry was perhaps even more poverty-stricken and more heavily mulcted by the Church and nobility than that in Eastern Germany.

During the Revolutionary Wars, Western Germany, like the Austrian Netherlands, Nice and Savoy, was overrun by the French armies, ostensibly carrying freedom to oppressed peoples but in reality endeavouring to save the fatherland from the hostile European powers of the First Coalition. For many of the French politicians war had been not only a means of obtaining tribute to solve the government's financial difficulties but a way of retaining power. These wars had led to the Terror and to the dictatorship of the Committee of Public Safety. By 1795 the revolutionary armies had broken the European Coalition. That year Prussia withdrew from the war and conceded to France the left bank of the Rhine. The wars, however, had produced a military system which was to lead to the defeat of civilian government and to the suppression of the activities of the Paris mobs, in other words, to the consolidation of counter-revolution.

Following Prussia's withdrawal from the war, her rulers continued their enlightened efforts to improve their administration and the lot of their subjects. These efforts increased with the accession of Frederick William III in 1797, but his achievements were restricted because of his unwillingness to enter into conflict with the aristocracy. Nevertheless the owners of the great estates began to find it profitable to abolish serfdom in pursuit of their aim to introduce capitalist methods of agricultural exploitation. In 1805 Prussia joined the Third Coalition but encountered disaster at Austerlitz and Jena. Following these defeats, in her efforts to reconstruct her power, she adopted French ideas in their Napoleonic form. Ably served by Stein, Scharnhorst, Gneisenau, Humboldt and Hardenberg, she reformed her municipal legal and educational systems, and she re-emerged as a member of the Grand Coalition which brought about Napoleon's downfall. Within her literary circles and among the products of her new military and educational systems there emerged the idea that she belonged to a great German nation. Elsewhere in Germany north of the Main, during the decade following the Peace of Basle (1795) life had gone on in much the same way as before and, under the continued influence of the Enlightenment, there was appreciable development in agricultural and domestic industries. South of the

Main, the French Revolution, in the form that it was imported by the French armies, had a much greater effect, Bavaria, Württemberg, and Baden becoming independent States allied to France.

In 1797 Austria, defeated in Italy, had signed the Peace of Campo Formio. In subsequent negotiations, there emerged a plan for compensating the German princes who had lost territory on the left bank of the Rhine from the ecclesiastical lands on the right bank. The execution of this plan enabled Bavaria, Württemberg, Hesse–Darmstadt and Baden to make considerable accessions. Subsequently (June 1806) they joined the French-sponsored Confederation of the Rhine consisting of fifteen nominally independent states. The old German Empire ceased to exist. Francis II renounced the imperial title and became Francis I of Austria. As a result of this new order the 300 or more German States were reduced to thirty-nine. To some extent the Confederation developed among the Germans, among whom there was already a highly developed sense of cultural unity, a political national feeling. The new order, however, cut both ways, for it also led to a determination of every State to preserve its independence. Many of these States followed the example of Prussia: they took Napoleonic France as their model and made extensive changes in their administration. The greatest changes came, however, on the left bank of the Rhine where the *Code Napoleon* and French administration were imposed and also in the new States created by Napoleon (Berg, Frankfurt and Westphalia) where the new order, though not complete, proved to be durable.

Throughout the Revolutionary and Napoleonic period, the Austrian hereditary lands, despite the reforming zeal of Emperor Leopold, remained more impervious to French influence than did Germany. Francis II, who succeeded Leopold in March 1792, was a benevolent but not enlightened ruler. Fully immersed in the problems of the war, he avoided conflicts with prescriptive powers; he banned subversive literature, and employed his police and espial system to hunt down subversive persons. Education he entrusted to the Church. From the middle classes, who found employment in commerce, the professions and the expanding bureaucracy, he met with little trouble. Of all his territories, Hungary was perhaps the most difficult to govern. Toward the Hungarians he was usually non-demanding and pliant: nevertheless he refused to yield on the language issue and he insisted that they should buy manufactured goods from Austria and pay upon them a heavy import duty; and in May 1812, following disputes over the issue of a new paper currency, he dissolved the Hungarian Diet which was not reconvened for over a decade.

On Austria's Italian possessions the effect of the French Revolution closely resembled that which it had on Germany, Belgium and Holland. Among the intellectual classes, the ideas of the Enlightenment had found a hearing and civil servants had endeavoured to introduce reforms only to provoke hostility, which hostility increased as the French *emigrés* spread news of the iniquities of the revolution in France. Italian intellectuals began to change their tune. When France overran Nice and Savoy, Sardinia made alliance with Austria and Britain. Naples, too, joined the First Coalition, as did Lombardy. Tuscany, Genoa, Venice, and Modena endeavoured to remain neutral. In all states, however, pro-French 'parties' were formed from Jansenists, freemasons, and *illuminati*, and their leaders, though harried by the ruling authorities, survived to welcome the French invasion of 1796 and to collaborate in the establishment of the Italian Satellite republic – the Cisalpine, Ligurian, Roman and Parthenopaean. All these republics (like the Helvetic republic in Switzerland) were given constitutions on the French model: nobility and the old legal institutions were abolished; church property was secularised; and the control of education was vested in the State. The constitutions, however, were very narrowly based and satisfied the ambitions of only small minorities. Against the French and their collaborators there were many risings; and when the armies of the Second Coalition entered Italy, the disgruntled Italians welcomed them, but only to find them as odious as the French. In 1800 Napoleon again invaded Italy. This time he set up (except in Rome and Naples) new satellite regimes including a large north Italian republic which he subsequently made into the Kingdom of Italy. The rest of the Two Sicilies – Naples – became a kingdom, at first under Napoleon's brother Joseph and later under Murat, who was married to Napoleon's sister. Everywhere the old regimes were destroyed and French administration introduced. The result was that thousands of Italians gained from the French military and administrative experience but they toiled as time-servers rather than as Italian unitarists and patriots. More conducive to the rise of Italian nationalism and patriotism was the widespread hatred of taxation and conscription, and perhaps, as the result of economic development, the growth of a new commercial and industrial class, which began to see the benefits of Italian unity. By way of contrast to this new bourgeoisie (which was very small) the old land-owning classes remained provincial and even parochial in outlook, as indeed did the industrial classes, which suffered considerable hardship from French economic policy and the British blockade.

Like Italy, Spain and Portugal came under the heel of the French armies but they escaped the experience of French administration. Both had come to a small degree under the influence of the Enlightenment: enlightened rulers and bureaucrats had attempted some reforms, which were largely blueprints of their good intentions. In the Iberian peninsula, however, there were groups of radicals who came not so much from the commercial and industrial classes, as from the smaller urban-dwelling landowners and from the army officers. In a country where the nobility showed little inclination to assume political power at a local level they established juntas in the provinces. They resisted the rule of Ferdinand VII, who had hoped to govern as the protégé of France, and also the government of King Joseph, Napoleon's brother. In March 1812 the central junta, which had first been organised in 1809, promulgated an extreme constitution, an instrument which harked back to the French constitution of 1793. Nevertheless Joseph had the support of the *Afrancesados*, who hoped, by co-operation with the French, to preserve Spain as a separate kingdom. The constitution was shortlived. In 1814 Ferdinand returned and he managed, with the help of anti-Jacobin elements, to abolish it. But he failed completely to suppress the liberalism generated in the revolutionary period, which remained to fight another day. Much the same is true of Portugal. Although the liberal revolt of 1808 had failed, the Portuguese liberals were to stage a revolt in 1820.

Such briefly was the effect of the French Revolution in the Iberian peninsula. In both Spain and Portugal, besides a militant liberalism there was a strong patriotism, which although separatist and provincial, evinced a profound hostility to alien intrusion. This patriotism of the masses was engendered by the clergy who were democratic and, in default of the nobility, the natural leaders of the people. A similar kind of patriotism was to be found, but in different conditions, in Russia. Here, outside governmental, military and intellectual circles, the French Revolution was to have little effect until the invasion by Napoleon in 1812. Like her fellow sovereigns Catherine II, already disillusioned with the *philosophes*, deplored the turn of events in Paris but displayed very little enthusiasm for a counter-revolutionary crusade. She banned the word "republic" from stage plays, prohibited republican fashions of dress, sent the publicist Novikov to prison and exiled Radischev to Siberia. Her successor Paul III, though not energeticaly reactionary, was certainly capricious and aroused much hatred. In 1801 he was murdered by military conspirators; and his son and successor, Alexander I, may have been implicated to some extent. What is certain, however, is that Alexander was highly critical of his father's rule and when he became Tsar he gathered around him his old friends whom Paul had sent away. Among them was his former tutor, the Swiss romantic and liberal, La Harpe, who, resenting Bern's control of his native Vaud, had welcomed the French invasion of Switzerland. There was talk of promulgating a charter to the Russian people but nothing came of it. Nevertheless Alexander organised new ministries of state (which were much resented by the nobility), attempted certain educational reforms, permitted masters to emancipate their serfs and forbade the sale of serfs separately from land. For the Poles, whose country had been partitioned for the third time in 1795, he showed some sympathy, but was disconcerted to learn that a Polish legion was serving with the French. For the French, especially after the Treaty of Tilsit (1807) he had profound contempt and he later became the inveterate enemy of Napoleon. That treaty, however, which was greatly resented in Russia, earned for him the reputation of being a Francophil. No wonder then that the nobility were hostile to the reforms planned by Speranskii, whose draft constitution and code of Russian law were never promulgated. To Alexander's reforming zeal, the renewal of the war put an end, and the burning of Moscow turned his thoughts to religion, just at the time when he became, in the eyes of his patriotic subjects, the Liberator of Europe.

Napoleon attributed his defeat to the Spanish ulcer, the treachery of Austria, the snows of Russia and the mud of Poland. But this explanation is superficial. His downfall was due to the exhaustion of France in men and resources; to the failure of the French imperial structure to match the British with its greater economic strength, its superior navy, its improved military organisation and its revitalised and well-paid Allies; to the forces of patriotism and nationalism, which at first redounded to the advantage of the French but later to her disadvantage; and to Napoleon's own military deficiencies, his lack of political sagacity and his restless ambition. As a dictator he eventually lost his *raison d'être*: his achievements in France were more or less complete; the regime he had created had given equal opportunity to all-the-talents, including hosts of time-servers and potential conspirators, even in his armies. It needed only a major setback in the field for the Talleyrands, the Fouchés and the Murats, to organise his enemies and his lukewarm supporters to bring about his downfall.

Unable to defend Paris, on which the allied armies had converged, Napoleon abdicated and Talleyrand, with the Tsar Alexander's blessing, became the architect of the Bourbon restoration. On 30 May 1814, Talleyrand signed the First Peace of Paris, which confined France to approximately her 1792 frontiers and deprived her of her European conquests. The reconstruction of the State system of Europe was left to the Congress of Vienna but in effect Europe was reconstructed by the four great powers, Austria, Great Britain, Prussia and Russia, who in January 1815 admitted France to their counsels. Roughly speaking these powers restored, where it seemed reasonable and expedient, the old state system. Great Britain and Austria worked, though not without differences, to contain France (and indeed Russia) by strengthening Austria, Prussia and Holland. Paying scant respect to any desire peoples may have had for self-determination, they joined the Austrian Netherlands (Belgium) to Holland, maintained a partitioned Poland, transferred to Prussia a large part of Saxony, an additional part of Poland, small parts of Holland and Hanover, a large part of the left bank of the Rhine (the rest went to Holland and certain German states) and Swedish Pomerania. They restored substantially the Austrian dominions and compensated the Emperor Francis for his loss of the Netherlands (which he had no wish to retain) by giving him Galicia in central Europe and Lombardy and Venetia in Italy, Habsburg rulers being placed in Tuscany, Parma, and Modena. They gave Lucca to a Bourbon, restored the Bourbons in Spain, re-established Ferdinand IV in the Two Sicilies, and returned the Papal States to the Pope. To Sardinia they gave Piedmont, Savoy, Nice and Genoa; in Germany they provided for a confederation of thirty-four states and four free cities under the leadership of Austria and Prussia. Denmark gave Norway to Sweden and received Lauenberg from Prussia. Switzerland was reconstructed as a federation, neutralised and guaranteed. Only one new state (if we except Napoleon's short-lived sovereignty of Elba) emerged from the labours of the Congress – the Septinsular Republic: these Ionian Islands had become inde-

pendent during the wars: placed under the protection of Great
Britain they became in all but name a British crown colony.

The transfer of populations from one ruler to another was not,
given prevailing conditions, so outrageous as it appeared to later
generations. Nationalism, except in relatively small intellectual
circles and among some who had been employed in the Napoleonic
system, was little more than a provincialism which, being satisfied
with a degree of local liberty and moderate taxation, saw oppression largely in the form of foreign armies. The Belgians, for the
most part, went quite happily along with the Dutch; Saxons and
Prussians, Piedmontese and Sardinians, rubbed along quite well
together. The Poles in the Congress Kingdom (it included about
half of the Prussian shares of 1793 and both the Austrian and Prussian shares of 1795) were at least satisfied to escape Prussian rule,
gratified to have a national army, and hopeful of the promised constitution. Italians who had come under a French occupation had
no particular yearning for unity. Most Germans were satisfied
with their local liberties and their provincial cultural centres.
Much indeed had to happen before there arose a widespread
demand for unity in Germany and in Italy, and when at length unification came, it was predominantly in the form of the expansion of
Prussia and of Piedmont–Sardinia. In 1815 the blessings of peace,
the hopes of gaining a better livelihood in the fields, the workshop
and the marketplace were of greater moment than the abstract
ideas of the French Revolution.

In November 1815 Great Britain and Austria, partly with a view
towards giving confidence to the new regime in France but primarily to provide for European security, concluded with Russia
and Prussia a treaty of Friendship and Alliance, which was a con-
tinuation of the wartime alliance. They defined the *casus belli*
clearly – the return of Napoleon or any member of his family to
France, or an attack by France upon a European frontier – and they
agreed each to maintain a standing army. One clause of the treaty
provided for periodical conferences to review the situation of
Europe. The Tsar, no longer a liberal, had wished for these conferences to provide the means by which the great powers would
intervene in any state which harboured revolutionary movements.
But the British minister Castlereagh would have none of this and
he subsequently combated various attempts to transform the
Quadruple Alliance of 1815 into a version of Alexander's visionary
Holy Alliance which had been signed by Prussia and (not without

levity) by Austria. Inasmuch as the so-called Holy Alliance meant anything, it was the determination of the three rulers concerned to display solidarity against revolutionary principles, and, as such, it came in for much invective from European liberals. The Austrian Minister, Metternich, had but limited use for it and he set greater store by the Quadruple Alliance, the real basis of the European Concert. To this select company of great powers Bourbon France was admitted in 1818 but not to the Alliance, which remained directed against her. It was not, however, the intention of Great Britain, nor indeed of Austria, to intervene except by diplomacy in French affairs. There was no intervention at the time of the July Revolution of 1830, nor at the time of the 1848 Revolution, which led to the return of a Bonaparte and the establishment of the Second Empire. By that time the world had changed. Although in the three decades, 1818–48, there were revolutionary movements in France, in 1830 the moderate liberals stopped the revolution halfway, and in 1848 when they themselves were under fire from extremists, from socialists and from the lower orders, the forces of counter-revolution, in which the former revolutionists were now to be found, were strong enough to hold their own. Foreign intervention, for which there was no great demand, would have been pointless and the ruling governments gladly accepted Louis Napoleon's word, for what it was worth, that the Empire meant peace.

In 1821, however, Austria intervened in Naples and Piedmont and in 1823 France intervened in Spain. In 1820 Murat's old Neapolitan officers, disgruntled because of lack of promotion, linked up with the *carbonari*, a freemason organisation, which, resentful of the government's alleged oppressive measures, demanded the Spanish constitution of 1812, administrative and land reform, and the abandonment of mercantilism. The great powers met at Troppau to discuss the situation, the British and the French being represented by "observers" only. Here the three eastern despotisms drew up a protocol threatening intervention in any state where there was revolt against the lawful government. Ferdinand IV, by feigning willingness to satisfy the revolutionaries, got away to Laibach (by now the seat of the conference) and formally asked for assistance. Much to Metternich's relief (the last thing he wanted was a Russian army in Italy) the mandate to put down the revolution was given to Austria, who dispersed the revolutionaries with very little difficulty and remained in occupation until 1827. This intervention provoked a military revolt in Piedmont. That too the Austrians put down. Elsewhere in Italy there were other disturbances and these were followed by sporadic revolts in later years. These, however, were ruthlessly suppressed and the names of the victims were to pass into the mythology of the Italian *risorgimento*.

The revolution in Spain, where, as in Portugal, the liberals were divided into moderates and extremists, had begun before, and, indeed, had provided an example for the revolutionaries of Naples. Earlier *pronunciamientos* in both Spain and Portugal had failed, but in 1820 the provincial *juntas* and the revolutionary army of Riego had acted simultaneously. As in Naples the King was forced to accept the constitution of 1812. But the revolutionaries were divided and royalist guerillas managed to install themselves in many areas. These royalists (and royalists generally) looked to France to bring about a counter-revolution and at length in 1823 the French, having obtained the previous year at the Congress of Verona the moral support of the three eastern powers, invaded Spain. As Chateaubriand reminds us, an ageing King of France succeeded where Napoleon had failed. From the lower orders the revolutionary dictatorship could count on no support: moreover it had made an inveterate enemy of the church, the ally of royalists more royalist than the King. From 1823 to 1833 Spain was governed by a ministerial despotism which was under constant pressure from extreme popular royalism. In 1827 the monarchy was faced with the Catalan revolt, one of the demands of the rebels being the restoration of the Inquisition. By that time the affairs of Spain and Portugal had become more than usually intertwined. In 1820 the Opporto garrison and lower officers in Lisbon had revolted. But, as in Spain, the revolutionaries were divided and the moderates failed to gain the acceptance of a moderate constitution. John VI, however, was unwilling to base his rule on reactionary (including popular) elements. After his death in 1826 the problem of the Portuguese succession added further complications to the already intricate politics of the Iberian Peninsula.

The Congress of Verona (1822), which dealt with the Spanish Revolution, had been originally planned to discuss the Greek revolt of 1821 against the Turks. The Ottoman dominions were generally considered to be the concern of the European Concert, above all because of the suspected designs of Russia. Metternich feared that Alexander would profit from the Greek revolt, that rebellion would spread to the eastern fringes of the Habsburg

Empire and lead to a Franco–Russian alignment which would destroy the European Concert. He fondly imagined that an organised subversive liberalism, with its headquarters in Paris, was working to destroy the Vienna Settlement and overthrow legitimate environment. There was indeed some communication among liberals throughout Europe, but there was only a modicum of concerted action. Each subversive movement was largely fashioned by the immediate environment.

This is particularly true of Greece, where the revolution was more democratic, more religious and more nationalist than elsewhere. In the regions where Greeks outnumbered Moslems the orthodox peasantry rose in support of the kleftic bands. Many of these klefts or bandits, who abounded in the Turkish Empire, driven from their time-honoured place in Turko–Greek society by Ali Pasha of Janina, had served with the French, British and Russian forces in the Ionian Islands where they had taken refuge. After the wars, like military classes elsewhere in Europe, they had become desperate men. No wonder then that they seized the opportunity of Ali Pasha's rebellion against the Sultan to regain their own. Some of them, who had already imbibed ideas from French revolutionary sources, were initiated into a conspiracy already long preparing in the Greek world under the influence of European ideas. The conspiracy, mainly the work of the Greek diaspora, had only a rudimentary organisation and it failed in two of the regions, the Danubian Principalities and Constantinople, where it had aimed to strike. Its activities, however, led to revolts (not all of which were successful) in what is now mainland Greece and in certain Greek islands. In these revolts on the mainland the klefts, supported by the people, played a leading role. The central direction of the rebellion (as far as it existed) passed into the hands mainly of westernised Greeks and it was these who over a decade or more of internecine strife fashioned a western form of government and attempted to introduce constitutional arrangements even more democratic than the constitutions of western Europe.

The Greek revolt was the first truly nationalist movement in post-1815 Europe. The Serbians indeed had already gone a long way to nationhood and with the Greek example to follow were soon to develop a sense of nationality. The Romanians too had become aware of their national identity but it was not until after the Crimean War that they were able to establish a nation state. Similar national movements developed elsewhere as a result of liberal ideas and above all romanticism which stressed the individuality of different peoples. Nevertheless the greatest urge leading to action was the desire to throw off alien and oppressive rulers. Such was the case of the Belgian revolt of 1830, of the Italian revolts of 1830 and 1848, of the Magyar, Slav and Romanian risings of 1848, and of the risings of the Poles in 1830 and 1863.

In the revolutions of 1848 the forces at work varied from place to place and the revolutionaries in the field had a variety of objectives. Liberals in the main were out to continue the work of the French Revolution which, they claimed, was incomplete. Romantics, however, tended to display nationalist aspirations. In almost all cases the revolutionaries found themselves confronted by weak governments which had become complacent. Most of the revolutionary activities took place in capital towns. There was no support in the countryside and little or no backing from industrial workers, who were as yet not concentrated (not even in Paris) in a factory organisation. These revolutions, once the ruling powers had recovered their nerve, were easily put down, a strange ending perhaps to a half century which saw the reiteration and proliferation of revolutionary ideas. Once the revolutionary wars were over, Europe passed into a relatively peaceful age. There was indeed, besides the disturbances already mentioned, the Decembrist revolt of 1825 in Russia (with its diverse and far-reaching aims), the Wartburg Festival of 1817, various military insurrections in France and an uprising in Lyons (1832), and riots and machine-breaking in England. But all these events were relatively unimportant. Much more important was the economic revolution which the French political revolutions had perhaps hastened and the far-reaching effects of which were most clearly discernible in Britain.

Between 1750 and 1850 the population of Europe grew considerably, the increase being greatest in Britain. The growth was largely due to a decrease in infant mortality and a fall in the death rate generally, which in turn were due partly to improved medical knowledge and partly to an increase in food supplies. After the turn of the century, famines in Europe became less common and their consequences mitigated by improved yields combined with better communications. These better yields and better communications were considerably more pronounced in England, Holland, Belgium, France and Western Germany than elsewhere. In England the enclosure of the land was more or less complete by

1820 and this process, which enabled landowners to adopt numerous improvements, amounted to what is not inappropriately called an agricultural revolution. Over the greater part of Europe that process was slow and remained incomplete at the end of the nineteenth century. This is particularly true of all those regions where the land was cultivated mainly by peasant proprietors, who resisted change and whose unit of production was too small to admit of the introduction of better methods. In Germany east of the Elbe, where feudal tenure obtained throughout the revolutionary and Napoleonic period, the land remained concentrated in relatively few hands, and in a later age and under generally changing conditions the great landowners made their estates more productive than the peasant holdings. This indeed is true of the greater French land-owners. Although the French Revolution had destroyed the feudal nobility, a landed aristocracy, augmented by recruits from the Third Estate, had survived, their lands having been augmented by the lands of the Church. Under the new order many peasants had increased the size of their holdings, the numbers of landless men increased, and these either became labourers on the great estates and larger farms or drifted into the towns.

What the revolution had done was to hasten a process by which, to use Carlyle's terminology, a 'cash nexus' was substituted for a customary relationship to society. This was the economic and social reality of the revolutionary doctrine of equality and individual rights. Equality meant not a right to an equal share of wealth, but freedom for all men to gain what they could, to sell their land and to enter freely into trades and professions. In practice this meant for an ever-increasing number of men the right to sell their labour where they could. In other words, status had been generally replaced by contract. Such men were to become no longer at the mercy of the vagaries of the season but at the mercy of the market, of varying demands, of slumps and foreign competition. Although the iron law of wages did not come into operation in the form of the predictions of the economists, nevertheless the laws of supply and demand were to keep earnings down in some places and in some trades below what many considered to be a reasonable subsistence level for a long time. But over the decades real wages tended to rise even though there were times when they were overtaken by inflation.

Changes in industrial organisations, even in England, seemed –

at least when viewed from the early years of the nineteenth century
– hardly so revolutionary as those in agriculture. In England they
had begun many generations earlier, and their origins are
complex. They derived in part from the great expansion of overseas
commerce in the sixteenth, seventeenth and eighteenth centuries,
from various technical inventions, from the existence of power fur-
nished by rivers and streams, from iron deposits and from a plenti-
ful supply of coal, the two last becoming of supreme importance at
a later stage. These conditions were not confined to England. In
late seventeenth- and eighteenth-century France there was considerable industrial development in response to the growing
demand for luxury goods from the wealthy classes and to a rising
demand generally for consumer goods. Owing however to the
restrictive practices of the guilds, growth was slower than in
England, where economic life was freer and where a flourishing
woollen industry had long been firmly established. In France (and
the same is true of parts of Germany and Italy) industrial growth
took place outside the towns, the labour force being drawn from the
country population which combined a barely subsistence agriculture with cottage industry. Cottage industry was indeed a feature
of Great Britain, but here, owing to agricultural changes (a greater
surplus of food and labour) there was an earlier and more pronounced tendency to bring the industrial worker under the factory
roof and there was a greater surplus of capital from agriculture
(and from commerce) to invest in industry.

Agriculture and industry reacted the one upon the other in many
ways. Improved agricultural production gave rise to increased
demands for manufactured goods, for improved tools, for iron
ploughs and machinery. These in turn increased the agricultural
output, which was already growing as a result of the introduction of
better seeds, better strains of animals, and better drainage. Of
great importance too was the improvement of communications
linking the countryside to the towns, which under the impetus of industrialisation and agricultural change began to grow in size and
number. Landless men began to drift in larger numbers into the
urban centres. New towns arose in the areas of cottage industry
and in time the "outworkers" ceased, except in certain regions, to
be associated with the land. This process was hastened when steam
power came to be substituted for water power – a process fairly
near completion in England by 1850, but not nearly so advanced in
Germany, France and America.

Following hard on the French Revolution and no doubt hastened in many ways by the political and social changes resulting from it, agrarian and industrial developments throughout the nineteenth century gradually destroyed almost everywhere what was left of the *ancien régime.* In certain aspects these developments appeared to be an emanation of the Enlightenment – the fulfilment of the idea that the rational application of knowledge could re-create society. This idea persisted during the revolutionary period and was developed in diverse ways by the political economists and the utilitarians in the post-revolutionary era. These developments combined with the ideas thrown out by the natural scientists led to conflicts with the churches, all of which, despite loss of land, had achieved, as leaders of counter-revolution, greater wealth, greater prestige, and even greater political influence than they had enjoyed in the eighteenth century.

The doctrine that political power derives from below redounded to the advantage of the churches – at least in the short run. In France and in Europe at large education remained in their hands and they exercised a constant influence in the cause of counter-revolution. Among the clerics there were fewer "free-thinkers" than during the earlier age. Even in England the established Church had become far less worldly and in the countryside the parson and the tory squire had become representatives of counter-revolution. Non-Conformists reinforced by those Anglicans who had gone outside the Church, had become fervent Evangelists: they recruited followers not only in the agricultural villages but in the urban centres. Between them, the established Church and the Non-Conformists gave the masses a sense of purpose – a service performed by the Catholic and Protestant clergy and above all by the missionaries of France, by the Pietists in Germany, and by similar religious movements elsewhere. The growth of literacy among the masses led as much to the reading of the Bible and books of devotion as to those organs of the expanding newspaper press which, where sufficiently free, disseminated a whole variety of ideas.

Because of the proliferation of ideas, the attitudes to the problems of the age were necessarily varied and often conflicting. The problems themselves, both those of immediate concern, that is to say those giving rise to political conflict, and those foreseen by men of longer vision, were numerous and often bewildering. Among those immediate problems – to mention only a few – were poverty, hours and conditions of labour, wages, prices, education, commercial policy, financial administration, the rights of religious communities and the legality of workmen's associations. Among the problems which were less amenable to political and administrative action were the increase of population, the uprooting of rural populations and their drift to ugly and squalid towns, the desecration of the environment, the spread of materialism and the decline of moral standards. All these problems were discussed at length in the literature of the age. Most writers served some movement or cause, invariably displaying a sense of mission and didactic purpose. Exactly what influence they exerted upon the perpetual unfolding of events must surely have been considerable. In the words of Byron,

> Words are things, and a small drop of ink,
> Falling like dew upon a thought produces
> That which makes thousands, perhaps millions think.

Byron, himself something of a Whig with strong radical leanings, a romantic by psychological necessity, a genius in the use of language (whether in poetry, satire or prose), was to find a ready-made audience not only in Great Britain but also on the Continent. Like Voltaire before him he was preaching largely to the converted. Those who have read David Mornet's substantial and brilliant monograph, *Les Origines intellectuelles de la Révolution française* (Paris, 1933), will always be exceedingly chary of attributing to one writer or group of writers the power to change the course of history. Mornet shows that the ideas to be found in the writings of Voltaire and of the French Encyclopaedists were already in the air, and the general conclusion to be drawn is that great literary works are not so much the generating power of the ideas they contain as the evidence for the widespread existence of those ideas. It is nevertheless probably true that, in preaching to the converted, a writer (and this must certainly be true of Byron) increases the number of his admirers, strengthens their admiration and makes that admiration more fervent and more likely to lead to political action.

2 Byron and England

The Persistence of Byron's Political Ideas

WILLIAM RUDDICK

"From the French revolution to the Spanish civil war", says Paul Thompson in *The Works of William Morris*, "there runs a long tradition of political poets; Blake, Shelley and Byron, Yeats and Spender: even to some degree Tennyson and Arnold."[1] He stresses the inevitability of Byron's being concerned, as a romantic poet, with political issues, but argues that Morris alone, among his list of political visionaries, "became a genuine political leader, and made a real impact on the English political scene".[2]

Dr Thompson's assertion poses a number of questions which must be considered in a study such as the present. One's immediate reaction may be to protest that the poet of *Childe Harold, Don Juan* (especially the English Cantos), and *The Vision of Judgment* cannot be dismissed in such a fashion. Yet when one begins to search for concrete evidence of Byron's "real impact on the English political scene" either in his lifetime or in the political lifetimes of his contemporaries or their immediate successors, one comes to recognise an unexpected dearth of positive evidence. Can Dr Thompson's assertion, then, be true? Certainly it has to be admitted that while on the Continent Byron's powerful scorn of oppression and his lyrical celebrations of the inevitability and beauty of national regenerative processes inspired liberal forces in half a dozen countries, and while at home his cries of impatience with the old and assertions of the need for change excited young readers and put heart into struggling working class self-educators, the majority of responsible people remained resolutely unconvinced by his words.

The direct influence of Byron's poetry and the example given by his death were immediate and powerful outside of England. At home such of his ideas and assertions as could be related to the domestic social and political situation were generally resisted or ignored. His political principles were either dismissed as irrelevant to the appreciation of his poetry or condemned as shallow and insincere on grounds largely arising from a knowledge of his personal or social situation.

In his 1831 review of Moore's *Letters and Journals of Lord Byron* the young Macaulay (himself a Whig and a member of the same Holland House political set to which Byron had belonged fifteen years earlier) devotes much space to Byron's poetical characteristics and moral character, but remains significantly silent on the political elements in his poetry. When other contemporaries chose not to ignore Byron's politics they made it clear that they thought them obviously insincere. That liberal sentiments should be voiced by a lord (and a lord not slow to parade the claims and enjoy the sweets of his nobility) was an indication of nothing more than frustrated egotism to Hazlitt:

> When a man is tired of what he is, by a natural perversity he sets up for what he is not. . . . His ruling motive is not the love of the people, but of distinction: not of truth but of singularity . . . we do not like Sir Walter's gratuitous servility: we like Lord Byron's preposterous *liberalism* little better. He may affect the principles of equality, but he resumes his privilege of peerage, upon occasion.[3]

At the opposite end of the political spectrum, a disbelief almost identical with Hazlitt's was voiced by Byron's friend Sir Walter Scott:

> On politics, he used sometimes to express a high strain of what is now called Liberalism; but it appeared to me that the pleasure it afforded him as a vehicle of displaying his wit and satire against individuals in office was at the bottom of this habit of thinking, rather than any real conviction of the political principles on which he talked.[4]

Hazlitt's and Scott's reactions are typical of a wide range of educated observers in Byron's lifetime and the years immediately following his death. Obviously a degree of hostility might have been expected from Tory commentators in the last years of the struggle against Napoleon, the difficult time of economic depression and political repression following the war, and the agitated period of bitterly polarised political attitudes which led up to the Reform of Parliament in 1832. But it is noticeable that there is no comparable body of writing upholding Byron's views on British politics to be met with on the other side. Friendly and hostile critics were equally sceptical. The greater depth and more direct expression of the political message in *Don Juan, The Vision of Judgment* or, indeed, the final Cantos of *Childe Harold*, failed to convince (or perhaps even be regarded by) Byron's early readers.

Before Byron's death in 1824 his poetry was beginning to lose its general popularity. The scandal of his broken marriage and the sensational rumours that attended it had been revived by the sexual provocativeness of whole sections of *Don Juan*. The poem by no means offended only the timid and appealed to the prurient: responsible, well-educated members of at least one provincial Literary and Philosophical Society (that at Newcastle upon Tyne) called a special meeting to vote for the book's removal from the library's shelves. The additional shock of what was generally thought to be a blasphemous political attack on King George IV (at a time when his personal popularity was beginning to recover from the scandals immediately preceding the death of his wife) stamped on responsible people's minds the image of Byron as an irresponsible and reckless satirist. His death at Missolonghi rescued his personal reputation, but it is noticeable that from that time on a distinction forms in the opinion of his contemporaries between Byron the hero of Greece, a man of action, politically and militarily effective, and the slapdash, self-regarding and self-dramatising poet of earlier days. Once more Sir Walter Scott voices the general opinion:

> Sir Frederick (Adam) spoke most highly of Byron, the soundness of his views, the respect in which he was held – his just ideas of the Grecian cause and character, and the practical and rational wishes which he formed for them. Singular that a man whose conduct in his own personal affairs had been anything but practical should be thus able to stand by the helm of a sinking state![5]

In the years up to 1832 Byron's liberal views on domestic policies and politics were generally written off as insincere. As Scott's and other testimonies show, his reputation as a prophet of European liberation stood very high, but a country which had had its own revolution almost two centuries earlier and was anxious to deal with the new problems caused by the growth of commerce and industrialisation through processes of adjustment if blank resistance could no longer be maintained was not in the mood for Byron's more radical warnings. For a time he offered a somewhat vague but exciting source of hope to the young, many of whom were more aware than their elders of the need for change and, like Byron in his last years, longed for it.

Tennyson's and Jane Welsh Carlyle's emotion at the news of Byron's death testifies to the hold which he had gained over the imaginations of young people. In the long run this generation would prove to have been powerfully affected by its early enthusiasm for Byron, but at the time his influence soon began to fade. For those in need of millenarial solace (the young and the self-educated working man in particular) Shelley's soon proved more sustaining. For the general mass of educated readers Wordsworth, Coleridge and, in due course, Keats all steadily gained ground. Bad imitations of the more sentimental and sensational elements in Byron's work did much to weary the public and the successive scandalous revelations concerning his private life both offended serious-minded readers and fixed in their minds an image of a self-willed and therefore morally defective poet. Also, though adolescents might still read *The Giaour*, critics found they had little new to say about his work.

The successive utterances of Thomas Carlyle show how Byron's stock slumped in the years following his death. In 1824 Carlyle thought Byron "late so full of fire and generous passion and proud purposes". By 1830 he had radically changed his opinion:

> No genuine productive thought was ever revealed by him to mankind; indeed no clear undistorted vision into anything; . . . but all had a certain falsehood, a brawling, theatrical, insincere character.[6]

Carlyle's remarks foreshadow those of a whole generation of critics who had little to say about Byron's thought (if they credited him with the ability to think at all) and were generally appalled by his moral character. Amid this general chorus of condemnation Matthew Arnold's very qualified praise in the *Memorial Verses, April 1850*

He taught us nothing, but our soul
Has *felt* him like the thunder's roll. . . .

is at least civil, though Arnold fails to recognise the essentially
intellectual basis of Byron's rebelliousness. For the re-birth of
intelligent sympathy (interestingly paralleled by the growth of interest in another, earlier political poet, Blake) one must wait for a
new generation of critics in the 1860s.

What made Byron rebellious was hardly understood at all by
readers before 1860. In part they were distracted by biographical
considerations, in part by their desire to read their own desires into
the poetry. Byron's poetry often invites audience identification
and the fact that his poems brought to the surface so many of the
concealed urges and pressures of the age increased their appeal.
For most readers Byron's earlier poems remained the best known
and most inviting. Their amorous or erotic charge diverted
Byron's readers from their own political frustrations to the consideration of frustrations of a more directly personal kind. This
process is clearly shown in an interesting passage from *The Revolution in Tanner's Lane* (1887) in which Mark Rutherford recreates
with great perceptiveness the consciousness of an urban craftsman
of the 1810s:

> In the evening Zachariah took up the book . . . he went on with
> the *Corsair*, and as he read his heart warmed. . . . Zachariah
> found in the *Corsair* exactly what answered to his own inmost
> self, down to its very depths.[7]

What stirs Zachariah so profoundly is not "the love of the illimit-
able, of freedom", though he stirs to its presence in the poem. He
hurries on to enjoy the depiction of strong and passionate love,
such as his own marriage has failed to give him. Essentially his
enjoyment of Byron is compensatory.

Such working class poetry from the first half of the nineteenth
century as survives shows that Mark Rutherford was accurate in
his act of historical recreation. *The Vision of Judgment* may have had a
temporary vogue in unauthorised cheap reprints for working class
radical consumption, but by comparison with the lasting popularity of Shelley's political poetry Byron's significance amounts to
very little. He influenced working class poets by offering them a vo-
cabulary of rhetoric through which they could voice their personal

aspirations and frustrations, but in his poetry they seem to have found nothing more.

As late as 1896 the (admittedly High Tory) critic George Saintsbury felt able to declare that in the years following Byron's death, though "Counter-jumpers like Thackeray's own Pogson worshipped 'the noble poet'; boys of nobler stamp like Tennyson *thought* they worshipped him, but if they were going to become men of affairs forgot all about him; if they were to be poets took to Keats and Shelley as models, not to him."[8] In fact, it would be truer to say that they may have forgotten Byron, or rejected him, with their conscious minds, but on a more fundamental level the consciousness of what he had done and stood for was still present, as will be shown. There were, it is true, certain reasons why his direct influence on English domestic politics and political thinking should have been slow to show itself. The basic belief which energises Byron's political writing is a positive certainty, akin to that of the French political writers of the late eighteenth century or the English radicals who were influenced by them, that society can revolutionise its nature through a rebirth or rediscovery of love and fellow feeling. Like Shelley, Byron looks forward towards a future golden age of fraternal liberty, but unlike Shelley his sense of what lies ahead is tempered by an ironist's understanding of the difficulties that lie in the path of progress. Byron has a far stronger sense (in many ways akin to that of Blake) of what the ingrained corruption of contemporary human society represents: he sees it, as Blake does, as the external manifestation of the dark, self-imprisoning side of human nature and its appetites. His assurance of future progress could not stimulate the young or the underprivileged as Shelley's did, for they are shot through with an irony which is easily mistaken for cynicism if one misses his underlying passionate commitment to truth and decency. His later poems seem to have been thus misunderstood till the latter part of the century.

Furthermore, in the period before 1848 English society at large was still in a state of reaction against millenarian visions and revolutionary predictions in any shape or form. The shadow of the French Revolution still lay on people's minds, and the realities of the present situation seemed to demand not perilous innovations but a slow and cautious process of social adjustment and political manipulation. For contemporary readers Byron's predictions of catastrophe and insistence on the need for a change of heart seemed either alarming or (as time passed and gradual change established itself as the new norm of government) old-fashionedly wide of the mark.

The main movements in politics and society in the first half of the nineteenth century show successive phases of political and economic readjustment in which the personnel who controlled the shaping of events stayed remarkably stable. Even after 1832, G. M. Young points out:

> The people of England still preferred to have their political experiments timed and directed for them by noblemen and gentlemen enjoying the confidence of the respectable classes.[9]

Byron's birth entitled him to take a place among the governors of his country, and for a short time after he entered the House of Lords he spoke and engaged in committee work. The subjects on which he spoke (class and religious justice and the need for parliamentary reform) foreshadow his liberal political utterances in *Don Juan*. At the same time, his involvement in Major Cartwright's Hampden Club and his easy entrée into the Holland House circle of Whig politicians suggest that if the course of his life in his London years had been different, he might well have taken his natural place among the generation of Whig politicians (manipulators of the system as much as reformers) who achieved the reform of Parliament in 1832 and made a start on the legislation to regulate and improve the conditions of the working classes which Byron's speech on the Frame-Work Bill of February 1812 clearly sees the need for.

But this was not to be: Byron's direct involvement in the processes of government, though highly creditable, was brief; too brief to have any very lasting effect on the attitudes of his fellows among the ruling classes. Nor was Byron by temperament a manipulator of the present situation at this stage (though in Greece he showed he could do so). His 1813/14 *Journal* shows this clearly enough. Byron longs to sway the British Senate as his admired friend Sheridan had formerly done: he has the poet's vision of the power of noble language to move a great assembly and produce a change of heart ("I coincide with you in opinion that the Poet yields to the orator"[10]), but his imagination was fed by memories of Greek oratory and his vision of the orator's role was essentially romantic and Grecian. In reality he was soon weary of the uphill work of his "senatorial duties" and distracted by the excitement of his amorous and social life.

The Member of the House of Lords was also the author of *Childe Harold*, who expressed such unorthodox sentiments as:

> Hereditary bondsmen! know ye not
> Who would be free themselves must strike the blow?[11]

During his years of exile the note of impassioned fervour for liberty was never lost from his poetry, but as his understanding of European politics (and of English politics seen in the larger context) grew deeper he achieved a new wittiness of presentation and of analysis which baffled his readers in the main, but was to be one of his most enduring gifts to the English liberal–radical tradition:

> I've no great cause to love that spot on earth,
> Which holds what *might have been* the noblest nation;
> But though I owe it little but my birth,
> I feel a mix'd regret and veneration
> For its decaying fame and former worth.
> Seven years (the usual term of transportation)
> Of absence lay one's old resentment level,
> When a man's country's going to the devil.
>
> Alas! could she but fully, truly, know
> How her great name is now throughout abhorr'd
> How eager all the earth is for the blow
> Which shall lay bare her bosom to the sword;
> How all the nations deem her their worst foe,
> That worse than *worst of foes*, the once adored
> False friend, who held out freedom to mankind,
> And now would chain them, to the very mind....[12]

The backward-looking tendency of this fine passage, inviting the reader (and the nation) to be true to the finest traditions of the race will need to be considered presently, for it was to prove a potent factor in Byron's reviving influence over the younger generation in the late 1830s and 1840s. But first the most immediate and striking manifestation of Byron's influence on Liberal thinking must be established.

Though the British public was slow to absorb the political message of Byron's late poetry, the clarion call to defend liberty overseas which is so striking a feature of even the early part of *Childe Harold* had an immediate effect on even those readers most scornful of the author's personal and artistic integrity. *Childe Harold's* lyrical and dramatic outbursts on liberty and the meaning of the Greek ideal of democracy for modern Europe did much to help those who strove to raise aid for the Greeks when their struggle for national freedom commenced. Byron's death at Missolonghi did the rest. Liberty and nationalism now had their voice and their martyr, and even those most hostile to Byron's views on home affairs found it almost impossible to resist. From the time of the Greek War onwards a new spirit of sympathetic willingness to intervene in, or guarantee the survival of, moderate liberal movements for national self-determination becomes manifest in British political thinking. Greece, Belgium, Spain, Italy in due course: all benefit from the change of heart, and each time young well-wishers, like Hallam and Tennyson visiting Spain in 1830, go forth with Byron in their hearts, if no longer in their hands, to observe and possibly to help a little.

Not all of Byron's passion for European liberty need be thought of as uniquely his own, or without precedent in earlier or other writers. But his dramatic urgency was new: he made the crisis seem urgent as well as important. And in linking the present nationalistic movements to the true spirit of antique liberty as he did in all his political poetry from *Childe Harold* onwards he helped effect a change of perspective very conducive to thinking men in the age of the Greek Revival and very capable of development in the High Victorian era of the Pax Britannica.

Sir Herbert Grierson saw Byron's thinking working on Mr Gladstone at one remarkable moment in his career:

> The spirit of Byron's poetry was the spirit in which Mr Gladstone approached the problem of foreign politics in the famous Don Pacifico debate, when, like Burke and like Byron, he insisted that the relations between nations should be the same as that between individuals, and governed by a regard for justice and humanity. For some years after the collapse of the Holy Alliance that cause did make some progress.[13]

Mr Gladstone belonged to the generation that grew up with Byron's poetry and was shocked by the news of his death. Like others of that group he had no high opinion of Byron's morals or muse in later years, but the passion with which Byron wrote on liberty and oppression had probably a lasting effect on him of which he was scarcely conscious. Grierson found "the spirit of Byron's poetry" in the Don Pacifico speech. One may also speculate on whether, without his boyhood reading of *The Prisoner of Chillon*, Gladstone might have thought of undertaking his memorable exploration of the prisons of Naples in 1850.

A body of poetry which inspires men to exercise justice, charity, and compassion in the affairs of weaker nations abroad is likely, once contemporary prejudices have begun to die down or be overcome, to turn men's attention to problems within a contrast-filled society at home. As the absolute resistance to change which so marked the post-war years grew weaker, and as the readjustment of political power in 1832 was seen to be working, the mental resistance generated by Byron's assertions of the imminence of revolutionary or radical developments began to die away. It is very obvious from the work of the new generation of writers that at least some aspects of the social and political message of Byron's later poetry began to be appreciated at least in the 1830s and, more widely, the 1840s.

The message of Byron's later poetry is clear enough for those able to face up to it. Byron sees aristocratic English government as being doomed by its own corrupt nature and its unwillingness to face change. He reminds his upper class readers of the lesson of 1789:

> A row of gentlemen along the streets
> Suspended, may illuminate mankind,
> As also bonfires made of country seats . . .[14]

Time is running out for the governing classes:

> I have seen the people ridden o'er like sand
> By slaves on horseback – I have seen malt liquors
> Exchanged for "thin potations" by John Bull –
> I have seen John half detect himself a fool.[15]

Nor is an impoverished proletariat the only threat to aristocratic power:

Cash rules the grove, and fells it too beside;
Without cash, camps were thin, and courts were none.[16]

Beneath the seemingly massive strength of aristocratic privilege
Byron sees, with a clarity that foreshadows Thackeray, the increasing power of commercial interests and new money. Against a
double weight of conformity – both the old aristocratic interest and
the newly rich, eager to join the aristocratic ranks and maintain its
privileged position – Byron can only set his deeply held conviction
that rottenness cannot last, that cant must destroy itself (like
Southey's attempt to rewrite history as High Toryism in *The Vision
of Judgment*) and that the forces of renewal which the French philos-
ophers had envisaged and the American and French revolutionaries set loose in the world most prevail. Republicanism could be
justified for good practical reasons:

The greater the equality, the more impartially evil is distri-
buted, and becomes light by the division among so many.[17]

But, more fundamentally, the new Liberal republican movements
in Italy, Germany, and Greece represented the undying human
will, energy and benevolence of nature which ancient Greece had
showed so magnificently to the world.

In his book *The Political Ideas of the English Romanticists* (1926)
Crane Brinton makes the point that Byron is "a true heir of the literary Jacobins" in his belief in Nature and devotion to liberty. But
he maintains that "his Liberal leanings are not those of a violent,
un-English rebel against society" and stresses Byron's desire for
"moderate" political reform. The point is arguable. Byron was a
natural aristocrat, accepting the rights and responsibilities of his
position and assuming that in any situation he would enjoy a position of eminence. Many of the stronger passages of satire or invective in his later poetry should doubtless be read as warnings to the
proud-hearted rather than predictions of inescapable political catastrophe. But to place him in the camp of the moderate Whig
reformers tells only half the story. Byron is a true Romantic Liberal
in that he believes an irreversible historic process is at work, renew-
ing society fundamentally in ways that require all men to subjugate
their personal interests to the common good. Even through the wry
satirical pose the true voice of feeling can be detected:

> I do not know; – I wish men to be free
> As much from mobs as kings – from you as me.[18]

There was enough appearance of radicalism in Byron's writings to trouble early readers, but in fact his chief gift to later Liberal thinking was not any single method of judging the English situation but rather a valuable tendency towards healthy scepticism: a willingness to get behind appearances, however treasured, and attitudes of mind, however reassuring, in order to reach the truth. Yet this scepticism was not withering or destructive to passionate feeling. Byron's belief in the sacredness of the cause of liberty and the value of all progress conducive to the well-being of mankind and the cherishing of the warmest feelings of the human heart was too quick and sensitive for that. Thus he appealed to the early Victorians (often far more than they realised) and warmed their belief in the value of compassion in political situations, as in their attempts at social reform.

In his own lifetime Byron was largely isolated from popular political movements. Neither Cobbett nor "Orator" Hunt interested him. He disliked them as, at the other extreme, he disliked the Benthamites, for stirring up facile enthusiasm by means of oversimplified, essentially canting, arguments. By social tradition he was close to the attitudes of Grey and the future Lord Melbourne and he could understand their methods. But in the last resort his vision was more radical and at the same time more ideal than theirs. As Crane Brinton maintains, "without Byron's comfortable enthusiasm for ideal liberty, it [the Whig party in its transformation to Liberalism] must have failed to hold together".[19] But to those who watched this transformation with impatience or sighed at its limitations when completed, Byron's vision still had a more radical and inspiriting message to offer.

Crane Brinton raises a further, related point in this context:

> The trouble with England, it seemed to the author of *Don Juan* was that it cared more for contentment than for the truth. . . .
> English society was built on cowardice. It was organised stupidity.[20]

In Byron's exposure of this stupidity through his pursuit of "cant", Brinton judges him to be a forerunner of such later analysts of class complacency as Matthew Arnold and George Bernard Shaw. The comparison is a fair one, reflecting the opposite face of Byron's Liberalism: his lively scepticism concerning the status quo. The bracing effect of this irony, and its adoption by other social commentators, were lastingly to influence Victorian and later English thinking.

In *Victorian Essays* G. M. Young maintained that in early nineteenth-century England:

> Public opinion and discussion were bound by conventions –
> moral, social, and religious – stricter, I should reckon, than in
> any European country enjoying the same amount of political
> freedom. . . . The breaking down of these conventions in
> England was one of the greatest services, and the most lasting, of
> the liberal mind.[21]

In this breaking down process Byron's poetry played a most significant part, helping to establish a tradition of polemic in which sceptical analysis fulfils a purifying role in the service of an underlying vision of society as it might be. This is perhaps Byron's most lasting benefaction to the English Liberal tradition. It can be found working healthily in English poetry, for example, from about the end of the 1830s.

As well as general scepticism, Byron offers the example of a close study of institutions. In this, too, he was to prove influential. The English Cantos of *Don Juan* expose the mechanism of political and moral control by which English society is kept in a state of immobility while remaining tolerably at peace with itself. Byron hammers home the point that comfort is not enough: systems built on deception or the evasion of reality are condemned by their own unreality. Like Don Juan's education they cannot endure – or be endured by – any fully living man. Reformed or destroyed, they must leave the way open for fairness, liberty and the individual vision.

Byron's method in the English Cantos of *Don Juan* may owe something to Fielding in its use of the satirical panorama of a hypocritical society, but Byron goes as far beyond Fielding in showing a world constantly at the mercy of flux and uncertainty in its political situations as he does in his depiction of human nature. The world, of course, tries to blind itself to its impermanence, preferring not to believe that its political and social institutions are in the grip of a dynamic historical process, but:

> Talk not of seventy years as age; in seven
> I have seen more changes, down from monarchs to
> The humblest individual under heaven,
> Than might suffice a moderate century through.[22]

In the same stanza Byron laments the fact that "change grows too changeable, without being new" – a clear indication of his desire for a new order, a change of heart.

It is interesting to see how the new generation of writers, who almost without exception slighted Byron the poet for reasons which were actually connected with his private life, were in fact absorbing the lesson of *Don Juan* during the 1830s and 1840s. They soon moved beyond superficial imitation of his social panorama technique, usually un-ironic and involving uncritical reanimations of the "Byronic Hero" figure, such as distinguish the "Silver Fork" novels of the 1820s and those of the youthful Disraeli. Thackeray, for example, applied an instantly recognisable version of Byron's "English Cantos" manner in *Vanity Fair*. He might not be able to offer any real alternative beyond the moral salvation of the individual, but both his satirical method and his belief in the survival of individual goodness in a world governed by cant are essentially Byronic (the cant, after all, had changed very little between Byron's period in English society and the 1840s). The analysis of social, political and moral pretence that one finds in Thackeray's work (or, less intensely worried over but still more broadly based in the political novels of Trollope) is clearly in a realistic tradition deriving from Byron's last poems. The extent to which he was becoming influential by the 1840s is also shown, with particular clarity, by the change in Disraeli's attitude to Byron in his novels of that decade.

Disraeli offers a very interesting example of Byronic awareness. A writer who was also a practical politician and a political thinker, he progressed from a crude obsession with the superficialities of Byron's manner (and with imitating the Byronic hero in his own art and life) to a more profound understanding of what Byron's late satires had been about. Disraeli belonged to the generation who (like Tennyson and Browning) outgrew their adolescent love of Byron's early poems and became highly sceptical of his ultimate importance (though, interestingly, if they lived long enough they advanced to a more mature awareness of his merits by the 1860s and 1870s: this happened in both Tennyson's and Disraeli's case).

Yet even as they rejected *Childe Harold* Byronism with their conscious minds their own work shows how much they derived from
him. In the late 1830s and early 1840s Disraeli was particularly
interested in Byron. In 1837 he published *Venetia, or the Poet's
Daughter*, a novel freely based on incidents in Byron's and Shelley's
life stories. In the 1830s he was also involving himself with the
"Young England" movement and the best-known of his three
novels relating to the movement, *Sybil* (1845), shows especially
clearly the consequences both of the new developments in Conservatism and of Disraeli's reading of Byron. *Sybil, or the Two Nations*
moves beyond Silver Fork imitation of Byron's English social
comedy to show a more truly Byronic picture of an irresponsible aristocracy in decay. At the same time the idea (and the ideal) of a
regenerate aristocracy is presented in a way that Byron would have
understood. An aristocracy must be true to its highest standards,
forward-looking, regenerating society on lines evolving from the
best traditions of the past, while not being obsessed (as Burke, for
example, had grown obsessed, and English Toryism after him)
with preserving every form and feature of institutions as now con-
stituted. Scott would have understood Disraeli's romantic concept
of aristocracy but not his lack of concern to preserve the maximum
possible of national institutions. The idea of aristocracy as a force
for regeneration, however, comes much more directly from Byron,
and probably from the study of his life as much as from his writings.
Through Disraeli an essential strand of Byron's thinking is welded
into the new Conservatism of the 1840s. Byron's ample legacy
could, indeed, be of service to both parties in this period of evolution, offering the Conservatives an ideal, the Liberals a habit of
sceptical thinking and both parties a generous willingness to
modify old ways in the service of human need and human affliction.

Disraeli's *Sybil* has its alternative title *The Two Nations*. The industrial novels of the late 1840s and early 1850s show another way
in which the public conscience was catching up with what Byron
had maintained almost forty years earlier.

In a letter to Lord Holland, written on 25 February 1812, immediately before his speech in the debate on the Frame-Work Bill,
Byron said "we must not allow mankind to be sacrificed to improvements in mechanism". In the debate itself he criticised the
behaviour of both the civil authorities and the mill-owners, who
had brought industrial strife upon themselves:

> Had proper meetings been held in the earlier stages of these riots, had the grievances of these men and their masters (for they also had their grievances) been fairly weighed and justly examined, I do think that means might have been devised to restore these workmen to their avocations, and tranquillity to the country.[23]

Here, in brief, is the basic assumption of Mrs Gaskell's industrial novels and one of the ideals of Disraeli and the Christian Socialists in that same period. By the middle of the nineteenth century Byron's Liberal and social reforming ideas, in all their variety, were becoming directly relevant to the condition of English society and, quite clearly, relating to the current preoccupations of its most socially concerned writers.

In his speech on the Frame-Work Bill, Byron considered the effects produced by the introduction of new processes of manufacture:

> By the adoption of one species of frame in particular, one man performed the work of many, and the superfluous labourers were thrown out of employment. Yet it is to be observed, that the work thus executed was inferior in quality; not marketable at home, and merely hurried over with a view to exportation. It was called, in the cant of the trade, by the name of "Spider-work". The rejected workmen, in the blindness of their ignorance, instead of rejoicing at these improvements in arts so beneficial to mankind, conceived themselves to be sacrificed to improvements in mechanism. In the foolishness of their hearts they imagined that the maintenance and well-doing of the industrious poor were objects of greater consequence than the enrichment of a few individuals by any improvement, in the implements of trade, which threw the workmen out of employment, and rendered the labourer unworthy of his hire.[24]

This remarkable passage points directly forward, in its combination of passionate concern for social justice to the poor with a controlled wit and, at times, sarcastic sharpness of expression, to the social criticism of William Morris in the last quarter of the century.

Morris's style, in his late socialist writings and in the pamphlets and essays on craft work and work satisfaction, derives from a number of sources: Carlyle, Ruskin, Kingsley and Maurice all contribute elements of thought and style. But the wit and attacking sarcasm of Byron, thought through and argued through with intellectual clarity and rigour, are found again at many of the most striking points in Morris's writing. So too are Byron's ideals of decency and fairness, of society needing to be regenerated in such a way that all men should be free to live without being exploited, without being miserable and without having their capacity for imaginative effort destroyed. "The Isles of Greece" and Morris's *Nowhere* are divided by many years and many streams of influence, but common to both visions is the impassioned delight of foreseeing a society in which a past of ideal beauty and liberty shall be restored. Both visions look backwards, to an idealised past, but they also point to the future, offering hope to an exploited and crushed majority. In Morris's work and in his political activities many of Byron's ideals, perhaps kept current and developed somewhat as an element in the thinking of John Ruskin during the intervening years, are revitalised and given fresh currency. Like Byron, Morris came to believe that "the *Poet* yields to the *orator*". Through his writings and through his political activities the example of Byronic passion and witty, ruthlessly logical earnestness were in turn passed on to be developed in the prefaces and polemics of George Bernard Shaw.

Already, by the middle of the nineteenth century many of Byron's ideals and methods are to be seen being exploited by prominent writers who gave them a wider currency even while in their public and private statements they denied the importance of the poet whose writings they had absorbed with great relish in their youth. It is, for example, interesting to see how the later Cantos of *Don Juan* could influence very different writers in the late 1840s, in ways which, though divergent, are linked by a strong charge of anti-aristocratic, anti-privilege social criticism.

Two novels published in the same year, 1847, will show the strength of Byronic influence. In *Jane Eyre* the adaptation of Byron's Norman Abbey material is quite straightforward. Mr Rochester's house party at Thornfield simply holds up an aristocratic group to be dismissed as inconsiderate, overweening and morally feeble by the governess, Jane, who compares her companions unfavourably with the true aristocrat Mr Rochester, a "Byronic" hero but one whose superior standing is finally justified not by wealth or social prominence but by real superiority of moral fibre. In *Vanity Fair*, Thackeray (whose remarks on Byron are, curiously enough, among the most unfavourable to have been recorded) applies the social panorama techniques of *Don Juan* Canto XI to English society at the period of Byron's greatest fame. Thackeray's awareness of Byron's example is made additionally clear by the way in which he expands material obviously taken from the Battle of Waterloo section of *Childe Harold* Canto III. He is perhaps the first English novelist fully to exploit Byron's satiric technique and the technique of the disabused authorial commentator to analyse, as Byron had more briefly done, the characteristics of a society in a state of social and moral flux and decay whose presence it refuses to admit and whose effects it attempts to both accommodate and mitigate through the practice of "cant". In Thackeray's writing or, at the same time, in certain parts of Dickens's novels (for instance the political parts of *Bleak House*) Byron's capacity for logically convincing satirical exposure of the forces that stand in the path of progress and fairness in society are to be found once more. At the same time, in such parts of Dickens's work as the extended examination of the workings of Chancery in *Bleak House* we find again the Byronic awareness that progress can only come about slowly because of the organic corruption of much of society (representing as it does organic corruptness within the human personality and the human heart) but that come about it will because goodness is also real and evil cannot help but destroy itself.

The creative writers of the 1840s and 1850s respond to elements in their own contemporary society which can be linked with preoccupations and assertions which they could find already developed or suggested by parts of Byron's work. At the same time, the younger writers both gave fresh currency to Byronic ideas and ideals, and developed their contemporaries' understanding of them. For example, Byron's healthy, flexible scepticism could serve the new generation of poets either in expressing their certainty of the inevitability of progress or, more subtly allied with Byron's passionate awareness of the mixed and contradictory nature of human responses, it could produce a fragile but illuminating vision of a truth superior to mundane preoccupations which could itself liberate by its very sense of reality. In the former category Browning obviously stands pre-eminent: his poems about Italy show very clearly indeed how well he understood the extent to which Byron's adoption of a seemingly eccentric viewpoint could open the way for the expression of warm feelings and Liberal enthusiasms. In the second category there are the delicate, self-mocking ironies of Clough's *Amours de Voyage*:

> Rome will not suit me, Eustace; the priests and soldiers possess it;
> Priests and soldiers: – and, ah! which is worst, the priest or the soldier?
> Politics, farewell, however! . . .
> No, happen whatever may happen,
> Time, I suppose, will subsist; the earth revolve on its axis;
> People will travel; the stranger will wander as now in the city;
> Rome will be here, and the Pope the *Custode* of Vatican marbles.[25]

Clough's apparent dissociation of himself from contemporary politics here is, in ways which clearly derive from Byron, a delicate but profoundly realistic presentation of the complexity of his response. It is a Liberal's response; aware of the gulf between what probably will happen and a desired ideal, but using such details as the idea of the Pope as "custode" played off against the classical ideal enshrined in the Vatican marbles to compare the inadequate present and imminent reality with the Golden Age which the fighters for Italian liberty long to see restored.

Browning and Clough, Disraeli, Thackeray and, in due course, Trollope, serve to show how an intelligent awareness of the potential within Byron's late poetry came into existence and was of service to men desirous of seeing progress take place within their society. The new phase of the struggle for Italian unity may have helped bring Byron's Liberal prophecies back into the public mind as being words fully thought out as well as rhetorically inspiring. But most of all, if the evidence of the writers can be taken as representative of the best thought of the age, Byron's ideas and perceptions were being found to possess a continuing relevance and perception. As the novelists found, Byron had shown how systems of political and social management could stand in the path of desirable reforms and changes. "Cant" stood in the way of necessary changes of thought. The poets longed to voice the Liberal enthusiasms of the heart. The critics of the economic state of England and its problems of class relations and individual lack of fulfilment could also find inspiration and practical help in Byron's writings and example. And as the century grew older it came to seem that Byron's most valuable gifts to newer writers were his courage to ask the needful question, and his refusal to accept the convenient or tactful answer, and his liberating, validating and cleansing wit.

Byron's Liberal opinions and frequently radical answers to problems of nineteenth-century English life and society (which he was frequently among the first to discern) found their way into the Victorian consciousness by a variety of routes, as the evidence of the writers shows, but it was not until almost the end of the century, when Liberalism was being forced to realise that the world was once more being assailed by major difficulties, that adequate criticism of his political poetry and its value began to be written. In a review of the Ernest Hartley Coleridge edition of *Don Juan*, published in the *Academy* in 1903, Francis Thompson gave the first convincing account of Byron's characteristics as a political satirist and caught the essential feeling of his Liberal faith:

> It must be remembered that *Don Juan* produces no impression of world-weariness. It is not a sigh, but a shout. Open it where you will, it flashes life. The negations and nihilisms with which it abounds are uttered as roundly as other men's faiths; there is no miserable infection of the utterance; no miasma or helpless ranting. . . . Byron sowed the spirit of questioning, and the courage of denial, deep in the hearts of men; and without these nothing can be done.[26]

The clouds thickened, the storm came, and in a post-war world faced by problems not unlike those which Byron had known, the real understanding of what Byron had given, and still could give, to the Liberal spirit under stress, came about. Sir Herbert Grierson's succession of fine interpretative essays appeared between 1920 and 1925. In the 1930s, as the Liberal spirit faced still more urgent threats, Byron's relevance seemed to increase. George Orwell was drawn to write finely and most characteristically on Byron in a social–political context and another critic who was also a poet turned to Byron as the recipient of his reflections on current problems, as well as a fit model for the tone of voice and reflective manner in which to express them. In his *Letter to Lord Byron*, W. H. Auden envisages Byron still alive in 1936, leading the fight against "the ogre" repressiveness wherever it is to be found:

Against the ogre, dragon, what you will:
His many shapes and names all turn us pale,
For he's immortal, and to-day he still
Swinges the horror of his scaly tail.
Sometimes he seems to sleep, but will not fail
In every age to rear up to defend
Each dying force of history to the end.

Milton beheld him on the English throne,
And Bunyan sitting in the Papal chair;
The hermits fought him in their caves alone,
At the first Empire he was also there,
Dangling the Pax Romana in the air:
He comes in dreams at puberty to man,
To scare him back to childhood if he can.[27]

The extent to which Byron has influenced English Liberal thinking and practice cannot easily be summarised. For much of the
nineteenth century the message of his poetry was obscured by biographical considerations which caused serious readers to distrust
his thought. Until the 1830s there was widespread resistance to his
criticisms of British society and the politics in which it engaged: the
combination of radicalism and prophetic fire was too much for
readers who were, by the third decade of the century, beginning to
respond to a comparable wit and prophetic energy (reassuringly
free, however, from Byron's visions of egalitarianism to come) in
the periodical criticisms of Thomas Carlyle. Yet from the first
Byron's passion for European liberty and his criticisms of Britain's
continental involvements in the age of the Holy Alliance were profoundly influential in stimulating men's attitudes towards supporting Liberalism abroad and, in due course, towards seeking for
social justice at home.

Well before any conscious understanding of Byron's political
writing can be found, the evidence of the novelists shows how his
practical demonstrations of the illogicality and self-interest built
into the old system were a powerful effect. By dramatising corruptness and narrow views Byron made men feel the truth of those
assertions which their conscious minds still rejected and stimulated them to cry out for social reforms.

But Byron was also a social visionary. His cleansing cynicism
might help men find reality in an age of manifold uncertainties, as

the evidence afforded by novels of the 1840s and 1850s makes plain. But his vision of what might and ought to be was also highly influential. In positing a regenerated state of society Byron leaves no privileged place for wealth or ancient titles. He demands that men should be free to fulfil themselves, in work as in love: that the imagination should be fostered and men's characters allowed to develop naturally and fully. Well before the general discovery of Blake's poetry his late poems are already offering the public many of the views on society and the importance of the individual personality which later generations associate most closely with the poetry of Blake. Through Ruskin and William Morris the line of Byron's social thinking and (equally important) Byron's social vision is carried on and developed. In the writing of Shaw it finds a voice whose capacity for truth-discerning wit and passionate commitment to justice are at last equal to Byron's own.

The full fruits of Byron's ideas and idealism were slow to reveal themselves. In the heyday of British Liberalism his was, perhaps, most markedly a humanising and liberating influence, helping men to find social and political truth beyond the confines of custom and accepted thought. But in the last quarter of the nineteenth century and in the twentieth Byron's wit, realism, egalitarianism and passion for social justice have proved an increasingly powerful influence in progressive English thinking. The degree to which Byron's poetry, born of an age of oppression, lived again as an inspiration to Auden and George Orwell in another age in which progressive Liberal ideas were once again in peril affords further testimony to the still vital power which his political poetry can be felt to contain.

NOTES

1. Paul Thompson, *The Work of William Morris* (London, 1967) p. 209.
2. Ibid.
3. William Hazlitt, *The Spirit of the Age* (Oxford, *World's Classics*, 1960) p. 116.
4. Sir Walter Scott to Thomas Moore. Quoted in S. C. Chew, *Byron in England: His Fame and After-Fame* (New York, 1924) p. 120.
5. Scott's *Diary*; entry of 8 September 1826.
6. Quoted in Chew, op. cit., p. 250.
7. Mark Rutherford, *The Revolution in Tanner's Lane* (London, 1877) pp. 22–5.
8. Quoted by Sir Herbert Grierson in *The Background of English Literature* (Harmondsworth, 1962) p. 70.

9. G. M. Young, *Today and Yesterday* (London, 1948) p. 26.

10. Byron; letter to John Hanson, 2 April 1807.

11. *Childe Harold*, Canto II, LXXVI.

12. *Don Juan*, Canto X, LXVI-LXVII.

13. Grierson, *Essays and Addresses* (London, 1940) p. 16.

14. *Don Juan*, Canto XI, XXVI.

15. *Don Juan*, Canto XI, LXXXV.

16. *Don Juan*, Canto XII, XIV.

17. Quoted by Grierson in *The Background of English Literature*, p. 170.

18. *Don Juan*, Canto IX, XXV.

19. Brinton, *The Political Ideas of the English Romanticists* (Oxford, 1926) p. 115.

20. Ibid. p. 157.

21. G. M. Young, *Victorian Essays* (London, 1962) p. 114.

22. *Don Juan*, Canto XI, LXXXI.

23. Peter Gunn (ed.), *Byron, Selected Prose* (Harmondsworth, 1972) p. 110.

24. Ibid., p. 108.

25. *Amours de Voyage*, Canto V, X.

26. T. L. Connolly (ed.), *Literary Criticisms by Francis Thompson* (New York, 1948) pp. 115–16.

27. W. H. Auden and Louis MacNeice, *Letters from Iceland* (London, 1937) p. 58.

3 Byron and France

Byron as a Political Figure

ROBERT ESCARPIT

Knowledgeable scholars, and especially scholars in comparative literature, usually admit that a postulate for Byron's literary reputation was the commercial success of *Childe Harold*. In spite of his often voiced wishes and of his repeated protests, that dubious masterpiece and involuntary best-seller (though not so good a seller as is often believed) is generally used to assess the weight and stature of the man in history and of the writer in literature.

Such a warped view of reality is neither a whim of destiny, nor one of those fortuitous deviations which may occasionally be observed in the literary fortunes of a writer. It is quite consciously and wilfully that some of the most essential features of Byron's character have been ignored or even erased by the cultural and literary apparatus of a social class on which he had been thrown by the chances of an improbable heritage and to which he never really belonged.

No publisher ever encouraged the satirical vein in the manner of Gifford which inspired Byron's first poems. On reading or re-reading *English Bards and Scotch Reviewers* or *The Curse of Minerva*, one cannot but admit that the success of *Childe Harold* stifled the voice of a great polemicist whose toned-down echoes are to be found in *The Vision of Judgment* or *The Age of Bronze*. After having been re-established by John Murray on account of his performance in the first two cantos of *Childe Harold*, and after having been engaged by Murray in his literary factory as a specialist of melancholy moods, of inconsequential revolt, powerless bitterness and mysterious exoticism, Byron later was amicably but firmly dismissed by his publisher and literary advisors when, having exhausted the poor resources of that vein, he tried to strike back through *Don Juan* towards the main stream of militant poetry which in his heart of hearts he had never forsaken.

Only after his death was it possible to salvage what he had been able to write of *Don Juan* and to integrate it as a minor contribution to the great papier mâché monument of conventional Byronism. Dead or alive, Byron is doomed to remain first and foremost the author of *Childe Harold*: that has been graven on marble over his tomb in Hucknall Torkard. In the so-called "complete works" which are put at the disposal of students and from which academic programmes are drawn, one would seek in vain his political speeches and those masterpieces of journalistic prose which are some of his journals and letters. Not until 1972 were sizeable extracts from those hitherto much ignored texts revealed to the public at large by the Peter Gunn edition of *Lord Byron's Selected Prose* in the Penguin series.

It is a moot point between scholars which, *Childe Harold* or *Don Juan*, is the better poem and which more truthfully expresses Byron's personality. It all depends on the way they are read and on the image of Byron which the reader projects on them: the meretricious symbol of a cheap romanticism or the harsh truth of a historical man. If we admit the second type of reading, we must admit, too, that Byron is present in every single word he wrote, in the most cacophonous of his verses, in the sharpest of his points, in the most humorous of his commentaries, in the darkest of his ruminations. No writer is less detached from his writings, and that lack of distance between the artist and his work may well lead us to wonder whether Byron is really a writer in the sense generally accepted by contemporary criticism.

Twenty-five years ago, I began my doctorate thesis in these words: "*On a parlé de Byron beaucoup plus qu'on ne l'a lu*" (Byron has been talked about much more than he has been read). That sentence could be understood in many ways, but it mainly referred to the irruption of Byron into the ideological environment of young Europe between 1825 and 1848. That irruption can hardly have been due to the bland, insipid, untruthful and misleading translation of Amédée Pichot, which more or less consciously blotted out Byron's revolutionary message. Byron imposed himself not so much through his writings as through his death in Missolonghi, a militant example which was so irrefutable that it could appear as a challenge as well as a token of remorse.

It is said that G.K. Chesterton answered once to a friend who was shocked by the harshness of French political caricature at the end of the nineteenth century: "Oh, but then you never died on the barricades!" During many years between 1820 and 1871, many young Frenchmen had to die on the barricades. In a way, directly or indirectly, Byron helped them die.

Truth to say, the effect of Byron on the so-called romantic generation was rather disappointing. In his unjustly forgotten work, *Byron et le romantisme français* (Paris, 1907), Edmond Estève has left very few stones unturned. His outlook is mainly literary, and in fact there is very little extra-literary influence to be found in the works of the main French romantics. All of them dreamed of writing a *"dernier chant de Childe Harold"*, and some of them wrote what amounted to it. In all these productions the reference to Byron appears as a form of wishful thinking. Each of these writers chose in Byron what was more suitable to his own mood: Hugo took the Eastern color, Vigny took the stoicism of the darker meditations, Musset took the flippancy of the satire without its pungency.

The case of Lamartine is somewhat different. Among the romantics he is, by his age, the nearest to Byron's generation and he had the chance of an active political career somewhat in the line of what Byron defined as his political ideal in his Journal of 23 November 1813: "To be the first man – not the Dictator – not the Sylla, but the Washington or the Aristides – the leader in talent and truth – is next to Divinity! Franklin, Penn, and, next to these, either Brutus or Cassius – even Mirabeau – or St. Just." That was roughly the political programme on which Lamartine failed in front of the rising tide of resurgent Bonapartism in 1849.

But Lamartine never had any opportunity to read Byron's Journal. Like many of his contemporaries he had been a victim of Amédée Pichot's deceptions. His first reaction on reading the 1819 translation (which did not include *Don Juan*) was to save Byron's soul. Byron was very indignant when he heard about it and strongly resented being called *"chantre d'enfer"*. Obviously Byron's death in Missolonghi was a revelation for Lamartine. It certainly was quite consonant with his preoccupations at the time. In his work on *Le Jocelyn de Lamartine* (Paris, 1936) Professor Henri Guillemin quotes a number of significant extracts of Lamartine's correspondence between 1826 and 1829. Some are wistful: *"Assister à cette résurrection d'un empire sur la terre des souvenirs* (i.e. Greece), *et y participer moi-même comme Lord Byron..."* Some are piteous: *"Si je n'étais pas marié, j'irais me battre pour les Grecs."*

In fact, Lamartine had a better excuse then he knew at that time for not going to Greece: actual revolutions were brewing in his own country, an advantage which Byron was denied.

Although we have little direct evidence, there is no doubt that the 1830 revolutionary generation was strongly marked by Byron's influence, but less in its national than in its international aspect. The "louis-philipparde" revolution was indeed a very limited upheaval as far as France was concerned. The new regime contrasted to the *Restoration* system only because the latter was strongly anachronistic and the Britain of young Victoria soon appeared far in advance of the France of the ageing Louis-Philippe. On the other hand, France became then the cross-roads and headquarters of all the revolutionary movements in Europe, bent on the freeing of the nationalities. And there Byron's living message was heard and commended. There are many examples of political exiles carrying it from France to their own countries. One of the most striking is that of José de Espronceda who got acquainted with Byron in Paris and later awoke a wave of partially political Byronism in the Spain of the forties. In the same way, one could trace an Italian, a German, a Polish and a Russian Byronism which originated in French intellectual circles between 1830 and 1848.

There does not seem to have been any direct Byronic influence on the 1848 revolution in France, although there has been no serious research in that field. The fact is that the new rising force of Marxism (quite mistakenly) ignored Byron. In a well-known passage Karl Marx himself pointed out Shelley as the true revolutionary of the famous pair. An involuntary prisoner of Romanticism, Byron was included in its negation by the scientific socialists. He was absent from the great upheaval which through 1848, the Commune, and the October Revolution, led from the era of hope to that of accomplishment. Only lately, thanks to the work of scholars such as Anna Elistratova, has he recovered in the USSR some of the prestige he deserved.

In France Byron fell a victim to the contradictions of the intellectuals of the mid-nineteenth century, who were robbed by Napoleon III of their illusions yet unable to choose between action and literature. In fact he had come too early, and the yet unaccomplished revelation of his unknown writings came too late. His political thought was strong and lucid, but no one knew. What remained of him was a kind of mythical image not unlike that of Che Guevara in the 1970s but it lacked the underlying strength of militant ideology and of organised action, such as that offered in our days by the revolutionary parties or groups. It only symbolised the still unorganised drive of the peoples towards their freedom and their independence. It took Byron his whole life to find his appointed place in the first skirmishes of the long struggle. We now know that place was not the one he deserved, and only now can we appreciate the full significance of Byron as a political figure.

Byron was a political figure even by his birth in the poor lower middle class, very near the workers which the industrial revolution had driven towards the towns and which the wild mechanisation of capitalist industry had doomed to unemployment and misery. As the penniless Lord Byron of Newstead Abbey, he was able to observe in 1811 the first Luddite riots in Nottingham and particularly the assault of the workers against the new knitting machines which deprived them of their work. He also was able to witness the ruthless repression which ensued.

The fate of the Nottingham workers was probably quite a minor issue for the Whigs and their leader Lord Holland. But the Bill introduced by the Tory government and tending to inflict the death penalty for the destruction of machines, was an excellent opportunity for a parliamentary skirmish. We do not know whether Byron volunteered to take this opportunity for his maiden speech. We do know that he took the job seriously. The Whig notables of Nottingham had provided him with a full dossier and an outline of the arguments he was to use, the gist of them being to strike at the harsh policy of the government towards the frame breakers.

A few days before the speech he wrote to Lord Holland, explaining that he preferred to use his own arguments, based on his own experience. And that is what he did on the 27 February 1812 in terms to which the House of Lords was not accustomed. It is less a matter of tone than of clear-headed social and political analysis, as will be evidenced by the following quotations:

> The rejected workmen, in the blindness of their ignorance, instead of rejoicing at these improvements in arts so beneficial to mankind, conceived themselves to be sacrificed to improvements in mechanism. In the foolishness of their hearts they imagined that the maintenance and well-doing of the industrious poor were objects of greater consequence than the enrichment of a few individuals by any improvement, in the implements of

trade, which threw the workmen out of employment, and rendered the labourer unworthy of his hire.

These men were willing to dig, but the spade was in other hands: they were not ashamed to beg, but there was none to relieve them; their own means of subsistence were cut off, all other employments pre-occupied; and their excesses, however to be deplored and condemned, can hardly be subject of surprise.

You call these men a mob . . . Are we aware of our obligations to a mob? It is the mob that labour in your fields and serve in your houses, – that man your navy, and recruit your army, – that have enabled you to defy all the world, and can also defy you when neglect and calamity have driven them to despair! You may call the people a mob; but do not forget that a mob too often speaks the sentiments of the people.

Considering that those words were uttered in 1812, before any theoretician of socialism had denounced the structures of monopolistic capitalism or described the mechanism of class struggle, one may think Karl Marx would have been likely to revise his judgement on Byron if he had known of them. On the other hand, one may easily imagine the effect of such a speech in a world such as ours, dominated by radio and television. In fact it had then practically no immediate effect. There was in it as much to be gained by the noble Lords of the opposition as by those of the majority, but there was much more for millions outside the narrow circle of the leading class. In that circle the speech was considered a success as a piece of oratory. The content was ignored, for the time being at least.

But memories endure. Byron made two more speeches in the House of Lords. One, again on behalf of the Whig party, was on the Catholic problem in Ireland. Its Swiftian irony is still telling in our days and some of its passages have remarkably modern accents. The third speech was a short intervention which Byron made of his own accord to sustain Major Cartwright's petition in favour of parliamentary reform. Although there was still some praise, criticism became increasingly louder. It was not voiced more openly at the time because Byron, two days after his maiden speech, had "found himself famous" thanks to *Childe Harold* and had chosen a literary career instead of a political one. But when in 1816 his separation led to social ostracism, his peers who hooted him out of the House of Lords certainly had more serious grievances against him than his having been abandoned by his wife.

Between 1813 and 1820 Byron's political ideas were less clear than they had been before. He was fascinated by Napoleon in whom he recognised the leader of an international revolution although he did not appreciate his dictatorial ways and did not wish to see him in Britain. He was both relieved and disappointed by his defeat. It was only in Ravenna, when he met the *carbonari* in Countess Guiccioli's entourage, that he began to evolve towards a new political attitude which is partially reflected in the first cantos of *Don Juan*. These were not appreciated by the British establishment and consequently by John Murray, who proved reluctant to pursue a literary experiment which was later vetoed by Countess Guiccioli on the ground of immorality. During eighteen months Byron gave way to that double pressure. Meanwhile he dabbled with the idea of revolution. He thought of joining Bolivar. He tried to help the *carbonari* but soon discovered they were poor revolutionists: "I always had an idea that it would be *bungled*," he wrote bitterly in his journal of 24 February 1821, after the failure of a general Italian uprising.

As far as Britain is concerned, his main grievances were more of a moral than of a political nature at that moment. On 7 February 1821, in the first letter on Bowles, what he denounces is hypocrisy: "The truth is, that in these days the grand '*primum mobile*' of England is *cant*; cant political, cant poetical, cant religious, cant moral; but always *cant*, multiplied through all the varieties of life." *Don Juan* is aimed at cant in general, although later, probably under the influence of Shelley, Byron tends to emphasise what he calls "cant political".

Later, when he broke off with Murray, he was drawn by the Hunt brothers towards a kind of republican radicalism that did not really appeal to him. The character of the English *milord*, which had become part of his acquired nature, could hardly be reconciled with the idea of an English republic. Nevertheless, in 1823, *The Age of Bronze*, which was printed by the Hunts in *The Liberal*, shows that Byron's pre-Marxian analysis of British society was still in force. In stanza 14 when he denounces precisely the cant of the landed gentry who hide under the magical word *rent* all kinds of oppressions and sordid interests, he very clear-sightedly describes a class policy founded on money and profit. Cobbett, who made similar remarks at the time, was probably less realistic than Byron.

But the main theme of *The Age of Bronze* is broader. It opposes to the governments of the Holy Alliance an impressive evocation of a worldwide revolutionary upheaval of the peoples struggling towards their freedom and independence. I personally have often wondered if, many years later, the translator of the words of the *International*, had thought of *The Age of Bronze* when he wrote:

> For Reason in revolt now thunders
> And at last ends the age of cant!

If he did not, this is another instance of that prophetic quality which characterises Byron's political thought.

At that time, Byron's political thought takes a loftier turn by becoming international. That is a trend which can be traced as far back as the first canto of *Childe Harold*, where he scolds the Portuguese for proving unable to assume the duties of independence. The new attitude, however, matured in Italy, as is shown by a passage in the Ravenna journal dated 18 Febuary 1821:

> It is a grand object – the very *poetry* of politics. Only think – a free Italy!!! Why, there has been nothing like it since the days of Augustus. I reckon the times of Caesar (Julius) free; because the commotions left every body a side to take, and the parties were pretty equal at the set out. But afterwards, it was all praetorian and legionary business – and since! – we shall see, or, at least, some will see, what card will turn up.

The remark on Caesar is most enlightening. Perhaps Byron, who knew Madame de Staël, was not unaware of her change of attitude when, after a lifelong fight against Napoleon's tyranny, she found that national independence came foremost and that freedom had no sense without it. For 150 years the world has been learning that lesson the hard way, and is still learning it.

That explains why in that very year of 1823 Byron accepted a kind of compromise with the British establishment through the Philhellenic Committee, although he had very few illusions in respect of the real purposes of those philanthropists, as his letter to John Bowring of 12 May 1823 shows:

> I need not suggest to the Committee the very great advantage

which must accrue to Great Britain from the success of the Greeks, and their probable commercial relations with England in consequence; because I feel persuaded that the first object of the Committee is their EMANCIPATION, without any interested views. But the consideration might weigh with the English people in general, in their present passion for any kind of speculation, – they need not cross the American seas for one much better worth their while, and nearer home.

John Bowring could hardly miss the lashing irony of that statement.

Ironical as he might have been, Byron was certainly clear-headed about the investment, as he was clear-headed about the political and military strategy. History does not tell if Winston Churchill took Byron's *Letters and Journals* with him to Yalta, but he might have taken a worse adviser.

But Byron had other reasons to fight for Greece. As soon as he heard that revolution was flaring up in that country which he knew well for having spent two years of his youth in it and to which he was always attracted, he knew that he had been appointed by destiny to take the lead. On that Odyssean *nostimon hêmar* – the Day of the Return – he forsook the pen for the sword.

And he did it in a most efficient way. The delegate from the Philhellenic Committee suddenly turned into a political and military chief who most completely took in hand an almost desperate situation. Some military writer, a specialist of revolutionary warfare, should some day seriously study Byron's activity in Greece. He would find good lessons in guerilla tactics. One may think Byron used that Skander Beg who was in the fifteenth century the father of Albanian independence as a model. Most characteristically, Byron was more pro-Albanian than pro-Greek. He did not let himself be blinded by the easy alibi of a new state to be founded. He thought and repeated that a people win their freedom over their oppressors, whoever they may be. He liked the Albanians because he knew them to be proud and indomitable. He distrusted the Greeks for their passivity, as he had previously the Portuguese. He was not far from preferring the Turks against whom he was fighting. Indeed his fight in Missolonghi was not that of the Greek politicians, but that of the independence of the people at large.

The disillusioned French intellectuals of 1850 had closed their Byron, but others were soon to open it again at the page of

Missolonghi when, after 1860, the awakening of the nationalities came to the front of world politics.

Jules Verne, who was born four years after Byron's death, affords us an excellent example of that new political Byronism in *Twenty Thousand Leagues Under the Sea* and in its sequel *The Mysterious Island*. Captain Nemo, an Indian prince fighting for the independence of his country, is an obviously Byronic character, and when he addresses the Ocean, he does it almost in the same terms as Byron in the fourth canto of *Childe Harold*. We see him help the Greek insurgents and fight British imperialism. When he reveals his identity, it is to Americans escaped from the War of Secession one of whom is a Black. And the mysterious island which is the last harbour and grave of *Nautilus*, is almost identical to Byron's description of the abode of the mutineers of the *Bounty* in *The Island*.

For generations that underground and often unconscious influence of Byron endured in French minds, and especially when came for France the time of revolutionary warfare under a more bitter oppression than Byron had ever dreamt of – that of the Nazis.

In Missolonghi Byron was one of the first to experience the ruthless realities of the kind of fight we still know in which are inextricably mixed the idealist and the mercenary, the militant and the military, the politicians and the adventurers, the peoples in arms and the calculated interests of the great powers. The army, at the head of which Byron found himself thrown on arriving at Missolonghi, strangely pre-figures the international brigades of the Spanish Civil War, a century later.

One could easily compare Malraux in 1936 with Byron in 1824. The former had the terrible misfortune of surviving that hour of glory – perhaps because his involvement was less deep, less total than Byron's. A squadron leader is not the commander-in-chief of an army doomed to suicide. But if one wants to understand Byron in Missolonghi, one must read Malraux's *L'Espoir*. One will find there both the lyrical illusion and the clogging atrocity of a mud-stuck war. I personally have always been struck by the uncanny resemblance of two orders of the day, one by Byron in Missolonghi, one by Malraux's hero Magnin trying to reorganise his fighter squadron. In almost identical terms they say the same: mercenaries will be paid off and the others will have to accept regular army discipline.

And, last but not least, if I may put forward my personal experience, when I had to abandon for a time my thesis on Byron in 1944 to throw myself into the adventure which was to transform, through fighting, the lyrically stampeding crowd of the Resistance forces into an efficient national army, Byron was my guide. Although they did not know it, some of the guidelines, that helped the stumbling soldiers of darkness to find their way through the blinding light of regained freedom, harked back through the years to the lonely figure in Missolonghi.

4 Byron and Germany

The Shadow of Euphorion

CEDRIC HENTSCHEL

No other British writer except Shakespeare has seized so tenacious a hold on the German imagination; and even Shakespeare has not been more lavishly praised or more avidly imitated. Whether as poet, legend, portent of social change or symbol of the human predicament, Byron's ascendancy in Germany is the more remarkable because it lacks that local connection which, in Greece, Italy, and Switzerland, gave his fame and after-fame an immediate appeal. Here, one accordingly feels, are works that must surely possess compelling genius if they can penetrate so widely into a culture to which Byron himself – despite the reiterated obeisances he paid to Goethe – remained largely unresponsive. A complementary argument suggests that the Germans themselves must be peculiarly susceptible to the blandishments of Byronism, in all its contradictory manifestations. There may well be truth in both these conjectures.

Byron was too deeply committed to Graeco–Roman civilisation and the lure of the Mediterranean and the Near East to sense a close affinity with any northern country other than Scotland. His acquaintance with German scenery was confined to his journey up the Rhine in May 1816 during the initial phase of his exile. The picturesque banks of the river, with their castle-topped crags, moved the Pilgrim to pen a few appreciative stanzas, for he found the changing views refreshing after the insipid flats of the Low Countries; yet they could not instil the exaltation which the Alps and Lake Geneva were later to excite in him. Byron's first-hand knowledge of Germany – the country, the language, the people – was thus slight; but like most cultivated Englishmen of his generation he had access to the brilliant analysis of Mme de Staël, whose *De l'Allemagne* he praised; and Byron's library furnishes a few ad-

59

ditional clues. It included several works on Prussian history, in particular biographies of Frederick the Great. He also possessed August Wilhelm Schlegel's *Lectures on the History of Literature* – he had got to know the author in Mme de Staël's Swiss salon – but seems to have had some difficulty in assimilating Schlegel's ideas. In a revealing comment on Schlegel's brother Friedrich, he attacks the cloudiness of thought often regarded as the besetting sin of the German intellectual: "He always seems on the verge of meaning; and, lo, he goes down like a sunset or melts like a rainbow."

Apart from the pervasive influence of *Faust* on his dramas (he had heard 'Monk' Lewis declaim passages from Goethe's master-piece in Switzerland), there are few references in Byron's own works to suggest more than a superficial concern with German literature and history. Light-hearted, though not always unami-able, ridicule is his stock response to Teutonic themes. In his amusing satirical poem, *The Waltz*, Byron acknowledges Britain's debt to Germany in certain non-literary fields:

> Imperial Waltz! imported from the Rhine
> (Famed for the growth of pedigrees and wine),
> Long be thine import from all duty free,
> And hock itself be less esteemed than thee.

This "Apostrophic Hymn" also makes disparaging allusions to the plays of Kotzebue and the weighty tomes of 'Heyne' – not the poet, but the famed Göttingen classical scholar, who was later to be identified by some critics as the model for Carlyle's Professor Teu-felsdröckh. Such trivia may half mask the paradox that Byron was indebted for material and atmosphere to some of the greatest names in German literature. While he viewed Goethe as the non-pareil and the Faustian quest often absorbed his own thinking – arousing a last echo in *The Deformed Transformed* – Byron had, since boyhood, also admired Schiller, whose *Robbers* and *The Ghost-Seer* quickened his interest both in the Hero as Rebel and in Venice as an incomparably evocative setting. Even the soporific Wieland, for the most part uncongenial, left his improbable mark on the Gul-beyaz episode in Canto V of *Don Juan*. Thanks to readily accessible translations in English, French and Italian, Byron thus owed not a little – including the theme of *Werner* – to German sources. The debt was handsomely repaid: the Works of Byron were to engage the minds of successive generations of German writers, thinkers and politicians.

When Byron found the waltz an agreeable theme for satire, Germany lay crushed at Napoleon's feet, and his main intent was to deride Britain's Hanoverian monarchy:

> Oh, Germany! how much to thee we owe,
> As heaven–born Pitt can testify below,
> Ere cursed confederation made thee France's,
> And only left us thy d – d debts and dances!

And he added, tongue-in-cheek:

> Of subsidies and Hanover bereft,
> We bless thee still – for George the Third is left!

Because of the mingled adulation and revulsion Byron felt for Napoleon, he must have had mixed feelings about Napoleon's conquerors; but the Coalition certainly afforded opportunities for Byron to ponder the strengths and weaknesses of Britain's allies, as when, in "the Summer of the Sovereigns" (1814), the author of *Childe Harold* was caught up in the excitement that attended the appearance in London of the King of Prussia, as well as Blücher and his own future foe, Metternich. It was largely on Metternich's account that, towards the end of his life, Byron began to draw an invidious distinction between the Germans and the Austrians. On 12 January, 1821, he recorded in his Diary:

> I like, however, their women (I was once *so desperately* in love with a German woman, Constance) and all that I have read, translated, of their writings, and all that I have seen on the Rhine of their country and people – all, except the Austrians, whom I abhor, loathe, and – I cannot find words for my hate of them, and should be sorry to find deeds correspondent to my hate; for I abhor cruelty more than I abhor the Austrians – except on an impulse, and then I am savage – but not deliberately so . . . .

An exception to the general ban was allowed in favour of "a great and goodly writer", the dramatist Franz Grillparzer, in whose verse-dramas Byron had noted "a high intellect". Ultimately his jaundiced view of the Austrians was however, extended to include all their associates, so that (as we learn from Trelawny) on his last voyage to Greece he spoke of the Bourbons and the Neapolitan Government as "the jackals and hangmen of the detestable Austrian barbarians".

Not that Byron's opinion of the North Germans mellowed with advancing years! Prussia, as encountered by Don Juan, evoked the familiar note of banter:

> From Poland they came on through Prussia Proper,
> And Königsberg the capital, whose vaunt,
> Besides some veins of iron, lead or copper,
> Has lately been the great Professor Kant.
> Juan, who cared not a tobacco-stopper
> About philosophy, pursued his jaunt
> To Germany, whose somewhat tardy millions
> Have princes who spur more than their postillions.

Fortunately, personal relationships have a way of overcoming prejudice – rising above cliché attitudes and collective antipathies – or else that awesome meeting of minds, the mutual appraisal of Byron and Goethe, could scarcely have led to reciprocal esteem and lent a powerful impetus to Byronism in Germany. If Goethe's European stature gives a ready warrant for Byron's veneration, Goethe's singular regard for Byron is less easy to motivate, especially if we recall E. M. Butler's pointed comment: "Though Byron was no Germanophil, he fell many degrees short of Goethe's Anglophobia."[1] Yet the rising tide of Goethe's "passion" is plainly charted. *Manfred* and *Cain* were both analysed and lauded; in the former Goethe recognised an ingenious variation on his own Faustian theme; and it was after reading *Cain* in 1823 that he confided to Chancellor Müller: "Byron alone do I admit to a place at my side." Goethe's versified greeting, which concluded with the fatherly exhortation

> And the way I've perceived him, so may he see himself!

reached Byron just before he sailed from Leghorn in July 1823 and was countered with a friendly reply. The way now seemed well prepared for a personal meeting – had Byron lived.

But all too soon Goethe was compelled to write his controversial obituary. This amounted to little more than an account of his own association – he called it, more intimately, his *Lebensverhältnis* –

with his lamented friend. It was first published in 1824, in the original German as well as an English version, in Thomas Medwin's *Journal of the Conversations of Lord Byron.* As a valedictory it bears anomalous features, lacking the spontaneous warmth of much that Goethe wrote or said about his favourite. He refers to himself obliquely as "the German admirer", and his cumbrous syntax and stilted phraseology evoked merriment among some of his German critics. Johann Gries went so far as to call the eulogy "this strange diplomatic note", adding that nothing had ever reminded him so vividly of the antiquated officialese practised in Ratisbon under the auspices of the Holy Roman Empire.[2] Was this aloofness possibly intended to mark Goethe's displeasure with Byron's countrymen? The unwonted tone certainly does suggest the fundamental ambiguity which underlay his "passion", though it might also be charitable to assume that Goethe was numbed by grief and could not, thus soon, come to terms with his loss.

Far from being extinguished, the relationship was to blossom further, posthumously, and to bear remarkable fruit during the eight years that Goethe still had left to live after Byron's death. Indeed, the Sage of Weimar was to intensify his Byron studies, showering especial praise on *The Vision of Judgment,* a work which may well have prompted his own treatment of the struggle between Mephistopheles and the Angels for Faust's soul at the end of his drama. Goethe was also to receive two further communications from Byron, from beyond the grave as it were – one wholly delightful, the other irksome. In March 1826, C. F. Benecke, the university librarian at Göttingen, sent him a package containing the personal dedication which had been annoyingly omitted from the first edition of *Sardanapalus.* And could there have been a more handsome acknowledgement of his powers than for Byron to address him as his *liege lord*? However, a jarring note was to be struck in 1829 when John Murray, roving the continent on a tour that was to engender the celebrated Murray Handbooks, himself delivered yet another dedication in Weimar, to add to the tributes already paid in *Sardanapalus, Werner* and *The Deformed Transformed*; for in his prefatory reflections on *Marino Faliero* Byron had dared to echo Mme de Staël's accusation that *Werther* had more suicides to answer for than the loveliest woman; and had not shrunk from heaping scorn on the Classical-versus-Romantic controversy – "terms which were not subjects of classification when I was in England".

By the time these irreverent sallies reached him, Goethe had already, and irreversibly, conferred upon Byron the ultimate accolade. Though he withheld the Second Part of *Faust* for posthumous publication, he deliberately excepted the Helena-Act from the general ban. Separately printed in 1827, it bore as a sub-title, "Classical-Romantical Phantasmagoria" – a curious irony in view of Byron's stricture; but there can be no doubt that it was Goethe's eagerness to reincarnate Byron symbolically in the figure of Euphorion, the son of Helena and Faust, which impelled him to allow this portion of his last major work to go to press ahead of the remainder.

In ancient myth, the winged Euphorion, son of the shades of Helen and Achilles, was slain by a jealous Zeus. In the folk-book, as in Marlowe's play, Faust had already replaced Achilles; but the allegorial significance now accorded to Euphorion–Byron, the fruit of this improbable union, was entirely Goethe's invention and one to which he had given much thought.[3] What, one wonders, would Byron himself have made of the heroic ancestry thus foisted upon him? Certainly the uneasy conjunction of Gothic and Classi-cal components, manifest in much of his earlier verse, suggests an unstable heredity. But Goethe went farther, sensing in the opposed paternal and maternal strains a formula for disaster: the death of Euphorion, when his wings refuse to bear him, is the poetic reflec-tion of Byron's death in Greece. In this way Goethe identified Byron's "meteoric" career not only with the rise and fall of many other ill-fated men of genius, but with what he regarded as the ulti-mate cause of their misfortune: the destructive and self-destructive powers inherent in their demonic temperaments. His comments on the demonic – a semi-mystical concept fraught with contradiction because it also embraces the positive aspects of genius – open vast perspectives. Indeed, however ambivalent its effects may be, the demonic plays a key-role in modern German letters.[4]

While it is clear that in his portrayal of Euphorion Goethe was both eulogising and passing judgement on Byron, it is less easy to define what precise relevance this symbolic figure held for himself. It is not in dispute that in part he equated Byron with the author of *Werther* – with his own youthful self, who had only narrowly escaped tracing the same impetuous path as Euphorion. Perhaps he was convinced that after the cathartic relief he obtained from writing *Werther*, he had succeeded in mastering the demonic and now held its opposed forces in precarious but stimulating balance;

yet his satisfaction may also have been tinged with regret; and it is when one tries to fathom the nature of this "regret" that his relationship with Byron, his *Lebensverhältnis*, appears most suggestive.

The paradox of Euphorion becomes more intelligible if we recall the nature of the flaws even admirers detected in Goethe's mature personality. There is the suggestion that he withdrew from the hurly-burly of life into his private citadel, and that even his duties as a courtier and administrator in Weimar were camouflaged aspects of the familiar Ivory Tower; or, to put it in the current jargon, that he was not overtly "committed" to social betterment. Travelling in Italy at the outset of the French Revolution, he was more preoccupied with Torquato Tasso's introspective musings than with the dynamic aspirations of oppressed millions. Except for the farcical one-act play, *The Citizen-General*, most of his writings associated with the Revolution remained mere fragments – "a good illustration of what the world calls his indifferentism", to employ a phrase used by Longfellow in an analogous context.[5] And the general charge of 'indifferentism' is often bracketed with the specific accusation of servility toward social superiors. So staunch a worshipper at the shrine as J. G. Robertson felt compelled to note Goethe's "obsequiousness toward the Duke of Weimar" as an unpleasant instance of "that peculiarly sentimental toadying to princes and princelets which was characteristic of German life and letters in the eighteenth century".[6] Perhaps there is a touch of this same attitude in Goethe's Byron–worship, neatly parried by Byron, one may feel, when he declared himself to be Goethe's vassal.

Of the many comments Goethe made about Byron and his works, two in particular stress that topicality of outlook which he was elsewhere inclined to regard as suspect. There is the assertion, reported by Eckermann in July 1827, "Byron is not antique and not romantic, but he is like the present day itself" – a verdict oddly similar to Shelley's belief that *Don Juan* was "something wholly new and relative to the age"; and there is the acute observation that Byron's poems are "pent-up parliamentary harangues". Did such comments perhaps imply a belated acknowledgement that Literature, being graced with many mansions, has room not only for the aloof and formal structures enjoined by classicism, but also for that committed writing that springs from rebellious iconoclasm? If Byron indeed 'converted' Goethe in this sense, it was not the least remarkable of his many conquests. Yet it may be that the aged author of the Second Part of *Faust* felt relief as well as anguish when he sent Euphorion to his doom; for a living, a triumphant Euphorion would have called in question the quietist pattern of his own later life and the validity of suppressing those demonic forces which could inspire as well as destroy. Goethe's praise is thus everywhere accompanied by silent self-questioning; and if his immense prestige reinforced Byron's afterfame not only in Germany but throughout Europe, it is equally true that in choosing to commemorate his dead friend in the pitiful figure of Euphorion, Goethe established an ominous precedent for the development of the Byronic hero in German literature and for the personal fate of the many writers who sought to mould themselves in what they mistakenly believed to be Byron's image.

Long before Goethe's death in 1832, the literary progeny of Byron in Germany – a motley throng, differing in their aspirations, capabilities and social provenance – were already deluging their publishers with a mixed bag of Byronic improvisations, in which narcissistic self-revelation vied with the pallid exoticism of pseudo-oriental verse-tales, while a predilection for the fate-tragedy cast a thickening gloom on the German stage. Some of these imitators, among them the youthful Heine, were not without promise. The frenzied Swabian poet, Wilhelm Waiblinger, also deserves mention. In his tragically brief life he produced work which forms a curious link between Byron and Hölderlin: his four epic romances in verse, *Tales from the History of Contemporary Greece*, appeared in the year of Byron's death, while Phaeton, the hero of his novel, has traits which were modelled on the demented Hölderlin. Waiblinger himself must have been unaware of the striking affinity between the legend of Phaeton and the legend of Euphorion: but hindsight makes the parallel uncannily apt.

At the opposite end of the Byronic spectrum we encounter the robust and diverting Count Hermann von Pückler-Muskau, who presents unusually pressing claims in the context of the present survey: he was more familiar than most of his countrymen with British institutions and British society, having gallivanted in London with the Regency bucks during a vain search for an heiress to prop up his ailing finances; he had discussed Byron with Goethe in Weimar; and, more significantly, his travels in Greece in 1836 enabled him to assess with authority the political consequences of Byron's climactic exploit.

Pückler-Muskau's observations are the more compelling because of the many Byronic touches in his own character. He differs agreeably from the general run of Byron's German disciples in being more sanguine than morbid in temperament, though he, too, was occasionally overtaken by fits of hypochondria: it was not for nothing that Immermann, that connoisseur of modish ridicule, taunted him with having learnt Spleen from a Master in London. In its infectious zest, roving diversity of interests, and its external trappings, Pückler-Muskau's mode of life aped Byron's with conscious fidelity. The Prince liked to dress up in oriental costume and to flaunt outlandish weapons, to travel *en grand seigneur* by coach or on horseback, accompanied by a retinue of servants. He had a weakness for exotic women of humble station whom he would rescue from servitude; one such black slave he personally gave to Lady Hester Stanhope in Syria, and he brought an Abyssinian girl back with him to Germany. Fond of dogs and fond of swimming, he took daily dips in the Nile – even close to the cataracts. Like Byron he spent lavishly. As a consequence he had to relinquish his great estate at Muskau, as Byron was compelled to sell Newstead Abbey. But there were traits in him which also suggest more positive correspondences. Anti-imperialists, both men disliked the appurtenances of the colonial system. And they were not merely opposed to slavery. Just as Byron objected (in *The Curse of Minerva*) to the rape of the Elgin Marbles, so Pückler-Muskau denounced the French for removing the ancient obelisk from Philae; and both showed concern for radical writers less privileged than themselves – Byron for Leigh Hunt, Pückler-Muskau for Heine.

The parallels must not be pressed too far. Pückler-Muskau's literary abilities were of a lower order. He possessed no skill in writing verse, although at its best the prose of his travel-narratives displays something of Byron's colourful vitality. But in two important respects his path was the more fortunate. Born three years before Byron, he was to enjoy a long life; and his obsession with landscape gardening suggests an enviable capacity to switch to more tranquil pursuits and so achieve an inner peace. To the end, however, he retained an air of Byronic panache. Above all he shared with his Master certain fundamental ambiguities, reserving to himself an elitist posture, based on birth and wealth, while proclaiming a libertarian message; and in the duality of his career – his constant "scribbling" sorting oddly with his unslaked thirst for action – he stands before us as a kind of Byronic *Doppelgänger*.

Of Pückler-Muskau's multiple works, the two lengthy journals of his travels in England and Greece are both haunted by Byron's shade. The earlier of these accounts, covering the years 1826–9, was soon made available in English.[7] Before setting off for London the author had paid his respects to Goethe in Weimar. A thwarted diplomat – he longed to be Prussian Ambassador in Constantinople – Pückler-Muskau was a consummate flatterer. He told Goethe he saw him as a spiritual Napoleon who had subjugated the whole of Europe but had "no Waterloo to dread". In cordial mood, Goethe found it a good moment to make yet another pronouncement on Byron:

> He afterwards spoke of Byron with great affection, almost as a father would of a son. . . . He contradicted the silly assertion that *Manfred* was only an echo of his *Faust*. . . . He very much regretted that he had never become personally acquainted with Lord Byron and severely and justly reproached the English nation for having judged their illustrious countryman so pettily and understood him so ill.

Byron's spirit was again invoked in Britain, though not always in an agreeable context. Riding past Newstead Abbey, Pückler-Muskau noted that the family seat (he wrongly calls it the birthplace) was "now much neglected"; and in London he was distressed to find the "hideous melodrama", *The Vampire*, falsely attributed to Byron. When the Countess H— took Lady Byron's part in the marital dispute, Pückler-Muskau sagely commented:

> I did not put implicit faith in this account, in spite of my great respect for the narrator. The soul of a poet like Byron is hard to judge; the ordinary standard is quite inadequate for it, and very few people have any other to apply.

There is thus ample testimony that Pückler-Muskau shared Goethe's enthusiasm for Byron. He hailed him as the greatest English writer since Shakespeare, while at the same time echoing Goethe's contempt for British snobbishness and hypocrisy. A less convincing tribute was his adoption of the pseudonym "Semilasso", for despite his self-proclaimed nervous disorders, Pückler-Muskau is miscast in the role of a devitalised, "semi-exhausted"

Byronic stereotype.

It was with rather keen anticipation that Semilasso decided to travel from North Africa to the Orient via Greece; we may be sure that Byron's adventures on Greek soil, a decade earlier, were vividly in his mind when he came ashore at Patras in December 1835. And for Pückler-Muskau, the seasoned political commentator, there was now an added attraction, for it was a Wittelsbach, Otto, the second son of Ludwig I of Bavaria, who now sat on the Greek throne. By a quirk of European politics, an interventionist mission had been thrust upon an untried German prince. Following the assassination of Kapodistrias, first president of a free Greece, in 1831, the protecting powers had agreed that a monarchy would be the most stable solution for a country still beset by warring factions. After a short regency, Otto had assumed the crown in June 1835, but his throne was never secure, and he was forced to abandon it during the revolt of 1862. This initial, royalist experiment, which Byron himself would have regarded with distaste – for we can scarcely accept Edward Trelawny's contention, expressed in a letter to Mary Shelley in August 1824, that he intended "to destroy the republic and smooth the road for a foreign King" – was thus doomed to failure; and yet the Wittelsbach connection with Greece, so well in key with the humanistic tradition of that royal house, does help to explain why Byron's legacy appealed not only to enlightened German men of letters, but also to the German establishment and aristocracy. But for Byron's sacrificial death at Missolonghi, there might well have been no battle of Navarino; and but for the defeat of the Turk, no German prince could have held sway over Greece. On the political plane, therefore, the German debt to Byron, however oblique, was considerable. Thus disarmed, even men of staunch conservative principles were prepared to concede that much might be forgiven a poet who had indeed voiced social heresies, but who had done so with abundant verve and wit, and who had, after all, laid down his life in a noble and profitable cause.

Not that Pückler-Muskau, whom Heine dubbed "the last knight-errant of the old aristocracy of birth", needed to turn such mental somersaults. Though reluctantly prepared to support a Bavarian monarch in strife-torn Greece, his own instincts were democratic. Markedly anti-clerical, he felt a sense of kinship with that rumbustious adventurer and fellow-radical Trelawny, of whom he was to draw an engaging portrait in the account of his

Greek travels. By the time the *South-Eastern Picture Gallery*, sub-titled *Greek Sorrows*, was published in 1840,[8] Trelawny had long since left Zante; but through his own encounter with Tersitza, Trelawny's Greek wife and sister of the guerrilla chieftain Odys-seus Andritsos, Pückler-Muskau was able to piece together the romantic story of Trelawny's escapades after Byron's unexpected death: his long, beleaguered stay in the inaccessible cavern on Mount Parnassas, his marriage to the young Greek maid, his near-murder by Mavrocordato's English hirelings, his slow recovery and his rescue by the Royal Navy after Odysseus had defected to the Turks. Pückler-Muskau tells the tale with every show of admir-ation for Trelawny's "invincible enterprise". His report is notable as one of the few authentic accounts that have come down to us con-cerning the early life of Byron's intrepid lieutenant.[9]

Apart from such biographical revelations, there is much in Pückler-Muskau's book that suggests the aura alike of Byron and E.T.A. Hoffmann. There are even passages of fictitious embroid-ery in which the author, mildly disguised as "Herr von Rosen-berg", is pursued by his *Doppelgänger*, Count Erdmann. Despite this romantic device, the *Greek Sorrows* also display realistic social observation of a high order and might even be claimed as a turning-point in the German attitude to Greece, which had too long been coloured by the antiquarian ideals of Winckelmann, Goethe, and Schiller and was out of touch with the harsh political and economic problems affecting the country. None of the earlier German huma-nists who had laboured to interpret Greek classicism had ever visited Greece; paradoxically, the strength of their abstractions often sprang from ignorance. Pückler-Muskau, who liked Turks and Greeks in almost equal measure, set out to redress the balance and to show what was hollow in the Greek cause and what social ills, from bribery to brigandage, required urgent remedies. To those who clung to a rarefied, Apollonian view of Greek culture he suggested with asperity that they were no longer living in "the age of Aspasia and Alcibiades"; and to those who still saw Hellenism undefiled and unadulterated he pointed out that the Athens of the day was "one quarter ancient, one quarter Turkish, one quarter neo-Greek, and one quarter Bavarian".

In presenting an unvarnished image of the contemporary Greek scene, Pückler-Muskau began to free the German spirit from that "tyranny of Greece" which E. M. Butler has analysed in a brilliant study.[10] His stature was sufficient to lend credence to his thesis in the loftiest circles; and after the eclipse of King Otto, the Germans, ever more disenchanted with the Greeks, began to intensify that pro-Turkish policy and increasing concern with the Orient which was ultimately to take Wilhelm II on his pilgrimage to Jerusalem and promote visions of a Berlin–Baghdad railway. Those who find literature inseparable from history may therefore see some correlation between the gradual decline of German Byronism, as the nineteenth century wore on, and the increasing strength of the Turkish lobby, which was to have pregnant consequences in both world wars.

If Pückler-Muskau shared with Byron a spacious, uninhibited quality more properly befitting the Europe of a past age, his social views, like Byron's and Trelawny's, presaged the advance of democracy. His impressive range is signalled by his association not only with a moodily Byronic poet like "Solitaire" Nürnberger, but with more politically motivated, anti-reactionary dissidents such as Heine and Laube. Though his roots lay in the Romantic epoch, he could not identify with the narrow, chauvinistic aspects of Romantic philosophy, as expounded by Fichte and Schleiermacher, and he thus emerges as a transitional figure, heralding the Young German movement. In a refreshing survey of the post-Romantic trend in German literature, C. P. Magill tells us that the critic

> making his way from the picturesque ruins of Romanticism towards the thriving *Kleinstadt* of Poetic Realism passes . . . through the war-scarred hamlet of Young Germany. He would feel little urge to tarry, were it not that his eye is caught, and held, by an edifice of Oriental splendour, which arises from among these humdrum dwellings like a pagoda in a Midland suburb.[11]

The "pagoda" is Heinrich Heine, towering above his contemporaries – writers such as Herwegh and Freiligrath, Wienbarg and Mundt – whose collective efforts, as Magill observes, can scarcely sustain that convenient but fanciful label: "Young German School". The authors so designated were certainly all prompted by strong social motivations and would, like Trelawny in 1830, "have rejoiced to behold the leagued conspiracy of kings broken, and their bloodhound priests and nobles muzzled, their impious confederacy to enslave and rob the people paralysed".[12] However, their singular ineffectiveness in bringing about social change – and only those who like Heine fled to France or like Herwegh to Switzerland could even freely voice their thoughts – highlights that difference in political background which stultified much meliorist endeavour and constricted German Byronism within tight bounds.

There was at least one other distinguishing factor. A notable constituent of Byronism elsewhere – the urge to achieve liberation from a foreign oppressor – was almost wholly lacking in Germany. It is true that on the threshold of the Byronic epoch Prussia had to help beat off the French invasion; yet Napoleon had become the ally of the Bavarians and the emancipator of the Rhineland Jews. In any case his reign was brief. Even before completing *Childe Harold*, Byron himself had occasion to ponder the defeat of the French despot at Waterloo; and Germany was thereafter to remain safe from the Gallic 'menace' till 1870. For the major part of the nineteenth century, if the German people had oppressors, they were to be seen plainly on the home-front: the petty but expensive monarchs, the junkers, the industrialists, the clerics, the servile automatons in the civil service. These Establishment figures and the social tensions and malpractices they begot were the obvious targets for literary satire and radical agitation. But in the Age of Metternich such personages were well protected by a rigorous and repressive system of internal security. Overt criticism was hence a dangerous game and, with the chronic want of *Zivilcourage* or public spirit, there were few who were prepared to play it. Here is a root cause of the anaemia sapping German Byronism in its political aspect. Only those who could escape abroad could write more freely.

The mingled apathy and reaction which set the tone in German society of the post-Napoleonic era, coupled with the failure of the revolutions of 1830 and 1848, augured ill for social reform. Lacking a foreign foe to pillory on the one hand and forcibly restrained from attacking internal abuses on the other, men and women of eager Byronic temperament were left with nothing to cultivate but their least productive foibles. They adopted dandiacal affectations. They posed as fallen angels, as doomed victims of a cursed generation – or even as vampires. Would-be titans, they remained pygmies – *Zerrissene*, or self-divided neurotics.[13] Fortunately, this is not the whole story. Some elements of German Byronism did find a lodging in more robust spirits, even though their careers may have pursued the same sad trajectory as Euphorion's. One thinks of playwrights such as Georg Büchner or Christian Dietrich Grabbe, whose raw but potent dramas hint at volcanic forces which were soon to be quenched by the cloying effusions of the *Biedermeier* period. It was left to a later age, namely to Gerhart Hauptmann in his compelling tragedy *The Weavers* (1892), to reproduce the urgency of Byron's social message in its original starkness.[14]

From a welter of Byronically tinged men of letters, it is not easy to select those who drew their inspiration directly, rather than obliquely, from the original source – who to our certain knowledge were well acquainted with Byron's works; but Grabbe and Heine both fulfil this criterion. Grabbe signals the revolution of 1830, as Heine occupies the doldrums that preceded and followed the upheaval of 1848. Idiosyncratic "loners", they can scarcely be bracketed in terms of quality unless it be conceded that Heine's early Byronic fantasies fall far below the highest peaks of his achievement and so do not wholly outclass Grabbe's uncouth dramas, in which magniloquence too often sinks into turgid bombast. Grabbe centred his plays around awesome potentates – Hannibal, Barbarossa Sulla and Napoleon – but it is his *Don Juan and Faust* (1829) which catches the eye of the Byron enthusiast. The idea of juxtaposing these twin heroes was probably suggested by Franz Horn, a Berlin literary historian, who had mooted the thesis that Hamlet, Don Juan, and Faust were complementary types; but we know that Grabbe bought Byron's works in English in 1826, and his play not only includes echoes of *Manfred* and *Cain* but, in its Roman setting, betrays the influence of *Childe Harold*. Grabbe had taken on an immense theme that might well have daunted a more mature writer. In the final act Mephisto claims Juan and Faust alike, so demonstrating that all endeavour, whether of the spirit or the flesh, attains the same dismal consummation.

In Heine the Byronic strain is most apparent in the early verse-dramas *Almansor* and *William Ratcliff;* the plots of these fate-tragedies recall both *The Giaour* and *The Bride of Abydos. The Book of Songs,* published only three years after Byron's death, also has Byronic components; and Heine doubtless had Byron in mind when, in *The Memoirs of Herr von Schnabelewopski,* he tried his hand, rather unconvincingly, at erotic anecdotes. Indeed, in this vein, as S. S. Prawer comments, Heine reminds one of "a sniggering schoolboy, rather than the Goethe of the *Roman Elegies* or the Byron of *Don Juan*".[15] And yet, if we consider the main burden of Heine's work, does not its fearless irreverence, its devil-may-care jauntiness, its deeply moral undertone come close to matching the true

Byronic spirit? Perhaps W. E. Henley had sensed this deep affinity when he claimed that Byron "had awakened Heine, inspired Schumann, and been saluted as an equal by the poet of *Faust* himself"; and that his voice had been recognised "as the most human and least insular raised on English ground since Shakespeare's".[16] George Saintsbury too, though no Byron lover, yet acknowledged in his *History of Nineteenth Century Literature* that Byron "had great power over Heine".

One of Heine's keenest admirers, Elise von Hohenhausen, dared to call him "the German Byron"; but there were other contenders for the title, especially in those northwestern regions of Germany which, by tradition, lay most open to English influence. It was in Hamburg that Heine had chanced upon F. Jacobsen's *Letters to a German Noblewoman concerning the most Modern English Poets*, published at Altona in 1820 and containing some of the earliest translations. In Westphalia Annette von Droste–Hülshoff and Ferdinand von Freiligrath both became enthusiasts, reading Byron in the original tongue. Freiligrath was to owe to Byron, no less than to Victor Hugo, much of that local colour with which he bedaubed his "poetry of the desert". For Annette the attraction was potent but brief; yet it is remarkable evidence of Byron's magnetism that Germany's foremost poetess should have been poring over *Manfred* in Münster at the same time that Goethe found himself enthralled by the same work in Weimar.

As elsewhere, so also in Germany Byron's untimely death in Greece aroused a fresh glow of approval for his poems. It was recalled that the hero of Hölderlin's mystical novel *Hyperion*, written as long ago as 1797, had essayed, like Byron, to deal a blow for Greek independence against the Turk. Hölderlin's idealistic aspiration had now become heroic reality. Tributes multiplied. Wilhelm Müller, himself a noted Philhellene, wrote a first tentative biography and also saluted Byron in verse; the figure of the freedom-fighter began to oust that of the melancholy Pilgrim. "I would sacrifice all the enjoyment of my life for a single year of Byron's woes," Börne declared in his *Letters from Paris*, thus conferring approval on "maladjustment" as a possible outward symptom of inner political maturity. Yet if we assess Byron's influence in Germany over a longer period, we cannot fail to note an unfortunate polarisation. His *literary* influence was increasingly dominated by the image of Euphorion, and though Goethe had associated this allegorical figure with valiant Faustian strivings, he had also demonstrated how the Promethean urge could lead to disaster; Grabbe's ill-starred Don Juan was by no means the sole Byronic hero to lurk in Euphorion's shadow. On the *political* front, Byron was chiefly remembered as the saviour of Greece, and generations were to elapse before his role as a champion of democracy was to receive proper recognition. This dualism, reflecting an essential ambiguity in Byron's own nature, occasioned dissonances in his reception; but it accounts, too, for Byron's ability to win plaudits from men of opposed political beliefs. Despite his onslaughts against the monarchy, he could beguile conservatives no less than radicals. Just as in England Byron drew admiration from Disraeli as well as from working men's guilds, in Germany his writ ran from Bismarck and the House of Wittelsbach at one political extreme to Ferdinand Lassalle at the other.

The Wittelsbach connection with Byron was originally prompted by a common interest in the history and culture of Greece. The rulers of Bavaria had long been noted as enlightened patrons of the arts and archaeology. King Otto's father, Ludwig I, had cultivated these pursuits in Italy and Greece, and his passion for all things Greek was such that he gave a Byronic twist to the name of his English favourite, Lady Jane Ellenborough, calling her "Ianthe". But it was in the reign of Ludwig's grandson, Ludwig II, the protector of Wagner, that the royal association with Byron was to assume a particularly intriguing shape. A Byronic aura clings to this homosexual psychopath, solitary in his extravagant castles, who at times seems more like the hero of a Gothic romance – an immature invention of Dr Polidori's perhaps – than a flesh-and-blood king. It was appropriate that his contemporaries should have called him "the last of the Romantics".

Ludwig's interest in Byron is amply attested. Inevitably, it was *Manfred*, with its operatic, well-nigh Wagnerian quality, that cast the first spell; and the incidental music Schumann had composed in 1849 proved an added attraction. Ludwig attended two public performances at the Residenztheater in Munich in 1868; and in 1877, and again in 1878, *Manfred* was included in the repertoire chosen for his private sessions at the Hoftheater. In the translation by A. Böttger the play came to enjoy a measure of popularity. Indeed, the archives of the Residenztheater list a total of forty-five performances. The evidence regarding a second Byron play, *Sardanapalus*, is to some degree speculative, yet the probable link with Ludwig is highly suggestive. We know that the king's Viennese friend, the actor Joseph Kainz, produced a translation of *Sardana-palus*. A production was planned but never staged. It is, further, common knowledge that the 209 *Separatvorstellungen* which Ludwig attended from 1872 onwards were centred on themes that gratified his narcissistic self-indulgence. His self-identification with the Sun King, Louis XIV, is notorious. But might he not have been mir-rored, in a manner equally apt and flattering, in Byron's striking portrait of the Assyrian monarch?

Sardanapalus is chiefly, but unjustly, remembered for its atmo-sphere of sensuous, Wildean licence: the king makes his entrance "effeminately dressed, his head crowned with flowers", to the accompaniment of his attendants' "lascivious tinklings". Despite the remoteness in time and space, it is tempting to draw a parallel between the sybarite of Nineveh and the sybarite of Hohensch-wangau. But any such comparison need not of itself imply a nega-tive judgement. As G. Wilson Knight has shown, Byron, in the play that Goethe singled out for especial commendation, also plumbs deeper levels where many Byronic conflicts are resolved: where "energy and eternity coalesce and we are aware less of con-flict than of essence".[17] Though Sardanapalus urges us to "eat, drink, and love; the rest's not worth a fillip", his dalliance with Myrrha is far removed from mindless hedonism. His views on the ruler's mission and the purpose of life enhance what we know of Byron's social criticism. Sardanapalus abjures conquest and reviles his "martial grandam, chaste Semiramis". His aims are pitched in favour of "mild reciprocal alleviation" and making his country "one wide shelter for the wretched". It is fascinating to conjecture what Ludwig may have made of this enigmatic epicene being. Did he see Sardanapalus as a reformer or simply as a con-noisseur who shared his own luxurious tastes? One of Browning's obscurest monologues, written in 1871, may half-illuminate the problem. In "Prince Hohenstiel–Schwangau, Saviour of Society" the musing, eponymous prince is usually identified with Louis Napoleon, Emperor of France, but the Bavarian associations inherent in the title suggest at least a hybrid figure, of which Ludwig II may well have been one component.

In the person of Sardanapalus Byron sought to fuse male and female attributes into an ideal whole. He thus wrestled with a problem which still has relevance for our own insufficiently emancipated age – as it had for the luckless King of Bavaria. Ludwig lacked the altruism of a Sardanapalus; but he may well have regarded the Assyrian as a prepossessing forerunner, not least in their common dislike of sabre-rattling. This pacifist strain at once set him apart from his great Prussian contemporary, Bismarck, and it is odd that Byron should have been a link between two such differentiated characters.

Despite his own immense successes, however, and Ludwig's abject failures, Otto von Bismarck, "the mad Junker", was highly wrought and far from unemotional. Like Ludwig he felt drawn toward Byron; but once he became absorbed in affairs of state he managed, like Disraeli, to slough off his early Byronic pose. Yet, as his biographer, Emil Ludwig, has noted, in old age he again gave expression "to the sense of *taedium vitae* in Byronic fashion". "My temperament", Bismarck himself declared, "is dreamy and sentimental".

Bismarck's flirtation with Byronic moods is attested in the love-letters he wrote in 1847 to his fiancée, Johanna von Puttkamer. It is true that he mocks his susceptibility as "all nonsense"; but there was an element of guile in his courtship. When he liberally adorned his correspondence with quotations from the Bible, Shakespeare and Moore – as well as Byron – his main aim was to show that, though a mere dike-reeve on the banks of the Elbe, he was no country clodhopper, but a gentleman with some pretensions to culture. Even so, it is apparent that the lines that he copied from "To Inez" struck a deeper chord in his own nature:

> What exile from himself can flee?
> To zones though more and more remote,
> Still, still pursues, where'er I be,
> The blight of life – the demon Thought.

Byron's superbly evocative description of a storm in the Alps could scarcely fail to kindle Bismarck's imagination:

> Far along,
> From peak to peak, the rattling crags among,
> Leaps the live thunder.

The urge these lines aroused in him was to plunge headlong on horseback into the foaming falls of the Rhine; but sanity prevailed over self-destruction, and to comfort his fiancée, we see him toning down the effect of the quotation with the comment: "A pleasure of this sort can only be indulged once in a lifetime." It was thus chiefly the "melancholy" Byron who attracted Bismarck, just as Metternich showed himself fascinated by Childe Harold's despondent musings over the fall of empires. In his elegiac meditations Byron touched on issues of fundamental human appeal, and these seemingly defused what both Bismarck and Metternich must have regarded as the unpalatable political content of much that Byron wrote in his less sublime manner. Moreover, where lesser men might have recoiled, these two statesman of supreme ability could respond to Byron within a framework of aristocratic elitism and acknowledge the skill of his satire, even though Byron's wit and invective were often directed against their own social order.

An equally fluid approach to Byron is evident in another great dogmatist of the Right, Friedrich Nietzsche, whose indulgence in mental acrobatics is so marked that he often appears the dupe of his own aphoristic style. His philosophy hovers uneasily between the opposed attractions of the Apolline and the Dionysiac view of reality. In his more balanced moods Nietzsche preferred the Apolline attitude, seeking a human condition in which equanimity should oust the messiness of unbridled passion: the highest art, he prompts us to believe, achieved by Homer, Calderon, Racine and Goethe, was the distillation of a wise and harmonious lifestyle. Yet Nietzsche also recognised the need "in certain phases of existence", and especially in youth, for a different kind of art, the product of "tension, excitement, antipathy against all that is regulated, monotonous, simple and logical".[18]

This wrenched psychological spectrum caused inconsistencies in Nietzsche's critical appraisal of European literature. When gravitating towards the Apolline ideal, he upholds strictness and rejects laxity in matters of form. Racine and Voltaire, he accordingly urges, are the models to which the correct dramatist must conform, while Lessing must be castigated for trying to substitute the Shakespearian mode, with its flouting of the classical rules. Yet in his unbuttoned moments Nietzsche is capable of swallowing the deliberate incoherence of *Tristram Shandy* and praising Sterne as a master of ambiguity. It was this elasticity in his criticism, however, which enabled him to appreciate Byron from varying – and even diverging – points of view. It is easy to see why the Nietzsche who fulminated against Christianity should have admired the author of *Cain*, so much so that in a letter to Erwin Rhode he once bracketed Byron with Schopenhauer as a formative influence. It was Byron's pessimism to which he first responded. In his *Human, All-too-Human*, he quotes those "immortal lines" which must also have appealed to the young Bismarck:

> Sorrow is knowledge: they who know the most
> Must mourn the deepest o'er the fatal truth,
> The Tree of Knowledge is not that of Life.

When he discovered *Manfred*, at the age of 13, Nietzsche detected in his own soul "all the dark abysses in this work". Later he was even to compose an overture to *Manfred* – a tribute to Byron's shade scarcely less remarkable than the advent of Euphorion in the Second Part of *Faust*: a work, incidentally, which Nietzsche asserted was far inferior to *Manfred*. Yet he also regarded Byron as a poet who, however emancipated in his ideas, maintained a strict sense of form and could thus – after some Procrustes-like adjustment – be accommodated within the Apolline scheme of things. Here Nietzsche was doubtless led into error by a failure to appreciate Byron's diversified approach to poetic style. Had he been aware of the revolutionary quality of *Beppo*, he would have realised that, even if Byron defended the poetic canons of the Augustans and disliked blank verse, he could grow restive in the shackles of tradition and, struggling free from the cramping conventions of poetic diction, was ultimately to become a notable stylistic innovator. But all in all there is a refreshing originality in the Nietzschean view of Byron. In its fusion of Apolline and Dionysiac characteristics it offers a rounded portrait, an awareness that Byron did not harp on one string but was master of many talents.

It is a commonplace of criticism that nineteenth century radicalism drew sustenance not only from the intellectual begetters of the French Revolution, but also from those trumpet-tongued poets, bent on anarchy, who were prominent in the Romantic Movement. While it would be misleading to identify Byron with any single school, the targets of his satiric genius – the anti-liberal forces of reaction rampant in post-Napoleonic Europe – placed him squarely in the radical camp. One would accordingly expect to note the effect of his opinions on some eminent German leaders of the Left. The evidence for any such effect is, however, tantalisingly meagre. The explanation perhaps lies in the tepidity of German radicalism, which only acquired full momentum after the First World War had shaken German society to its foundations. Earlier, the braver spirits having been banished abroad, the would-be reformers who remained on German soil were compelled, for fear of reprisals and loss of livelihood, to pitch the threshold of their social criticism at an egregiously low level. The Swabian poet Ludwig Uhland typifies this listless approach. Though he was expelled from his Chair of German Language and Literature at Tübingen for harbouring "dangerous" ideas, his verse strikes the present-day reader as neo-feudal, rather than iconoclastic, in its naïve patriotism. In his poem "The Good Old Right" he apostrophises:

> The Right that like a pillar strong
> The prince's house upholds;
> And safe against intruding steps
> The peasant's cot enfolds.[19]

For writers forced to reach an accommodation with *Biedermeier* paternalism, Byron's vehement acerbities held scant appeal. However, in the heyday of Marx and Engels, an anomalous Byronic hero briefly emerged in Germany in the singular figure of Ferdinand Lassalle. Marx, whom he visited in London in the year of the Great Exhibition, wrote that Lassalle believed himself to be "not only the greatest scholar, the deepest thinker, the most brilliant investigator, but also a Don Juan and a revolutionary Cardinal Richelieu". A dandy, resplendent but doomed, dying as the result of a duel when not yet 40, Lassalle combined classical scholarship and legal acumen with political agitation in a hectic career which won him the grudging respect of Bismarck. His fate stands in sharp contrast to the successful path trod by Disraeli who, climbing from somewhat similar origins, outgrew his early Byronic phase. Lassalle on the other hand, perhaps goaded like Nietzsche by the spirochaete of syphilis, exaggerated his innate titanism to the point of self-destruction.

Lassalle's knowledge of Byron must be largely assumed rather than documented;[20] but in his blank-verse play *Franz von Sickingen* there are strong Byronic undercurrents when the author tries to show how reformist zeal leads to self-immolation. Recalling how Curtius leaped into the gulf to save Rome, Lassalle's protagonist asserts:

> The best must hurl themselves in Time's fell rift.
> Their bodies only serve to seal it up once more.

Their bodies only are the wondrous seed
From which the plant of universal freedom,
Expanding, founds a green and fertile world.
This is the curse that rests on all true men,
Consigning them and all who side with them
Daemonically to sinister destruction.

Lassalle's brief stay in London reminds us that the two greatest German dissidents of all time, Marx and Engels, lived for decades in Byron's homeland and thus had unusual opportunities to acquaint themselves with English literature, as well as with the slums that were to provide ammunition for their social theories. Engels's researches, indeed, produced a *locus classicus* in the appraisal of Romantic poetry, in the assertion proclaimed in *The Condition of the Working Class in England* (1845), that it was "the workers", rather than the middle classes, who were familiar with the poetry of Shelley and Byron in unexpurgated form:

> Shelley's prophetic genius has caught their imagination, while Byron attracts their sympathy by his sensuous fire and by the virulence of his satire against the existing social order. The middle classes, on the other hand, have on their shelves only ruthlessly expurgated 'family' editions of these writers. These editions have been prepared to suit the hypocritical moral standards of the bourgeoisie.[21]

Eager that German workers should share in this enlightenment, Engels even translated some of Shelley's poems. He also had a shrewd liking for "The Vicar of Bray", which he believed provided an instructive key to the course of English history. Marx, too, was evidently familiar with Byron's works, and we know from his *Herr Vogt* that he could savour the robustness of the epitaph on Castlereagh:[22]

> Posterity will ne'er survey
> A nobler grave than this:
> Here lie the bones of Castlereagh:
> Stop, traveller, –!

In pursuing the tortuous path of German Byronism from Goethe

in Weimar to Pückler-Muskau in Athens, from Heine in Paris to
Nietzsche in Basel, from Lassalle in Breslau and Berlin to Engels in
Manchester, we have only cast casual glances in the direction of
Austria. Understandably, the Austrian share in the movement
was more limited in scope. For Austrian officialdom Byron was
long to remain a nefarious foreigner who had dared to foment rebellion in the Italian provinces. The indirect success of his intervention in Greece seemed no less ominous to a regime which sought at
all costs to hold a ramshackle empire together under Habsburg
domination. If Greece could throw off the Turkish yoke, might not
the Czechs or the Hungarians be provoked into similar centrifugal
action, leaving Vienna exposed as a limbless trunk? Such was the
fear of contagion from the Greek example that even so reliable a
member of the Austrian ruling class as Count von Prokesch-Osten,
who had served as Ambassador in Athens from 1834 to 1849, was
forbidden to publish his account of the Greek uprising against the
Turks till 1867.[23] Only Metternich himself, on his unassailable
perch, could afford to see in Byron the poet as well as the rebel; and
we have Grillparzer's testimony that the statesman who controlled
Europe's destiny for decades could recite by heart the whole of the
Fourth Canto of *Childe Harold* in English. Metternich may also
have been intrigued by the elaborate accompanying notes, con-
scientiously supplied by John Cam Hobhouse. As he memorised
Byron's thoughts on the decline of Venice and Rome, did he, one
wonders, draw the obvious moral and ponder how long the Habsburgs could be spared their own ultimate eclipse?

Even Metternich could not suppress nationalist aspirations in
all corners of the Habsburg empire; and those Austrian writers
who had been fired by the Greek example could at least emulate
Byron by espousing the cause of the Poles. Here was a semi-
legitimate outlet, for they could direct their animus against Russia,
while ignoring, if they were wise, the parallel roles played by
Austria and Prussia in the subjection of Poland. The German poet
Count August von Platen, himself a devotee of Byron, had
expressed sympathy for the Polish insurrection of 1830, and he was
supported by the most gifted of Byron's Austrian disciples, Nikol-
aus Lenau. Endowed with a lyric talent of the highest order, Lenau
yet cuts a rather sorry figure in the chronicle of Byronism. Like
Grabbe, he sought grandiose themes – a *Faust* and *Don Juan* were
among his more ambitious projects – but his inveterate nihilism,
which even a pioneering spell in America failed to alleviate, held

scant hope for the victims of the Immortals. Occasionally, it is true, Lenau indulges in banter which echoes the sprightly tone of *Beppo* – as when he terms a churchyard saunter "lemonade for the soul"; and perhaps such levity hints at greater wisdom than the necrophilistic gloom which characterises much Byronistic pastiche. But insanity claimed Lenau in the end, and he furnishes yet one more example of a Byronic epigone who was unable to cope with reality and was doomed to share the fate of Euphorion.

While German-speaking Austrians were either loyal to the Habsburgs or, if not, found themselves muzzled, more fluid conditions prevailed in the outlying parts of the Empire, where the literature of revolt against Austrian oppression was expressed in a welter of Balkan and East European tongues. In Prague as in Budapest (the capitals of subject nations), Byron's message had immediate political relevance. The Hungarians in particular, ever sensitive to external cultural influences, responded with enthusiasm to the challenge. In the insurrection of 1849 they drew inspiration not only from Byron but from Lamartine – and even from the liberal Pope Pius IX, who had reasons of his own for disliking the Austrian presence in Italy. It is nevertheless remarkable that two major figures in the Hungarian revolt, Lajos Kossuth and the poet Sándor Petőfi (1822–49), should both have heeded Byron's clarion call. In his youth Kossuth was even reputed to bear a facial resemblance to Byron; but it was Petőfi, with his impetuous patriotism and his incandescent verse, whose career, ending untimely on the field of Szegesvár, pursued the same ill-fated trajectory as Byron's. Further Byronic echoes abound in Hungarian poetry. Karl Postl, himself a refugee from Austrian oppression and the confining discipline of the Holy Cross Order, who as "Charles Sealsfield" developed an impressive talent as an historical novelist, regarded János Arany, perhaps the greatest Hungarian poet of the nineteenth century, as Byron's *Geistesverwandter* or "spiritual brother". And the tale could be continued into our own century.[24]

If the vicissitudes of the Austro–Hungarian Empire lent added impetus to Byronism in the political context, while also enlarging its geographical bounds, as the nineteenth century wore on, aspects of Byronism hitherto neglected came under increasing scientific scrutiny. Where a literary phenomenon has sufficient substance, it tends to be interpreted afresh by each generation; so it was with Byron – and the accretions that time and legend have fastened to his name. Much of this interest was biographical: the attempt to fashion, with the aid of new analytical techniques, a convincing psychogram or 'pathograph' of an elusive and abnormal personality which tended to defy neat labels. Inevitably Byron's chequered ancestry and the riddles surrounding his marriage loomed large in the discussion. Collectively such investigations showed the pervasive influence of Darwin and Freud. The new, naturalistic mood in Byron studies began with Karl Bleibtreu (1859–1928), who devoted three plays to his enigmatic theme: *Lord Byron's Last Love* (1881), *His Daughter* (1886) and *Byron's Secret* (1900). In the second of these dramas in particular, Bleibtreu made great play with the role of heredity; indeed, *His Daughter* is sometimes acclaimed in histories of literature as the first "Darwinian tragedy" to be written in German. Not that Bleibtreu can be credited with true innovation: he had, after all, merely given a Zolaesque twist to the Fate Tragedy, which had long been entrenched in the German Romantic tradition. More recently new depths of morbidity were to be plumbed by the psychoanalysts. Thus Ernst Kretschmer concluded that Byron should be ranked, together with Michelangelo, amongst the *geniale Vollpsychopathen* or "profoundly psychopathic men of genius", but then had some difficulty in reconciling his unique achievement with his ominous grouping, especially as lesser men such as Grabbe and Lenz were included in the same category.[25]

It says much for the integrity and resilience of Byron's original message that, despite the clutter of pseudo-scientific interpretations imposed upon it, it could still influence German political thinking a century after its author's death. It would, indeed, be difficult to imagine a more apt conclusion to the pattern we have been exploring than the career of Ernst Toller – poet, dramatist and revolutionary – who instilled a new immediacy into the Byronic ideal and whose example in the twenties helped to inspire some of the committed literature of the thirties in Britain as well as Germany. As an activist in the forefront of a communist revolutionary movement, Toller differed from those radical writers who were content to be mere theoreticians. For a brief period during the abortive uprising of November 1918 he was actually the head of the Munich Soviet Republic. Sentenced to four years' imprisonment, he sought outlets for his social beliefs in a series of dramas, one of which, *The Machine-Wreckers*, recounted the story of the Nottingham Luddites.[26]

In the Prologue to *The Machine-Wreckers*, Toller describes the

passage through the House of Lords of the notorious Bill prescrib-
ing the death penalty for workers guilty of industrial sabotage.
There is a tense confrontation between Byron, Castlereagh and the
Lord Chancellor. Defending the wreckers, Byron berates his
fellow-peers in a speech which Toller adapted from the original
argument:

> And one thing more I say to you, my lords,
> For wars your purse was ever open wide;
> A tenth part of the money that you gave
> To Portugal in "service of mankind"
> Would have sufficed to still the pangs at home
> And give the gallows peace. I saw in Turkey
> The most despotic rule the world has known,
> But nowhere dearth in plenty such as here
> In Christian England.
> And what is now your remedy for the ill?
> Hanging, the nostrum of all penny-quacks
> Who burrow in the body of the State!
> Is not the law bespattered to the crown?
> Shall blood be shed until it steams to Heaven
> In witness of your guilt? Is hanging medicine
> For hunger and despair?

In rebuttal, Castlereagh argues that the House has been listening
to "a poet's voice and not a statesman's" and then develops a chil-
ling Malthusian thesis:

> The more the infant ranks are thinned by Death,
> The better for our children and our land.

Byron alone votes against the Bill. His solitary gesture of defiance
achieves nothing for the moment, but he retains the respect of his
foes. In the words of the Lord Chancellor: "Your *beau geste*, my lord,
we must admire." With the collapse of the Weimar republic
Toller's own active role in German politics was at an end; his
suicide in New York in 1939, four years after Kurt Tucholsky's
suicide as an exile in Sweden and three years before Stefan Zweig –
that penetrating analyst of the demonic – died by his own hand in
Brazil, was part of the mounting toll taken by the Third Reich.
Such deaths seem to confirm the view expressed by Ferdinand

Lassalle in his *Franz von Sickingen*, as a modern adaptation of primitive myth, that mankind achieves progress by advancing over the sacrificial pyres of its bravest spirits: personal tragedy, self-willed, may result in collective good.

It is not easy to attempt an overall evaluation of Byronism in Germany, whether in the field of politics or the field of literature. The data are too varied to be neatly docketed. Moreover, the concentration of argument on a single man of letters, however eminent, runs the risk of becoming obsessional and so distorting the picture. Byron's influence may have been formidable, but his was not a voice lifted in isolation. Even if we restrict our enquiry to an Anglo–German frame of reference – itself an artificially limiting factor – we are bound to note that Germans were also influenced by the thoughts and actions of other Britons sympathetic to Byron's ideals. Did not Swinburne follow in Byron's footsteps in championing the cause of Italian liberty?[27] Yet more evocative of the shades of Byron and Euphorion alike is the story of Clement Harris who, as his memorial in Athens attests, "died fighting for the cause of Greece at the battle of Pente Pigadia on the 23rd April 1897". Except that he was a musician, not a poet, Harris's career closely echoes Byron's. He, too, sat as a boy in meditative mood on Peachey's tomb in Harrow churchyard; and when, on his first visit to Greece, he chanced on a book in his hotel, the first heading to catch his eye ran: "The Last Days of Byron". But it is not simply Harris's death in battle against the Turk which awakens our interest. The strangest parallel of all is, surely, that Harris was later commemorated in elegiac verse by the foremost German poet of his day, Stefan George, in the same way as Byron had been canonised by Goethe. George's poem "Pente Pigadia", dedicated to "Clemens" (the author preferred the German form of the Christian name), was first published in 1904 and later included in *The Seventh Ring*, where Harris was immortalised as one of an illustrious band, along with Mallarmé, Verlaine, Villiers de L'Isle Adam, Nietzsche and the Swiss painter Boecklin.[28]

It would be difficult to accept – however urgently his *Doppelganger*, Harris, may coax us towards such a belief – that Byron, with his huge vitality and baffling idiosyncrasy, was merely a type-figure. Moreover, it is a safe assumption that Byron was greater than any of his disciples – and perhaps, one might pessimistically add, than most of his German devotees and imitators put together. Here our circular argument returns to its beginning: the quietest

German temperament, the sentimentality of the regional cultures, the bumbledom of the petty monarchies and the largely conservative flavour of German internal politics throughout much of the nineteenth century all tended to blunt the edge of social criticism. Byron doubtless exercised an attraction over politicians of all parties; but his social message was unacceptable in the reactionary camp and could only be echoed by more progressive spirits if they were prepared to incur official displeasure. In his complementary role as a champion of nationalist rather than social aspirations, Byron could evoke little resonance in the closed societies of the *Duodezfürstentümer* or in the self-sufficient German Reich, under Prussian hegemony, which succeeded them. Only the oppressed minorities in the Austro–Hungarian hinterlands could answer Byron's call with heartfelt conviction.

Reviewed against this frustrating background, German Byronic literature, wide in compass and varied in treatment, is no mean achievement. If it fails to reflect Byron's genius to the full, this is mainly because of its obsessive preoccupation with the figure of Manfred. "Manfred, like Faust and Hamlet", one German panegyricist declares, "is the man of genius, the superman whose enraptured eye takes in all the beauty of the world and whose yearning for the highest, the perfect existence, for a divine life is, nevertheless. so great that all the pleasures which the world can offer are incapable of filling his heart."[29] It is easy to see what prompted so generous a response to Manfred. It was both plausible and flattering to perceive Byron's hero as a link in a dynasty of titans stretching from Goethe's Faust to Nietzsche's Superman. But perhaps there was also a more humdrum, linguistic reason why German Byronic literature became more closely aligned with the posture of Manfred than with the posture of Don Juan: both in its rhetorical sublimities and its Wordsworthian profundities, the language of *Manfred* lends itself more readily to imitation in German (and, one might add, to translation into German) than does the colloquial style typical of Byron's later manner. While Goethe admired *The Vision of Judgment*, he disliked *Don Juan*; and a general survey of Byron's reception in Germany suggests that many engaging aspects of his character – his devastating wit, zest for living and sheer sense of fun – failed to be met with perceptive understanding. With the comparative neglect by German translators and editors of his prose, and especially of his revealing letters, the image of Byron fashioned in Germany inevitably lacked the warmth and conviction inseparable from a full and unvarnished portrayal.

In the Anglo-Saxon countries Byron's stature is still growing and acquiring new facets; and after a period of relative decline, a similar claim might now be made regarding his reputation in Germany, where the recent inauguration of a Byron Society seems to prelude a revival of interest. However limited Byronic associations with Germany may be, when Goethe placed Byron at Shakespeare's side in his literary pantheon, he launched a controversy which has beguiled critics to this day. But Byron's role was not confined to literature. As he loved to stress, he was also an *agent*, and though his sights were fixed on targets in the Mediterranean world, the convulsions of history in which he played a part were to have repercussions north of the Alps, far beyond the frontiers of Italy and Greece. If Byron's overt actions and inspired pen had not helped to kindle the Greek revolt, the Greek crown which was to elude his own head might not finally have graced a Bavarian skull. The consequences for Germany's cultural heritage might have been considerable. The outstanding contribution made by the Wittelsbachs to Bavarian affluence and enlightenment is well known; but would the partiality of the royal house for all things Hellenic have assumed such sumptuous proportions in the nineteenth century, had not Greece become for some decades a dynastic extension of their own homeland? Would Ludwig I have directed his architects to turn Munich into "the Athens of the North" without this impelling motivation? Can it be that the present-day saunterer on the Königsplatz, as he marvels at those impressive classical façades and, later, admires the archaeological treasures so beautifully displayed behind them, finds himself in the presence of one of Byron's less recognised but more enduring monuments?

NOTES

1. E. M. Butler, *Byron and Goethe: Analysis of a Passion* (London, 1956).
2. See "*Goethe im Briefwechsel zweier Freunde*" (i.e. B. R. Abeken and J. D. Gries) by Hans Gerhard Gräf. *Jahrbuch der Goethe-Gesellschaft*, vol. V, 1918, p. 251.
3. Conversing with Eckermann on 5 July 1827, Goethe explained why he had chosen to identify Euphorion with Byron: "To represent the most recent age of poetry, I could scarcely use anyone except him, for we have simply got to accept him as the greatest talent of the century... Moreover he entirely

suited the part because of his unappeased temperament and his fighting spirit, which were to prove his undoing at Missolonghi." But Goethe liked to fuse several layers of meaning in his flights of imagination; so it is no surprise to find him enlarging the horizon when he again spoke to Eckermann on 30 December 1829: "Euphorion is no human, but an allegorical being. He is Poetry personified – which is tied to no time, no place and no person."

4. For an analysis in depth, see Stefan Zweig's study of Hölderlin, Kleist and Nietzsche, *Der Kampf mit dem Dämon* (1925). Zweig rightly sets the mature Goethe, "the opponent of all vulcanicity", in a polar relationship to his three tragic protagonists; but he goes too far when he suggests that Goethe was "the arch-enemy of everything demonic".

5. See Longfellow's *Hyperion*, Book II, Chapter 8, where Goethe is also called 'Old Humbug' and 'Old Heathen'! Longfellow visited Frankfurt in 1836. Though Goethe had died four years earlier, his character was still the subject of lively controversy.

6. J. G. Robertson (ed.), *Torquato Tasso*, Introduction, p. lvi (Manchester, 1918)

7. Following the German edition of 1830–31, an English translation was published in 1832 and given the title: *Tour in England, Ireland and France in the Years 1826, 1827, 1828 and 1829, with Remarks on the Manners and Customs of the Inhabitants, and anecdotes of distinguished public characters. In a series of letters by a German Prince.* Already by July 1833 the translator, Mrs S. Austin, could inform the author that eight editions had been printed. A new and revised English edition was published in Zürich as recently as 1940.

8. *Südöstlicher Bildersaal – Griechische Leiden*, edited by K. G. Just, was republished in Stuttgart in 1968.

9. H. J. Massingham's *The Friend of Shelley*, the first detailed memoir of Edward Trelawny, appeared in 1930. In his Introduction, Massingham complains of the paucity of biographical material. Thus he could only offer a brief footnote (p. 272) on Trelawny's divorce from Tersitza; but Pückler–Muskau had already written a plausible account in 1840.

10. E. M. Butler, *The Tyranny of Greece Over Germany. A Study of the influence exercised by Greek art and poetry over the great German writers of the eighteenth, nineteenth and twentieth centuries* (Cambridge, 1935).

11. C. P. Magill's "Young Germany: A Revaluation" was a contribution to *German Studies presented to Leonard Ashley Willoughby* (Oxford, 1952), pp. 108ff.

12. Massingham, op. cit., p. 232.

13. The Germans themselves sometimes concede that there can be *too much Byronic literature*: a verdict with which we must agree, if we stretch that elastic term so as to include the lachrymose attitudinizing of the lesser *Weltschmerzler*, who hailed *Byronismus* as an opportunity to agonise over sentiments originally portrayed with far greater skill in *Werther*. Cf. W. Leifer, *Rhein und Themse fliessen zueinander*, (Stuttgart, 1964), p. 193: "Als Byronismus war diese Haltung der von Goethe vermittelten Werther-Stimmung nahe. Daher ist Deutschland überreich an Byron-Literatur."

14. Even if Hauptmann did not consciously echo Byron in his social drama, the plight of the Silesian weavers shows striking parallels with that of their Nottingham counterparts.

15. S. S. Prawer, *Heine: The Tragic Satirist* (Cambridge, 1961), p. 36.

16. W. E. Henley's comments on Matthew Arnold's Byron anthology, first published in the *Athenaeum* in June 1881, were reprinted in his *Views and Reviews* (1890).
17. See G. Wilson Knight's assessment, "Byron: the Poetry", in his *Poets of Action* (London, 1967), p. 238.
18. *Menschliches, Allzumenschliches*, II, par. 173 (1877–9).
19. Quoted from *The Songs and Ballads of Uhland*, trans. by W. W. Skeat, 1864.
20. In his article "Lord Byron und Lassalle" (*Neue Rundschau*, 1911, vol. 2), Emil Ludwig mooted profound similarities between the two men. He however stigmatised them as *Scheinrevolutionäre*, or pseudo-revolutionaries. There is an interesting reference to Byron in Lassalle's *Arbeiter-Lesebuch* (1863): "How does Lord Byron, the famous English poet, define madness? He asserts it is the harmonisation of incompatibles."
21. See *The Condition of the Working Class in England*, trans. by W. O. Henderson and W. H. Chaloner, 1958, p. 273.
22. According to the dubious warrant of Edward Aveling and Eleanor Marx, Byron, had he enjoyed a normal lifespan, would have turned into "a bourgeois reactionary". Both Marx and Engels, it appears, regarded Shelley as a more wholehearted revolutionary than Byron.
23. The work was published under the title *Geschichte des Abfalls der Griechen vom türkischen Reich im Jahre 1821*. Censorship was relaxed in Vienna after the Prussians had defeated the Austrians at Sadowa in 1866.
24. Of Endre Ady, who died in 1919, Paul Ignotus recently claimed that he "basked in almost Byronic splendour when ostracized or ridiculed". (*Times Literary Supplement*, 8 August 1976).
25. See Kretschmer's *Geniale Menschen*, 4th edn., 1948, p. 18.
26. *The Machine-Wreckers*, in an English version by Ashley Dukes, was first published in 1923 and re-issued in 1935 in *Seven Plays by Ernst Toller*. The work had a mixed reception when performed in Berlin in July 1922. Even the "Red Count", Harry Kessler, dismissed it in his Diary as "untalented rubbish, which can only compromise the views he (Toller) presents, just as the untalented, trashy Munich Soviet Republic compromised republican ideas in Bavaria". *The Machine-Wreckers* may not represent Toller at his best; but his early exploration of the Luddite theme may have prompted his later treatment of revolt in the German Navy. Cf. his *Draw the Fires* (1930).
27. Hatred of tyranny was not the only parallel with Byron. As Franz Blei, the Austrian critic noted after a memorable meeting with Swinburne in Meran, the "fleshly aspect" of Swinburne's poems caused "a puritanical scandal" such as Britain had not seen since Byron's day.
28. Harris had studied music at the Schott'sche Konservatorium in Frankfurt. For a full account of his Diaries and his connection with Stefan George, see Claus Bock, *Pente Pigadia und die Tagebücher des Clement Harris* (Amsterdam, 1962).
29. Hermann Türck, *The Man of Genius*, 1914, pp. 179–80; first German edn., 1896.

5 Byron and Greece

Byron's Love of Classical Greece and his Role in the Greek Revolution

E. G. PROTOPSALTIS

Peter Gossler describes the visit made to Athens in 1810 by a large group of artists and architects from Northern Europe.[1] They conducted studies of many archaeological sites and observed, or participated in, the iniquitous sale of ancient works of art.[2] Lord Byron was in Athens at the time and was well aware of the part played by his fellow Englishmen and other foreigners in the mercenary trade in works of art. In his immortal verse, Lord Byron vehemently denounced the plundering of the ancient Greek monuments.[3]

Of all the famous foreigners who visited Athens while it was still under Turkish rule, no one attached his name and life to Greece as did the English gentleman, George Gordon, Lord Byron, who, from 1809 to 1810, with his friend John Cam Hobhouse, crossed the land of the Greeks from its uppermost northern border to the islands of the Aegean. This was Lord Byron's first visit to Greece. He spent a long time in Athens, attracted by the ancient glory of the "dawn-crowned city", by the wonderful monuments of classic art and by Theresa Makri, the gentle maiden of Athens who inspired the romantic poet with the purest feeling of love ("Maid of Athens, Ere We Part").

During his stay in Athens, Lord Byron visited the historic places of the city one-by-one and with his seminal imagination he recreated the dramatic phases of ancient Greek history. He often climbed up to the Acropolis and spent many days walking from one end of the sacred rock to the other, gazing and daydreaming. The echo of his steps sounded to him like the re-echoing of ancient times and reminded him of all he had learned at Harrow School and Cambridge University of the unique greatness of the ancient Greeks.

Byron deeply admired the ancient temples, the altars, the graveyards, the pillars, but he grieved to see the maimed statues

and stolen monuments and to hear of the terrible deeds of the civi-
lised Europeans who, arriving as admirers and worshippers of the
ancient monuments, turned into common thieves of ancient works
of art. Ambassadors, consuls, legal representatives of large or
small European countries, merchants and others, tore through enslaved Greece and, on their own or in co-operation with the conquerors, secretly or otherwise, snatched any valuable marble
works of art they could lay their hands on; thus there developed the
most rewarding but vulgar trade of all time. No other worshipper of
ancient Greece was as furious about the sacrilege and as ashamed
of his thieving fellow Englishmen as was Lord Byron. Was it he
who, hinting at the villainy of the greatest of these sacrilegious
people, Lord Elgin, carved the words "*Quod non fecerunt Goti, hoc
fecerunt Scoti*" on the artless block which initially replaced the stolen
Caryatid?[4]

What did the poet find in Athens? He who had been brought up
with a classical education, with the history of Greece, with the
miracle of the ancient Greek civilisation, he who knew of the
renowned land of Aeschylus, of Pericles and of "the residence of
the gods" found a pitiful town in the midst of which rose the
gleaming-white Acropolis to remind the educated vistor of the difference between the ancient greatness and its tragic decline. He
came to Athens guided by the vision of the temple of Demos, of Ario
Pago, the last democracy of the world, where the most perfect type
of a free and responsible civilisation developed. And he found the
descendants of the ancient Athenians, now pitiful slaves of barbarian conquerors, uneducated, poor, and oppressed.[5] A visitor to
Greece was confronted with the same picture wherever he travelled
in the ancient land. The impressions he carried away with him
were sad and the thoughts of present and future Greece were pessi-
mistic. Under the influence of these feelings, Lord Byron wrote
these verses which seem to form a sepulchral epigram:

> Cold is the heart, fair Greece! that looks on Thee,
> Nor feels as Lovers o'er the dust they loved;

Such was the general impression most visitors to enslaved
Greece formed at the time. But they were not able to grasp the
strength these Greeks had developed. Only a few years before the
1821 national rising, foreigners saw the Greek people as weak,
powerless and repressed, and the idea of national freedom quite

dead. Lord Byron, however, did not mock this degraded race as other less faithful foreigners had done, but preserved the spark of love and devotion towards the young Greeks in his heart; and this spark, which had come into being through the revolution and its first achievements, rose to a flame which enveloped this gentle phil-hellene.

During his first trip to the East (1809–11), Lord Byron spent approximately one year in Athens. About the middle of 1811, he returned to England. He believed he would retire from his adventures and enjoy his fortune and his title while writing poetry; but he could not. His restless, free, and brave spirit would not allow him to live in a restrictive, puritanical society. That was why he sought the joy of living elsewhere, in warmer climates, in brighter countries where the people and the sun smile all the year round. In 1816 he left England forever to settle in Northern Italy. In Venice, that idyllic city, with its rather loose morals, he lived a life of entertainment and pleasure until 1819, when he fell in love with Teresa Guiccioli, his "last attachment".

Love adventures, however, were not always Lord Byron's ideal pastimes. His restless and continually unsatisfied spirit always sought something new. For a while he thought he had found what he was seeking when he joined the Italian *carbonari* movement which acted against the Austrians and their agents. He worked with zeal in this secret society, even assisting with financial aid. Teresa Guiccioli's brother, Pietro Gamba, helped him turn the Palazzo Guiccioli, his Ravenna residence, into the headquarters and armoury of the revolutionaries. What was it that pushed him towards this new kind of adventure? Could it have been the love he felt for the political freedom of the Italians, or was it his boundless thirst for new adventures, for emotional involvement, for glory?

The ideals of the Italian revolution soon deteriorated. During the Laibach convention in 1821, the Austrians, in a matter of weeks, managed to repress through force all the insurrections in Italy. Lord Byron's thirst for adventure had lost its object. For a while he thought of going to a new continent, to America, where he was already well-known. What kind of emotional involvement could the vast and distant continent offer a man who sought danger, quick glory and stirring adventure?

Before the Italian revolution was suppressed, there opened a new scene in eastern Europe with the Greeks as protagonists, fighting for their political and national freedom. An unhappy people, with a vast spiritual inheritance, they had begun their struggle for freedom or death against an almighty Empire. They fought for the ideals and rights that Lord Byron himself worshipped. These descendants of the ancient Greeks, after so many centuries of slavery and now ready for any sacrifice, sought to gain with the sword their national freedom and their ancestral inheritance. Lord Byron worshipped Greece and was very liberal in his ideas. What more could he ask than to be a friend and supporter of the Greeks?

Towards the end of February 1823, Lord Byron began thinking seriously about Greece. Nothing could have attracted him more. The state of the Greek people, the heroic and historic country where the action was taking place, the danger of unequal opponents – all these attracted the English poet. The revolution was still a rising by a despairing people, with no external help or support, fighting with faith but with no certainty of outcome, aware of the opposition of the major Christian Powers of Europe. This is exactly what enchanted Lord Byron enough to lead him to stand up against the official governments of Europe and their powerful kings. How this attracted him!

Emperors and their ministers, supporters of class-distinction, friends of the Sultan, supporters of the Ottoman Empire, all adhered to the recent treaties because they wished to preserve the status quo in Europe, even if that meant that Christian people remained enslaved to conquerors of a different faith. On the other hand, this popular poet, as handsome as Adonis, as corrupt as Alkiviadis, presented himself as the friend of these enslaved people, the protector of the rebelling Greeks. Luckily, as his friend Hobhouse wrote to him, the English had already begun to take an interest in supporting the Greeks by founding the Philhellenic Society, of which many of Lord Byron's friends were members.

On 13 July 1823, Lord Byron left Genoa for Greece. He had with him, apart from a few loyal servants, the outlandish Edward Trelawny, the Italian doctor Bruno and his secretary and confidential adviser Pietro Gamba, brother of Countess Guiccioli. From the diary of the trustworthy Gamba we derive authentic information about the journey and Lord Byron's life up to his death.[6]

The passengers had their horses, arms, and ammunition with them as well as two guns from the *Bolivar*, Byron's schooner, which he had left in Genoa harbour. Once at Leghorn, he sought advice and letters of reference from Ignatio, the Bishop of Hungaro–Wallachia and Metropolitan of Arta, then in exile at Pisa, who held great influence over Greece, especially the mainland, and over its political and military powers.

Ignatio supplied Lord Byron with the necessary details on the most important Greek leaders of the army and government, especially on Mavrocordatos and Marco Botsari. In a previous letter of 29 July 1823 he had informed Mavrocordatos of Lord Byron's intentions and had drawn his attention to the English Lord's personality.

> The English Lord is coming to see the Greek state of affairs and to give him a helping hand. He has many contacts and is a member of the committee formed in London in aid of the Greek people. He has important friends and could help if he is impressed and if the Greek people win him over with their pleasant attitude.[7]

But because he knew Lord Byron's unstable character and his restless way of living, the Bishop wrote a second letter a month later and drew Mavrocordatos' attention to these points in the character of the poet:

> I have introduced you to Lord Byron who should be in Zakinthos by now. Do whatever you can to please him, not so much because he could give financial aid and real help, but mostly because if he fails he could do more harm than you could ever believe. Let the government show all proper welcome and honour to this man because his recommendation and his testimony are of the greatest value.[8]

During his journey, Lord Byron read the popular first volume of Langaze's memoirs and discussed with his travel companions the declining splendour of Napoleon Bonaparte's spirit while he lived through the final bitter days on St Helena. On 3 August 1823, he arrived at Argostolion where he met the well-known philhellene Colonel Napier, Governor of Cephalonia. After a pleasant trip to Ithaki, he returned to Argostolion, where he hired forty soldiers from Souli who had been uprooted from their homeland by the savageness of Ali Tepelene twenty years previously. These soldiers he sent to Missolonghi and received in return a warm letter of thanks from Marcos Botsaris dated only a few hours before this man met with a heroic death on the borders of Carpenision.

While in Argostolion, Byron received a letter from London which appointed him the main representative of the English Phil-hellenic Society of London. He was also informed from Greek sources of the political dissension among the rebelling Greeks. This dissension had begun at the second National Conference at Astri, had hindered a smooth political development, and was fast leading to civil war. Ignatio had especially recommended two Greek leaders to Lord Byron and these two held the English Lord's admiration most. They were Marcos Botsaris and Mavrocord-atos. The former, however, had fallen on the battlefield and the latter had escaped to Hydra after being cruelly threatened by Kolokotronis. The two factions in Greece were struggling to win Lord Byron – and his money – over to their side and did not hesitate to accuse one another in order to appear the rightful leaders of the rebelling Greek people.

George Praidis, while in Cephalonia on a mission, wrote a letter on 26 September 1823, to Ignatio who was in Pisa:

> ... Lord Byron is here. Upon arrival he heard about our dissen-sion and the accusations against Mavrocordatos, but he took no notice, because the people who informed him were not trust-worthy. He at once sent two people to Peloponnese[9] and to the government to take a close look and to inform them of his arrival and of his position as trustee of the Committee of London. They met with Hypsilanti and Kolokotroni and Papaphlessa at Tri-politsa and were told that Mavrocordatos was an enemy to Greece and that if he had remained an extra day in Tripolitsa, they would have put him on a donkey and sent him away from Greece. The Greek leaders told them to write to Lord Byron and advise him that if he wished to help Greece, he should neither seek Mavrocordatos nor listen to his advice but rather to dis-patch the boat, with arms sent from England, to Nauplion.[10]

Faced with this state of affairs in rebelling Greece, Lord Byron found himself in a difficult position. Gamba wrote in his diary,

> The person who gave us this information added that ... the Greek people are more interested in defaming each other than in obtaining independence for their country. The good thing is that they are not threatened very much by their enemies; the civil

wars are more dangerous to them than the Turkish attacks against them.[11]

Consequently, Lord Byron decided to remain in Cephalonia for a while in order to obtain more exact information about people and parties and until some kind of order was established on the confused political scene of rebelling Greece. He gave as much aid as he could to the needs of the revolution and, as a representative of the London Philhellenic Committee, he paid much attention to pressing needs, especially those of finance. He avoided getting involved in the political factions and attempted to persuade the leaders of the Greek revolution to unite and not waste money provided by the Philhellenes. He wrote to the "Executives" and the Parliament on 30 November 1823,

All I am seeking is the welfare of Greece and nothing else. I will do my utmost to achieve this; but I do not and never will consent to the deception of the English people or even of certain persons in England as to the true state of matters in Greece. The rest, gentlemen, depends on you. You have fought gloriously; now you must be honest towards your fellow countrymen and towards foreigners. Then it will not be said – what has already been said two thousand years ago – that Philopimi was the last of the Greeks. . . .[12]

On 15 October 1823, the Parliament, of which Panoutzos Notaras was then President, asked Lord Byron to finance the revolution with 30,000 dollars of his personal money and to take an interest in Missolonghi.

. . . because it is deemed necessary to dispatch Alexandros Mavrocordatos, a good patriot and chairman of Parliament to Missolonghi to organise things there and generally in the Western Districts of Greece. We beg your excellency to give voluntary assistance in any possible way, in cooperation with Mavrocordatos who knows their exact needs, to that part of Greece which . . . already suffers more than any other area in Greece.[13]

On 29 November 1823, Mavrocordatos was taken to Missolonghi in a warship commanded by Captain Pinotzi, and he took over the direction of Western Greece. Lord Byron, who apart from taking heed of the recommendation, had formed his own personal opinion of Mavrocordatos, was willing to meet and co-operate with him at Missolonghi. John Orlandos, who was heading for London with Andreas Louriotis to make arrangements for the government loan and who went through Argostolion to talk with Lord Byron, thought it necessary to inform Mavrocordatos, who was in Missolonghi, as to the English Lord's character. In a letter of 1 November 1823, he wrote:

> As Lord Byron has told us, he wishes to meet you. Before this meeting takes place, I wish to tell you a few things about his character. Lord Byron is a philhellene and even though he may want to aid Greece, others influence his feelings. This is probably the cause of his everchanging decisions. . . .[14]

On 4 January 1824, after an adventurous and dangerous journey, Lord Byron and his companions, having been formally invited by the Greek Government and by Mavrocordatos, arrived at Missolonghi where he was warmly welcomed by the army and the people. His appearance, dressed as he was in a magnificent scarlet uniform, relieved and encouraged the Greeks, who thought him as beautiful and impressive as Ares.

Lord Byron's presence encouraged the whole of rebelling Greece during that very difficult period of the Greek revolution; for apart from internal disturbances, they sadly lacked financial aid. They all looked upon him as a panacea. The central government sought loans for the enlargement and maintenance of the fleet. John Orlandos wrote from Cephalonia to Mavrocordatos at Missolonghi on 13 November 1823: "I hope your meeting with Lord Byron will secure us a loan of an extra ten thousand dollars, because all that he has loaned us to date suffices only for two months' wages of our crew."[15]

Emmanuel Antoniadis, representative of Crete, repeatedly asked Lord Byron for a loan of 10,000 dollars to save Crete.

> With tears in my eyes I dare to beg of you, Sir, to listen to me while I warmly plead with you, on behalf of Crete, for the benefit of mankind, knowing that by helping you will save the people of Crete and give the island a better chance. You will find that the Cretans will display all due gratitude and respect. . . .[16]

Anagnostis Monarhidis, representative of Psara, in a letter to Mavrocordatos of 3 January 1824, asks for a small loan from money given by Lord Byron, for the island's small fleet to enable it to move in defense of Euboea. "I am in no doubt that you wish to prompt the above said charitable Lord Byron to grant a certain amount as a loan in aid of Euboea, which island without doubt will succumb to slavery ... worse than the first unless help can reach there in time."[17]

Mavrocordatos, on the other hand, desiring to found a lawful state and a worthy army in Western Greece, wanted to introduce Lord Byron to the essential Greek cause. He based his thoughts on Lord Byron's love for Greece, on his love for liberty, on his love for glory, on his wish to be famous in England and the rest of the world, and, finally, on his financial power. On 16 January 1824 he wrote to Theodore Negri in Salona: "As far as Lord Byron is concerned, I can only tell you that he is quite willing to help our cause; he is prepared to do anything which he thinks beneficial ...."[18]

Lord Byron indeed became greatly involved in serving the cause of the Greek revolution in co-operation with Mavrocordatos. He accepted the leadership of the campaign against Nafpakto even though he was no soldier, hoping that the various independent partisans who were not too willing to take orders from Greek leaders, would do so from him. He also drafted and paid the wages of 500 fighters from Souli who, since the death of Marco Botsari, were drifting around in poverty in Missolonghi and Eastern Greece.[19] He also aided the organisation of a small body of riflemen and helped, at first in co-operation with Colonel Stanhope, to finance two newspapers in Missolonghi, *The Greek Chronicle* and *The Greek Telegraph*.

Despite daily disappointments which sometimes verged on actual suffering – especially concerning the disobedient fighters from Souli – Lord Byron's work at Missolonghi was fruitful and creative. On 26 January 1824 Mavrocordatos was pleased to write to the Greek government:

> As far as his lordship is concerned, he is ready to do whatever the Greek Government wishes. He is quite willing to go to Peloponnese if you ask him, even though he has accepted leadership of the campaign against Nafpakto, and would do anything you ask of him. He has undertaken the payment of 500 soldiers from Souli and is quite willing to either keep them with him when he

goes on a mission or send them off on their own wherever you wish. . . . [20]

It is obvious that Mavrocordatos spared no effort to make Lord Byron's difficult work in Missolonghi a little easier for him. Lord Byron's appointment as Commander General of operations against Aetolia is recorded in the Mavrocordatos Archives:

To the temporary ruling party of Greece.
From the Director General of Western Greece.

(a) His excellency Mr Lord Byron is appointed Commander General of the Greek forces in Aetolia.
(b) The fighters from Souli who are under the command of K. Botsari and Kitso Tzavella are under his lordship's direct leadership.
(c) The general army camp is to be moved near the fort of Nafpakto, whose seige is to be tightened and whose occupation is to be attempted.
(d) A force of riflemen under Captain William Parry is to be placed under his lordship's order.
(e) The war council is to be with his lordship at the General War Camp and is to be at his service.
(f) The prefects of Lidoricio, Karavvari, Melandrino, Apokouro and Venetico will be responsible to the Commander General for everything concerning the campaign.

Missolonghi . . . February 1824[21]

Much to Lord Byron's disappointment, the campaign against Nafpaktos had to be postponed for want of preparations and was finally cancelled. Lord Byron, now in a state of continual unrest, was low-spirited and anxious because of the swarm of problems that confronted him for solution. His biggest problem was the continuing turmoil within the walls of Missolonghi. The untameable fighters from Souli, although intrepid and invincible on the battlefield, were disorderly and unmanageable in the city; and because Lord Byron had built his hopes on these Suliotes, their attitude caused him much anxiety. Furthermore, these fighters were the only remaining military body in the city ever since the meeting of the partisans, arranged by Mavrocordatos, had failed.

All these different problems which Lord Byron faced daily, his disputes and quarrels with Stanhope, certain difficulties from outside Greece, especially the criticism from the wise and influential Greek living in Paris, Adamantios Korais, who was suspicious of Byron's and Stanhope's growing influence in Greece, greatly disturbed Byron. Korais, in warning the Greeks about Byron, quoted a fragment from Epicharmus: "Think clearly and proceed with caution."[22] This remark disturbed Byron and created in him an unhappiness and pessimism which was reflected in all his work but never once reduced his zeal for the Greek cause.

In this state of mind Lord Byron wrote, on 22 January 1824, the admirable verses of "On This Day I Complete My Thirty-Sixth Year".

'Tis time this heart, should be unmoved,
   Since others it hath ceased to move:
Yet, though I cannot be beloved,
    Still let me love!

My days are in the yellow leaf;
   The flowers and fruits of Love are gone;
The worm, the canker, and the grief
    Are mine alone!

              *   *   *

But 'tis not thus – and 'tis not here –
   Such thoughts should shake my soul, nor now,
Where Glory decks the hero's bier,
    Or binds his brow.

The Sword, the Banner, and the Field,
   Glory and Greece, around me see!
The Spartan borne upon his shield,
    Was not more free!

Awake! (not Greece – she *is* awake!)
   Awake, my spirit! Think through *whom*
Thy life-blood tracks its parent lake,
    And then strike home!

              *   *   *

If thou regret'st thy youth, *why live?*
   The land of honourable death

Is here: – up to the Field, and give
Away thy breath!

Seek out – less often sought than found –
A soldier's grave, for thee the best;
Then look around, and choose thy ground,
And take thy Rest.

It seems certain that from that day forward Lord Byron was seeking both an "honourable death" and "a soldier's grave", for he had decided to remain and die for Greece. Where else would he find a more beautiful "grave of glory"? Since then he often repeated to his friend Gamba: "Others can do as they wish. They can return but I will remain here; that is certain." The same persistent thought was expressed in his letters to friends, as though he had a premonition he would not leave Greece alive.[23]

The continual efforts to found a body of riflemen were a pleasant creative occupation for Lord Byron and his secretary Gamba. This small body of men allowed him to believe that he could soon realise his hopes, because the success of the plans for the siege of Nafpakto depended on these riflemen.[24] In appreciation of their efforts, Alexandros Mavrocordatos, issued an order on 22 February 1824, appointing Lord Byron colonel of the rifle battalion and Count Pietro Gamba, his lieutenant. To show its highest appreciation, the High Court at Kranidi decided – either on its own accord or at Mavrocordatos' suggestion – to grant to Lord Byron the honorary citizenship of Greece. John Kolettis, a member of the Executives, wrote to Mavrocordatos on 5 March 1824: "I will send you Byron's citizenship papers."[25] A few days later, on 29 March 1824, Lord Byron was proclaimed citizen and benefactor of Missolonghi.[26]

On March 22, 1824, Lord Byron received a message via Leghorn and Zakintho informing him that the Greek Loan had at last been granted and that he was appointed director of the trio who were responsible for the distribution of the money in Greece. With this loan in mind, Lord Byron made many plans, mainly concerning wars at sea. On March 11, 1824, Mavrocordatos wrote the following to the government:

His lordship thinks that now that we are sure of the loan, we should speed up the completion of the fleet and if it is not yet needed at Hellispondo, two parts should be sent out: one to join the fleet which is already here and the other to join the Egyptian fleet which is now somewhere near Crete.[27]

But the fighting between pro-government and anti-government factions had already begun, the major dispute being which of the two parties would administer the money of the loan. In Salona, in March 1824, Theodore Negri and Odesseas Androutsos called a general meeting and, having Stanhope on their side, invited Lord Byron, Mavrocordatos, and others, thus giving the impression of a general reconciliation. In fact, their aim was to isolate Mavrocordatos and gain Lord Byron's friendship and trust. Lord Byron, strongly in favor of national unity, had decided to go to Salona. But by 27 March he was prevented from going by ill health, impassable roads and unfordable rivers.[28]

Lord Byron's health was rapidly deteriorating. He first experienced an attack on 15 February 1824.[29] Mavrocordatos, in a letter to the government later in February, wrote: "Lord Byron has experienced some sort of paralysis but is now in good health. This, for the time being, should prevent him from realising the campaign against Nafpakto, if it is still planned and if it has not been postponed for other reasons."[30]

During March Lord Byron's health continued to be precarious, and early in April he experienced another attack and from then on his health worsened. His doctors, Millingen, Bruno, the German Eric Treimber and Loukas Vagia, sought in vain to save his life. During his illness and especially during his last days there was much anxiety among the people of Missolonghi. On 17 April, Mavrocordatos wrote a letter of desperation to the government:

A stroke of bad luck which cannot be remedied is threatening us and generally the whole of Greece. This is Lord Byron's dangerous state of health. He is breathing his last and the doctors can do no more for him. That is why I departed during the night, to reach Colonel Stanhope as soon as I could, to inform him of his lordship's condition, so that he may reach him in time. . . .[31]

During his final hours, Byron's thoughts turned to his daughter, his sister, his friends, his men in attendance, and more often, to Greece. "Poor Greece . . . I gave her my time . . . my fortune . . . my health. Now I give her my life. What more can I do?"[32]

On the afternoon of 19 April, the Monday after Easter, Lord Byron died. Grief and astonishment struck the people of Missolonghi, Western Greece, and the whole Greek population. In the minds of the Greek people, who idolised Byron and his military ability, the loss was irreplaceable. His love for Greece was thought to be boundless, his financial means inexhaustible, his powers superhuman. A few days earlier, the Sultan, at a meeting of the Divan, had proclaimed Lord Byron an enemy of the Ottoman Empire because of his pro-Greek activity.

The honours paid to the dead Lord Byron were analogous to the grief of the Greek people. A jar containing his lungs and viscera was deposited in the Church of San Spiridion and later removed to the Church of St Nicholas near the walls of Missolonghi. The funeral service was conducted by the Archbishop of Arta, Porphirios. Spiridon Tricoupis, the politician and historian, delivered a spontaneous eulogy which was first published in the *Greek Chronicle* and later in many other newspapers throughout Greece.

In addition to the proclamation issued in Missolonghi by Mavrocordatos on the day of Lord Byron's death, which referred to the honours paid to him, the Temporary Government of Greece, seated at Nafplion, issued another proclamation on 22 April 1824, now at the Mavrocordatos Centre, which announced that the first of May was to be a day of mourning for the whole of liberated Greece, "in memorial of the loss of the excellent man Lord Byron". It also described activities of political and military leaders all over Greece in honour of the dead Lord Byron. The first lines of the proclamation betray the emotional state of its composers:

> Because Lord Noel Byron ceased to walk on the Greek soil he had loved so much and for so many years, he has left for the land of eternity leaving great unhappiness in all Greek hearts; and because Greece is forever indebted to him for all his good deeds in her favour, the Nation should name him Father and Benefactor and mourn his death. . . .[33]

Peter Gamba, in describing Lord Byron's death, wrote:

> He died in a foreign land among foreigners, but had he passed away in any other land, he wouldn't have been more loved nor more sincerely mourned. Such was the devotion, mixed with awe and enthusiasm, which he inspired in those around him. . . . All Greeks, regardless of age and status, from Mavro-

cordatos to the most insignificant civilian, mourned for
him. . . .[34]

In the prologue of a book dedicated to one of Lord Byron's oldest
friends, John Cam Hobhouse, Gamba wrote:

> On the day of their victory, the Greek people did not forget their
> benefactor and showed that they felt deeply obligated to that
> great man and that their appreciation will last until his name
> shall cease to be mentioned among the nations of the world.[35]

The words of this Italian gentleman could well be repeated by
any Greek, contemporary or of subsequent generations. The
Greeks are eternally grateful to this philhellene poet, not for his
military success, nor for his financial aid (which his relatives and
inheritors repeatedly sought to retrieve from the Greek Committee
in London),[36] but for his sincere love for Greece and its people. By
means of his verse he praised the ancient glory of Greece, mourned
the miseries of her slavery, and finally gave his life in the struggle
for her national liberation.

One hundred and fifty years after his death we can, I think,
safely say that Lord Byron owes a part of his posthumous fame and
glory, independent of that associated with his poetry, to Greece.
Lord Byron became an integral part of the Greek nation and en-
rolled his name in the eternity of Greek history.

Lord Byron's death, at so young an age, coming at the time of
Greece's war for independence, when people in Europe and all over
the world were fighting for liberty, gave new status to the ideal of
freedom. That is why liberals all over the world regard Lord Byron
as a pioneer in the democratic restoration of the social and political
independence of all people, regardless of geographic boundaries.

One could repeat and perhaps agree, though with some reserva-
tion, with what Eleftherios Venizelos said at Newstead Abbey in
July 1931, in paying tribute to Lord Byron:

> Had Lord Byron not come to Greece to die, during Easter of
> 1824, while gazing at the Missolonghi lagoon, the battle of
> Navarino in 1827 might never have taken place. The countries of
> Eastern Europe might have waited many more years to gain
> their freedom and the history of a substantial part of Europe
> might have developed differently.

NOTES

1. Peter Gössler, "Nordische Gäste in Athen um 1810", *Archaeological Newspaper*, vol. 1 (1937), p. 69.
2. E. G. Protopsaltis, *George Christian Gropius and his Work in Greece* (Athens, 1947) , p. 78.
3. Lord Byron, *Childe Harold*, Canto II, xi-xv.
4. J. Gennadios, *Lord Elgin and Those Before Him in Greece and Athens in Connection with the Snatching of Ancient Works of Art* (Athens: Estia Press, 1930) p. 78.
5. G. Konstandinidis, *The History of Athens* (Athens: Filokalias Press, 1876) p. 565.
6. Pietro Gamba, *Relation de l'expedition du Lord Byron en Grèce* (Paris, 1825). Translated into Greek by B. Anninos and included in the "Historic Notes" published in Athens 1925. First English ed. London: 1825).
7. Alexandros Mavrocordatos, *The Historical Archives of Alexandros Mavrocordatos* [Hereafter referred to as *H.A.M.*] Edited by E.G. Protopsaltis (Athens: Academy of Athens Press) vol. 3, p. 355.
8. Ibid., p. 420.
9. Hamilton Browne and Edward Trelawny.
10. *H.A.M.*, vol. 3, pp. 514–15.
11. Pietro Gamba, *Byron in Greece*, 2nd ed. (Athens: Galaxios Press, 1966) p. 28.
12. Ibid., p. 45. See also *H.A.M.*, vol. 3, p. 609.
13. *H.A.M.*, vol. 3, p. 552.
14. *H.A.M.*, vol. 3, p. 569.
15. *H.A.M.*, vol. 3, p. 569.
16. *H.A.M.*, vol. 3, pp. 526–27; vol. 4, p. 178.
17. *H.A.M.*, vol. 4, p. 44.
18. *H.A.M.*, vol. 4, p. 71.
19. Pietro Gamba, *Byron in Greece*, pp. 66–7.
20. *H.A.M.*, vol. 4, p. 100.
21. *H.A.M.*, vol. 4, pp. 117–18.
22. *H.A.M.*, vol. 4, p. 132 (Letter by K. Gerostathi to Mavrocordatos, February 4, 1824).
23. Pietro Gamba, *Byron in Greece*, p. 81.
24. *H.A.M.*, vol. 4, p. 190.
25. *H.A.M.*, vol. 4, p. 233.
26. *Greek Chronicle of Missolonghi*, 12 April 1824. See also A. Ligniadis, *The First Loan of Independence* (Athens, 1970), p. 243.
27. *H.A.M.*, vol. 4, p. 248.
28. A. Ligniadis, *The First Loan of Independence*, pp. 233ff.
29. *Greek Chronicle of Missolonghi*, 6 February 1824.
30. *H.A.M.*, vol. 4, p. 160.
31. *H.A.M.*, vol. 3, p. 319.
32. Pietro Gamba, *Byron in Greece*, pp. 153–4.
33. *H.A.M.*, vol. 4, p. 342.
34. Pietro Gamba, *Byron in Greece*, p. 155.

35. Ibid., p. 9.
36. *H.A.M.*, vol. 4, p. 9 (Letter by Count Palma to G. Koundouriotis, 21 November 1824).

6 Byron and Italy

Catalyst of the *Risorgimento*

GIORGIO MELCHIORI

It may be an overstatement to maintain that Byron had a direct influence on Italian political thought in the nineteenth century, but his importance in defining and disseminating some of the principles of the new liberal ideology in England should not be underrated. Liberalism closely patterned on the English model was the leading doctrine of many of the Italians who brought about the *Risorgimento*, culminating in the unification of Italy.

Byron's liberalism was, of course, tinged with radicalism, an attitude which became clear when, going to Italy in the late months of 1816, he found a country where liberal principles could prevail only through revolutionary change. It is significant that one of the first poems he wrote – in December 1816 – shortly after his arrival in Italy, when he was still thinking in terms of English politics, should be the "Song For The Luddites":

> As the Liberty lads o'er the sea
> Bought their freedom, and cheaply, with blood,
> So we, boys, we
> Will *die* fighting, or *live* free,
> And down with all kings but King Ludd!
>
> When the web that we weave is complete,
> And the shuttle exchanged for the sword,
> We will fling the winding sheet
> O'er the despot at our feet,
> And dye it deep in the gore he has pour'd.
>
> Though black as his heart its hue
> Since his veins are corrupted to mud,
> Yet this is the dew

Which the tree shall renew
Of Liberty planted by Ludd!

This seems to contradict the non-committed and irresponsible life led by Byron during his first two years in Venice. The reasons that had prompted Byron to leave England for good are well-known. Perhaps the clearest statement of the way in which the poet himself saw them is to be found in an entry in his Journal written on 23 November 1813 nearly three years before his momentous decision:

> If I had any views in this country [England], they would probably be parliamentary. But I have no ambition; at least, if any, it would be *aut Caesar aut nihil*. My hopes are limited to the arrangement of my affairs, and settling either in Italy or the East (rather the last), and drinking deep of the language and literature of both. . . . Past events have unnerved me; and all I can do now is to make life an amusement, and look on while others play.[1]

But this is exactly what he did not do. After refusing to play a part in English politics, he became involved (though perhaps not immediately) in the Italian struggle for unification and independence. It is true that personal participation in the struggle was prompted by his liaison with Teresa Guiccioli whose father and brother, the Counts Ruggero and Pietro Gamba, were local leaders of the *carbonari* movement in the Pope's northern provinces. But, even before meeting Teresa, Byron had been thinking and writing about his political views, which had not changed since he had written the page of the Journal in 1813 which I have quoted before. On that very page he had attacked "the dull, stupid old system – balance of Europe – poising straws upon kings' noses, instead of wringing them off!"
And he added:

> Give me a republic, or a despotism of one, rather than the mixed government of one, two, or three. A republic! – look in the history of the Earth – Rome, Greece, Venice, France, Holland, America, our short (eheu!) Commonwealth, and compare with what they did under masters.

It is easy to see how the very history of Venice – a Republic in which the Doge could ally himself with the people against a corrupt oligarchy of aristocrats – tallied with Byron's views. Commenting on Otway's *Venice Preserv'd* in a letter to John Murray on 2 April 1817, he wrote:

> The story of *Marino Faliero* is different, and, I think, so much finer, that I wish Otway had taken it instead: the head conspiring against the body for refusal of redress for a real injury, – jealousy – treason, with the more fixed and inveterate passions (mixed with policy) of an old or elderly man – the devil himself could not have a finer subject, and he is your only tragic dramatist.

The two Venetian historical tragedies, *Marino Faliero* and *The Two Foscari*, written between 1819 and 1821, with no love interest and no metaphysics in them, are thoroughly political plays; they can be placed side by side with his *Prophecy of Dante*, written at the same time as witnessing his involvement in politics; the tragedies are the expression of more general views; the *Prophecy*, written as Byron states in the introductory sonnet, at the instance of Teresa Guiccioli, but in fact reflecting the attitude which the poet was sharing with her father and brother, is strictly linked with the specific issues at the basis of the *carbonari* movement. Indeed, even after the failure of the *carbonari* rising, and the removal of the Gambas from the Pope's dominions to the more enlightened Grand Duchy of Tuscany, the Grand-ducal authorities were worried by the *Prophecy*, because it was "most decidedly not written in the spirit of our Government, or of any of the Italian Governments," as, in it, "Lord Byron makes Dante advocate democracy and the independence of Italy for the salvation and good of the country"; they feared that the students at the famed University of Pisa would rally round the supporter of such unseemly principles.[2]

Apart from the link represented by Teresa Guiccioli, it was inevitable that Byron should be befriended by the Italian liberals the moment he set foot in Italy; but his immediate influence was not as great as that which his whole personality made after his death in Greece, when the national movement for the unification of the country got really under way. The Italian *Risorgimento* did not originate as a people's liberation movement: it was prompted instead by different intellectual élites in a number of small states, with different rulers, statutes, and traditions. The leaders were highly educated men, from the higher classes, who, being aware of a community of culture, felt the need to create a national consciousness in the people. Though they operated within a European rather than a narrowly nationalistic Italian context, they were conditioned to a certain extent by local situations, by the greater or lesser degree of freedom of expression and of access to information in the different states. The ideals of the French revolution had taken no root in them, because the brief period of Napoleonic rule in the Italian states had not been an improvement on the previous condition of foreign domination.

Besides, some potential members of this élite were too strongly linked with the local ruling classes not to prefer a conservative attitude; and, even more important, there was the religious question, the strong grip of the Catholic Church and of the moral – and political – principles it stood for, not only on the common people who had been in its thrall for centuries, but even on some of the most enlightened spirits. To what extent could they disagree with the judgement passed years later on Byron by the most authoritative Catholic philosopher and political thinker, Vincenzo Gioberti: "He helped the Greeks in his time, but he was, and is, a curse to the whole of Europe, as long as his writings will survive, which teach blasphemy and corruption."[3]

What was Byron's reputation in Italy when he went to settle there? What kind of information circulated among Italians on the rich English Lord who had descended on them, accompanied by a remarkable menagerie and a doubtful fame as a high-class rake? His poetry was known only to small circles of liberal-minded men of letters in Milan, Florence, and Turin; the rest was excited gossip going the rounds of the arisotcratic drawing rooms. Professor Martha King has admirably documented the way in which Byron's work became the mainstay of the supporters of the Romantic ideals among Milanese intellectuals.[4] *The Giaour* appeared in an Italian version by Pellegrino Rossi in 1818, eliciting enthusiastic essays from the Milanese poet and critic, the liberal Abbé Lodovico di Breme. At the same time Silvio Pellico, the poet, dramatist, and patriot (now best known for his moving Memoirs of a long term of imprisonment for political reasons in an Austrian fortress, *Le mie prigioni*), stated that the verse tales were not truly representative: the greatness of Byron's poetic genius was best seen in the plays he had started writing in Italy; and Pellico provided the first Italian translation of *Manfred*, which from that moment became the model of the Romantic hero, self-searching and self-tormented, breaking through the bonds of conventional morality and religion. In Italy, then as now, literary movements, as well as philosophical and ethical issues, are never separated from political ones; such a hero would appeal to the most independent spirits, those who pursued the ideal of a united country, free from the oppression of the Austro–Hungarian Empire and its quislings, from the Bourbons, the Pope and the Church. Byron's involvement in the *carbonari* movement and the attempted rising in the Romagna against the papal rule in 1821 fits perfectly into this pattern.

But after that date there was some kind of rift between Byron and his Italian admirers. On Byron's side, the failed revolutionary attempt made him highly critical of the ineffectual behaviour of the Italian patriots. He had been waiting hourly to play a major part in a revolution. The Ravenna diary for the early months of 1821 is full of excitement: the entry for 24 February gives the full measure both of his enthusiasm and of his disillusion:

> The secret intelligence arrived this morning from the frontier to the Carbonari is as bad as possible. The plan has missed – the Chiefs are betrayed, military, as well as civil. . . .
>
> Thus the world goes; and thus the Italians are always lost for lack of union among themselves. What is to be done *here*, between the two fires, and cut off from the Neapolitan frontier, is not decided. My opinion was – better to rise than to be taken in detail; but how it will be settled now, I cannot tell. Messengers are despatched to the delegates of the other cities to learn their resolutions.
>
> I always had an idea that it would be *bungled*; but was willing to hope, and am so still. Whatever I can do by money, means, or person, I will venture freely for their freedom; and have so re-peated to them (some of the Chiefs here) half an hour ago. I have two thousand five hundred scudi, better than five hundred pounds, in the house, which I offered to begin with.

The disaffection, as I said, was reciprocal. On the Italian side, an episode which occurred next year, when Byron and the Gambas had been forced to move their residence to Tuscany, alienated many sympathisers. During a rather futile quarrel between Byron's party and a certain Masi, a cavalry sergeant in the Tuscan Grand-ducal Army whom Byron had taken for an officer and a gentleman, a servant of the English Lord rushed out of the palace he had rented in Pisa and wounded the sergeant in the groin; Byron sent a surgeon and offered money in reparation. but it was refused. The episode was artfully misrepresented and inflated by the Tuscan authorites, anxious to get rid of the inconvenient foreign resident and his subversive friends.[5] And even Byron's sympathisers found it awkward to adduce extenuating circumstances for what was made to appear as the typical behaviour of a proud feudal lord surrounded by a host of hired ruffians. So in 1823 Byron left for Greece under a cloud. Much of his real influence dates from after his death in the cause of Greek freedom, when he became a kind of underground hero for those Italians who were hoping and later fighting for national unity.

Two attitudes are clearly discernible in the Italian appreciation of Byron after 1824: on the one hand the whole-hearted celebrations (frequently anonymous, for obvious reasons); on the other the half-hearted acknowledgements of a poetic genius coupled with moral irresponsibility. A good starting point for a survey of the evolution of the Byron image in Italy can be the anonymous *Stanze alla memoria di Lord Byron*, published in Leghorn in 1825.[6] It is a poem of thirty-one octaves (the stanza form of *Don Juan*), preceded by a short biography and followed by an ample commentary. Stanza XIV is perhaps the most significant; Byron is compared to Homer:

> *Quando dei forti Padri il cieco vate*
> *Cantava ai figli le immortali gesta*
> *Fu di onor luce; ma tra le onorate*
> *Polvi dei tuoi cercar scintilla, e desta*
> *Farti da morte, a darti libertate,*
> *Oh prode Grecia, opra divina è questa!*
> *Byron tu il festi, e tra gli eterni allori*
> *Si appaghi Omero de' secondi onori.*

[When the blind bard sang to the children the immortal feats of their Fathers, he was honour's beacon; but to look for the sparks still hidden in thy honoured dust, and to awake thee from death, to give thee liberty, O valiant Greece, this is the work of a God! Byron did this, and Homer must be content to take a second place among those crowned with eternal laurel].

The unknown author seems to consider Byron as being (adapt-
ing Byron's own comment on Ugo Foscolo, the great poet who preferred exile in England to honours in Italy under Austrian rule)
more of the ancient Greek than of the modern Scot[7] – and he
remarks in his introduction:

> The occasion of his death is the most beautiful laurel shadowing
> his monument. It is as if, while he had already reached one way
> [through poetry] the temple of immortality, he wanted to try
> another path to ascend to it. Death caught him while he was
> lending a helping hand to raise and place again on the ancient
> pedestal the worshipped mistress of all nations, Greece.

The author is unnamed because, even under the benevolent rule of
the Archduke of Tuscany, it was somewhat dangerous to celebrate
a poet who had died for the freedom of an oppressed country. At the
time and for many years to come no mention was made in biographical notices of Byron's association with the *carbonari* –
unless under such formulas as the following (applied not to Byron
but to young Count Gamba, who in his turn lost his life in Greece):

> New events which it would be useless to recall here, caused
> severe measures to be taken against young Count Gamba, so
> that he had to leave Tuscany within three days, and it was hoped
> that Byron would follow his friend.[8]

Mention of a movement for the liberation of Italy was taboo. But
Byron's death in Greece served an extremely useful purpose for
Italian patriots, who could express their own feelings by referring
to his fate; while no attack on the Christian oppressors of Italy
would have been tolerated, no censorship could suppress a condemnation of Turkish rule over a Christian nation. The identification of the fates of Greece and Italy is the major result of the
effect of Byron's death at Missolonghi on Italian public opinion.

The interest in the life and work of Byron extended considerably.
While by 1842 there circulated in Italy literally hundreds of different translations into prose or verse of all the works of Byron, as
early as January 1825 the *Antologia del Gabinetto Viesseux* in Florence,
one of the most authoritative and well-informed literary periodicals in Italy, published ample extracts from *Byron's Conversations
with Captain Medwin*, from the 1824 Paris edition,[9] and this became

the main source of information on Byron's character and ideas for his Italian admirers.

Within this frame of reference special attention should be given to the librettos of operas, in the first half of the nineteenth century, which appear to be based on Byron's works, testifying to the popularity of the poet outside the narrow circle of the *letterati*. It should be underlined that, because of its immense appeal to a large section of the population, opera had become a vehicle for the expression of liberal ideals. Opera performances were not restricted to such famous theatres as the Scala and the Fenice, but were given in many provincial towns; everywhere they became the occasion for patriotic and anti-Austrian demonstrations. Improbable or absurd as most opera librettos may seem, the sheer excitement of the music made the feeling run high. Byron himself was involved in a quarrel at the Scala in Milan, just after going to Italy for the first time, when he rescued his friend, Dr Polidori, from the consequences of a violent argument with an Austrian officer whose headgear was blocking the view of the stage.

The two Venetian – and political – plays of Byron were set to music by two of the greatest and most popular of the opera composers of the century; true, Gaetano Donizetti's *Marino Faliero* (1834) is based on the adaptation of the French playwright Delavigne, with far too many sentimental interpolations;[10] but Giuseppe Verdi's *The Two Foscari* (1844) squarely poses the problem of republican freedom. Finally, the case of an opera by Gioacchino Rossini may well be considered emblematic. The opera was called *Mahomet the Second*, and when first performed in Naples in 1820 it was a signal failure, but when six years later – six years that had seen the emergence of a movement for Italian freedom, and Byron's death – the opera was revived in Paris, with a new French libretto by L. Balocchi and A. Soumet under the Byronic title *Le Siège de Corinth*, it was a thundering success. The plot was not based on Byron's *Siege of Corinth*, and the change of title could be taken as a rather callous way of cashing in on topical events and popular feeling about them. But the significant fact is that, not only the sophisticated audience of the Parisian Opéra, but also, shortly afterwards, the popular audiences of the Italian theatres were able to see the topicality of it, and the Byronic references, and to be moved by the famous choruses of the besieged Corinthians, inviting them to sacrifice life itself in the name of freedom and of the fight against the oppressor.[11] They sounded not only as evocations of the heroic struggle of the contemporary Greeks, but clarion calls for the divided and oppressed Italians.

By 1826, then, the association of Byron with the fight for Italian freedom was well established, and Byron was regarded, in the words of the Abbé di Breme, as a new Tyrtaeus. The most impressive evidence of this is given by Giuseppe Mazzini, the thinker and man of action, the most passionate propounder of the ideal of a free and united republican Italy and the original moving spirit of the *Risorgimento.* Mazzini was a man with considerable literary interests, and one of his early essays, written in 1830 for *The Monthly Chronicle* (he was a political refugee in England), but published in neutral Switzerland on the eve of the first war for Italian independence, is a comparative study of Byron and Goethe. One passage in it is particularly significant and material in establishing the Italian view of Byron:

> We don't know whether Goethe will enjoy a greater share of our admiration as an artist than Byron, but we know, and we have no hesitation in stating, that Byron will enjoy a greater share of our love as a man and as a poet. . . . It could be said that Byron wished to take upon himself the aspirations, the sufferings, the struggles, the whole load, in order to raise us up – to raise us, his brothers. He never deserted our cause, he never lacked human sympathy. Surrounded by slaves and by their oppressors, wandering through countries in which even memory was suppressed, witnessing the progress of the Restorations and the triumph of the principles of the Holy Alliance, he never swerved from his courageous opposition, but maintained, in the face of the world, his faith in the rights of the people, in the ultimate triumph of freedom, and in his duty to promote this by every means in his power, and whenever the opportunity offered. At Naples, in the Romagna, wherever he saw a spark which might break into flame, he was ready to come to the fore, ready for the fight. His inmost soul was the receptacle of splendid ruins, of proud thought and actions; he stigmatized cowardice, hypocrisy, injustice, wherever they appeared. Such was Byron's life, furiously tossed between present ills and future hopes. Often uneven, at times skeptical, but always suffering, even when he seemed to smile; always loving, even when he cursed.[12]

This judgement of Mazzini's is the more important if we consider that it was quoted, in full, thirty years later, in the handbook on the history of English Literature by Enrico Sollazi, the only one available to Italian readers for a generation.[13]

But Byron, in the 1820s and 1830s was not only appreciated by a liberal and highly literate thinker: he was part of the education of a stateman – the stateman whose name is frequently coupled with that of Mazzini as the other founding father of Italian national independence: Camillo Benso Count Cavour, who was to become Prime Minister of Piedmont. They pursued the same end through completely opposite means: Mazzini, a thinker and an idealist, through the enthusiastic theorization of a free republican regime; Cavour, a politician and a diplomat, through patient negotiations on behalf of a traditional monarchic system. A descendant of an ancient aristocratic family, Cavour was trained from adolescence for the diplomatic service and, according to family tradition, was in his early youth a cadet in the military academy. The notebooks and commonplace books that he kept while serving in the army between 1827 and 1832 have come to light only recently.[14] They are mainly crammed with extracts from the works of French, English, and Italian historians, political thinkers, economists, and the like, but there is one devoted exclusively to the English poets. Out of twelve entries in it, one is from Matthew Prior, two from Pope, and all the rest are from Byron's *Childe Harold's Pilgrimage*. The eighteen-year-old cadet had selected passages either in a sententious or in a lighter vein (for instance, on the nature of woman) accompanying them with such comments in English as "very excellent precepts". But in another notebook, a couple of years later, we find, besides the transcription of an anonymous Italian poem on the fight of the Greeks for freedom, this note in English by Cavour himself:

> What Lord Byron says in defense (*sic*) of the abused Greeks can be said to the justifidation of all the other nations, who groan (*sic*) in bondage, and are reproached for the vices that their tyrants (*sic*) have given them.

There follows a transcription of Byron's own note to stanza 33 of Canto II of *Childe Harold*:

> At present, like the Catholics of Ireland, and the Jews throughout the world, and such other cudgelled and heterodox people,

they suffer all the moral and physical ills that can afflict humanity. Their life is a struggle against truth; they are vicious in their
own defence. They are so unused to kindness, that when they occasionally meet with it, they look upon it with suspicion as a dog
often beaten snaps at your fingers if you attempt to caress him.
'They are ungrateful, abominably ungrateful.' This is the
general cry. Now, in the name of Nemesis: for what are they to be
grateful? Where is the human being that ever conferred a benefit
on Greek or Greeks? They are to be grateful to the Turks for their
fetters, and to the Franks for their broken promises, and lying
counsels. They are to be grateful to the artist who engraves their
ruins, and to the antiquary who carries them away: to the traveller whose janissary flogs them, to the scribbler whose journal
abuses them! This is the amount of their obligations to
foreigners.

Immediately after Cavour quotes part of stanza 76 of the same
Canto:

> Hereditary Bondsmen! Know ye not
> Who would be free themselves must strike the blow?
> By their right arms the conquest must be wrought?
> Will Gaul or Muscovite redress ye? No!
> True, they may lay your proud despoilers low,
> But not for you will freedom's altar flame.

The young Cavour, in transcribing young Byron's shrewd and
compassionate observations on those Greeks that he was later to
try to rescue from bondage, was obviously thinking of his own compatriots, the Italians. The quotation is revealing of the feeling and
thought of the future statesman; he must have remembered
especially the last quotation in later years, when he actively promoted foreign alliances in order to get help for the unification of
Italy, but never trusted them fully: he relied on the national spirit of
independence, while convinced of the importance of securing sympathy for the Italian cause.

After the statesman, the historian. The first full-length critical
monograph on Byron's life and work was published in Milan in
1833. It was presented as a discourse addressed to the members of
the literary club (Ateneo) of Bergamo, and it tried to give a
balanced view of Byron's achievement and character.[15] The mono-

graph is the work of Cesare Cantù, who was to become the most authoritative and learned liberal historian of the last century, the first chronicler of the *carbonari* movement. It is well-informed and well-written, giving careful accounts of all Byron's poetical works and discussing his political thought. But its main quality is the awareness of the emergence of the Byron myth, and Cantù's ability to place it – at such an early stage – in a correct literary–historical perspective. *Manfred* is seen as Byron's most significant work, and an appendix reproduces side by side a scene from *Manfred* (III. i) and one from Schiller's *Robbers*, as expressing the new spirit of the age.

The historian's balanced view of Byron, as representative of a new climate of thought, must have been disturbing to the conservative forces ruling the country. His posthumous fame was much more dangerous than his participation, when alive, in national liberation movements. He could no longer be ignored. The only way to counter-balance his influence was to make a pretence of recognising his importance, while subtly discrediting his achievement. A typical example of the use of these tactics to exorcise Byron's ghost can be found in *L'Album*, a weekly journal devoted to "literature and the fine arts", published in Rome under the Pope's rule. In the section "Historical Memoirs" of the issue of 7 September 1839 the journal decided to face the Byron question by publishing an anonymous article, "Lord Byron's Sojourn at Pisa".[16] As the title suggests, it is concerned nearly exclusively with the deplorable episode of the wounding of Sergeant Masi, and while pretending to extenuate Byron's part in it, it manages to evoke all its unpleasantness. When it comes to summarise the subsequent events of Byron's life, the tone and approach are characteristic: Byron was tired of his fate: the West had nothing else to offer him; wishing to leave Europe, he hesitated between Greece and America; he decided for Greece because there was in it some show of glory. His pilgrimage was desperate: he left Europe as one leaves life when at the end of one's tether. There is no mention of the struggle for Greek independence: Byron's death is merely the suicide of an exhausted sensualist. And what could be more Jesuitical than the final summing-up:

> Byron was the expression of an age when human suffering, forgetful of the life to come, wanted to remake everything and break up everything. Byron's poems will never die because they teach

posterity what torment it is to lack faith. The songs of the British
poet often ring like harmonies from the Deep, and one would say
that his Muse inhabited Tartarus – that dark Tartarus
described by his fellow countryman Milton. In such cases Byron
appears as the interpreter of the bad side of the human heart. But
he knew also the high, the generous side, and this is why some
noble souls are still fond of him.

The same periodical returned to the subject ten years later, in
March 1849, when the experience of the ill-fated Roman republic
founded by Mazzini was showing that in Rome, too, there were
people ready to give their lives in the name of freedom. *L'Album*
published a longer and fairer biography of Byron,[17] though still
presenting his going to Greece as an attempt to compensate
through action for the failure of his poetic powers.

By this time Byron was definitely on the map of Italian culture.
Differences in political opinions might still affect the appreciation
of his work for a time, but even before 1870, when the unification of
Italy was achieved with the abolition of the temporal dominion of
the Pope – rendering pointless the pious arguments used against
him – his greatness was beyond doubt. There circulated in Italy
hundreds of translations of separate poems of his, and the first
translation in Italian prose of the complete works of Byron, by
Carlo Rusconi, was published in Padua as early as 1841–2; but the
most popular and frequently reprinted translation of all the works
is the five-volume edition published in Turin, in the Nuova Biblio-
teca Popolare, in 1852; it includes prose and verse translations by
different hands.

It would be beside the point to survey the formidable accumu-
lation of Byroniana in Italy in the latter part of the nineteenth
century, and the emergence of the decadent view of the Byronic
hero. Our concern is with the political influence of Byron in Italy,
and this must be limited to a time of stress and struggle, the beginning of the *Risorgimento*. It can safely be said that the complex and at
times contradictory human and poetic personality of Lord Byron
acted as a catalytic factor for the Italians at the crucial moment of
their national history. This is shown by the fact that two widely
divergent but extremely important political personalities –
Mazzini and Cavour – were both affected by Byron's writings.
What greater contribution to political thought and action could be
expected from a poet?

NOTES

1. All quotations from Byron's *Letters and Journals* are from the Prothero edition (1898–1901). I wish to register my great debt to L.A. Marchand's *Byron: A Biography* (1957) and especially to Iris Origo's *The Last Attachment* (1949).
2. See L.A. Marchand, *Byron: A Biography* (New York, 1957) p. 949.
3. Quoted in Guido Muoni, *La fama di Byron e il byronismo in Italia*, Milano, 1903. Other relevant studies of Byron's influence in Italy: A. Porta, *Byronismo italiano* (Milano, 1923); also the Byron centenary issue of *La Cultura*, vol. III, no. 6, 15 April 1924, with essays by Mario Praz, Umberto Bosco, etc; and G. Melchiori, *Byron and Italy*, Byron Foundation Lecture 1958, Nottingham, 1958.
4. M. King, "Early Italian Romanticism and the Giaour", *The Byron Journal*, vol. 4, 1976, pp. 7–19.
5. For an extensive account of the incident and its consequences see C.L. Cline, *Byron, Shelley and Their Pisan Circle* (London, 1952).
6. *Stanza alla memoria di Lord Byron.* In Livorno, per le stampe di G.P. Possoleni, 1825, 31 pages.
7. In a letter from Ravenna to Murray, 8 October 1820, Byron says of Foscolo: "He is more of the ancient Greek than the modern Italian."
8. From the anonymous "Soggiorno di Lord Byron a Pisa", *L'Album*, vol. VI, no. 27, 7 September 1839, p. 213.
9. *Antologia, Giornale di scienze, letter e arti.* Firenze, Gabinetto Viesseux, V. vol. xvii, no. 49, January 1825, pp. 32–64.
10. Donizetti had written another Byronic opera the year before, but in this case the subject, *Parisina*, is by no means patriotic.
11. The lines of the most famous of these choruses may be quoted as typical: "*Questo nome che suona vittoria Scuota ogni alma e la guidi a pugnarr E vedrassi sul campo di gloria Il sepolcro cangiarsi in altar.*"
12. The essay, written originally in English, was included in a poor Italian translation (not by Mazzini himself) in vol. IV of *Scritti Letterari di un italiano vivente* (Lugano, 1847).
13. *Letteratura inglese del prof. Enrico Solazzi*, Manuali Hoepli, 1879, pp. 178–80.
14. *Tutti gli scritti di Camillo Cavour*, raccolti e curati dal Carlo Pischedda e Giuseppe Talamo, Torino, 1976; quotations from pp 171–72.
15. Cesare Cantù, *Lord Byron. Discorso di Cesare Cantù ai signori soci dell'Ateneo di Bergamo*, aggiuntivi alcune traduzioni ed una serie di lettere dello stesso Lord Byron ove si narrano i suoi viaggi in Italia e in Grecia. Milano, 1833.
16. "Memorie storiche: Soggiorno di Lord Byron a Pisa", *L'Album: giornale lettarario di belle arti.* Rome, vol. VI, no. 27, 7 September 1839.
17. "Byron", signed S.V., in two instalments, in *L'Album*, vol. XVI, nos. 4 and 5, 17 and 24 March 1849.

7   Byron and Poland

Byron and Polish Romantic Revolt

JULIUSZ ZULAWSKI

Byron was never there. Yet, his adventurous Don Juan once rode
through that country, and the author remarks:

> But should we wish to warm us on our way
> Through Poland, there is Kosciusko's name
> Might scatter fire through ice, like Hecla's flame.

Poland – then partitioned – was often mentioned in his conten-
tious and polemic poetry directed against the cynical Congress of
Vienna and its offspring: the Holy Alliance – used by the great
"guarantors of peace" as a weapon to subjugate so many European
nations.

In The *Age of Bronze* Byron exclaimed:

> Poland! O'er which the avenging angel passed,
> But left thee as he found thee, still a waste,
> Forgetting all thy still enduring claim,
> Thy lotted people and extinguished name,
> Thy sigh for freedom, thy long-flowing tear,
> That sound that crashes in the tyrant's ear –
> Kosciusko! On – on – on – the thirst of war
> Gasps for the gore of serfs and of their czar.
> The half barbaric Moscow's minarets
> Gleam in the sun, but 'tis a sun that sets!

And then, in the same poem:

> But lo! a Congress! What! that hallow'd name
> Which freed the Atlantic! May we hope the same

122

For outworn Europe? With the sound arise,
Like Samuel's shade to Saul's monarchic eyes,
The prophets of young Freedom, summon'd far
From climes of Washington and Bolivar;
Henry, the forest-born Demosthenes,
Whose thunder shook the Philip of the seas;
And stoic Franklin's energetic shade,
Robed in the lightnings which his hand allay'd;
And, Washington, the tyrant-tamer, wake,
To bid us blush for these old chains, or break.
But *who* compose this senate of the few
That should redeem the many? *Who* renew
This consecrated name, till now assign'd
To councils held to benefit mankind?
Who now assemble at the holy call?
The blest Alliance, which says three are all!
An earthly trinity! which wears the shape
Of heaven's, as man is mimick'd by the ape.

But it is not my concern at the moment to quote every line he wrote in defence of freedom in so many of his poems and poetical tales, in *Childe Harold's Pilgrimage*, in *Don Juan*, in *The Prisoner of Chillon*, and so on. What I want to do now is to describe and explain, as far as I can, the unbelievably great influence he has unknowingly exerted on Poland's Romantic poets of the first half of the nineteenth century, forming, as everywhere, their poetical mood, and discovering for them, which proved much more important, a certain practical style of belligerent writing that they adopted to express, in their own poetry and for their own aims, their patriotic attitude. But how did this come about? There were many contradictory shades of poetic and dramatic tunes in Byron's writings. And, for that matter, most of the Romantic poets of Europe at that time stood for freedom against any kind of oppression. Why did Byron, more than the rest of them, become so attractive to Polish writers?

As far as I know, the first translation of his works into Polish was done by an active politician, Wladyslaw Ostrowski, in 1818. It was *The Bride of Abydos*. Before 1820 the distinguished and influential poet, Julian Ursyn Niemcewicz – at one time Kosciuszko's aide-de-camp in the first Insurrection in Poland – translated the poem "Fare Thee Well", and Karol Sienkiewicz translated "The Chain

I Gave". In 1820 Bruno Kicinski published his translations of *The Corsair* and *The Siege of Corinth*, and in the same year in a literary journal in Vilna there appeared an anonymous translation of *The Lament of Tasso*. In 1821 Stanislaw Jaszowski brought out the first translation of some fragments of *Childe Harold's Prilgrimage*, and Ignacy Szydlowski published in 1822 his translation of *Parisina*, and in 1823, of *The Giaour*.

In short, these are Byron's works translated into Polish during his lifetime. But he was widely read in these years by our poets – in his own language, or in French translations. In January 1822, Adam Mickiewicz, the greatest poet of Polish Romanticism, wrote from Vilna to his friend in Belin: "Germanomania was followed by Britannomania; with a dictionary in hand I edged my way through Shakespeare like a rich man from the Gospel entering heaven through the eye of a needle, but now for my pains it goes much easier with Byron, and I have made much progress. I think I shall translate *The Giaour*." And again in November 1822: "It is only Byron that I read, and I throw away any book written in another spirit, because I detest lies."

He did translate *The Giaour* later on (in fact as one, and the best, of four other translators). Some of its lines, for instance,

> For Freedom's battle once begun,
> Bequeathed by bleeding Sire to Son. . . .

entered the Polish consciousness for good, and still are well-known by people who do not even realise that these were Byron's words. In the preface to his translation of this tale, Mickiewicz wrote:

Every day the readers may become convinced about Byron's influence on contemporary literature, because they see the colour and the impress of this great poet in all the later poetical works. . . . Byron's characters are endowed with conscience. And that is what distinguishes chiefly our author from the writers of the past century. The bygone age was a sophist, not knowing the difference between good and evil, it had only taken practice in petty reasoning, and its chief aim and ambition had been to find an explanation to everything, or to blab about everything. . . . Byron was the first poet who would not be satisfied with such sophistic condemnation of thought and feeling. He had always had before his eyes the great problems of the world, the problems of the fate of the human race and of the future life. He had tackled all the basic moral and philosophical questions, he had coped with all the cruxes and difficulties of dogmas and traditions, he had cursed and fumed like Prometheus, the Titan, whose shade he loved to evoke so often.

This influence on Polish literature grew after Byron's death in besieged Missolonghi, and the flood of published translations was only a partial confirmation of the spreading acquaintance with the essence of his writings. It was a real, measurable influence, penetrating deeply into the imagination of both great and minor poets of the first and most eruptive period of Polish Romanticism. The second of Poland's leading poets of that period, Juliusz Slowacki (who himself did not give us any translation from Byron at all) wrote one of his most important – and most polemical – poetic tales on the *Don Juan* pattern. Besides, most of his earlier work was distinctly "Byronic". The same is true of young Mickiewicz, who wrote a poem *pro domo sua* after *English Bards and Scotch Reviewers*, although the latter had never been translated into Polish. A similar influence of Byron's writings is found in the works of the third leading poet of that period, Zygmunt Krasinski, and of many minor authors up to the 1860s.

In drama, they were impressed above all by the mysterious composition of *Manfred* and that of *Cain*; in poetical tales, by *The Corsair* and *The Giaour*; in polemic poems, by Byron's polemics. Even when they travelled, they often followed Byron's route with an edition of *Childe Harold's Pilgrimage* in hand as an emotional guide, and in their writings they used to adopt his attitude towards history and the landscape. Slowacki, who from his journey to the Near East (after the failure of the Polish insurrection against Russia in 1831), brought back a beautiful, very sad, and patriotic poem full of recollections of Byron's personality, on another occasion, a couple of years after Byron's death, wrote from Switzerland to his mother in Poland: "With Byron I climb the mountains."

But at the same time the process of introducing Byron into Polish literature by means of translations went on. Up to the end of the nineteenth century the best Polish poets, and many dozens of minor ones, translated his works. *Childe Harold's Pilgrimage*, in its entirety, had four various translations, *The Giaour* also four, *The Bride of Abydos* three, *The Corsair* two, *Lara* also two, *The Siege of Corinth* three, *Parisina* five, *The Prisoner of Chillon* two, *Manfred* as many as seven, *The Lament of Tasso* two, *Beppo* two, *Mazeppa* four, *Don Juan* two, *The Prophecy of Dante* one, *The Two Foscari* one, *Cain* five, *Heaven and Earth* one, *Werner* one, *Marino Faliero* one, *The Island* two.

Many short poems of Byron have been translated in the course of the nineteenth century, and afterwards, by a host of poets. And some new translations continue to appear even now *The Curse of Minerva*, *The Vision of Judgment*, and *The Age of Bronze* have been translated in their entirety just lately by myself, by Czeslaw Jastrzebiec Kozlowski, and by Wlodzimierz Lewik, respectively, but were known by our Romantics as well. *Hebrew Melodies* – treated at that time as symbolic songs of solidarity with any oppressed nation, therefore with Poland too – had several translators. It may be of interest to add that the manuscript of "Oh Weep for Those" from *Hebrew Melodies* is still in Czartoryski's Museum in Krakow (Byron had met prince Czartoryski and prince Radziwill in Lady Jersey's house in London in June 1814). *The Dream*, which exerted a very deep influence on the structure and idea of some most famous Polish works, and *Darkness*, were both translated by Adam Mickiewicz. I have just recently completed the first translation into Polish of *The Deformed Transformed*.

The poets of Polish Romanticism very soon discerned the real value and significance of Byron's writings in the midst of human slander and his own mysteriousness. Two years after Byron's death, Mickiewicz – while on punitive deportation in Russia – wrote in a letter to a poet-friend: "Those fumes, ashes, phantasmas and devilries that are detected in Byron's poems by journalistic critics trying to explain ideas and imaginations that are obscure to themselves with a heap of empty words – it is time such practices should give way to more serious and thoughtful remarks."

So, let us turn back to our question: Why has Byron become so attractive for Poles, and what – instead of those "phantasmas" – have they found in him? Perhaps the answer to this question could also explain to some extent the attitude of other people and nations who followed – or condemned – him all over Europe at that time.

Generally speaking, as a poet, Byron wrote along two main lines. One leads to the image of an individual surrounded by a hostile world and trying in vain in such a world to resolve the moral problems of his life or the riddles of the destiny of mankind. The other was a direct polemic aimed at current events. Both expressed the same attitude: an uncompromising criticism of the existing "establishment" marked by hypocrisy in human relations, political swindles, the short-sighted brutality of the police-states, the institutions of the "prison of nations" set up by the Congress of Vienna and the Holy Alliance as a pattern of a *"détente"* between the great powers, intolerance and discrimination; and of encouragement to get rid of all of it, to liberate, to set free the identity of human beings and the identity of nations. What is more, he gave expression to this attitude throughout his life as a man of action.

In 1842 Mickiewicz wrote in a letter to a poet-friend:

> Is our poetry to be shut up in books and remain bleak prose in ourselves? Brother, it is time to make poetry. . . . Do you think that poor Byron would write so many grand strophes had he not been ready to give up his title and London for Greeks? The secret of his power as a writer lay just in that readiness. . . . There is a greater cause in front of us. . . .

With all that, Byron was not a "romantic idealist". He was rather wide awake, under no illusions, critical in his writings, and practical in action. He never approached the problem of man, or nation, or any social problem, in general terms. Each specific situation – of an individual human being, an individual nation, or any definite case of social conflict – he treated separately, in its actual circumstances, from the point of view of ordinary justice and decency. He never defended any rationalistic doctrines – but simply the weak against the strong. When he fought for or against something, it had always a name of its own, it was always determined by him as such. It was never idealistically vague. His vital experience, and clear view of history, his disillusionment, and his knowledge of human nature – all this enabled him to act in a practical and effective manner, both in poetical polemics and political enterprises. His "romantic realism", as it were, certainly distinguished him from the then "romantic idealists".

Polish Romanticism arose as a reaction against the classics of the Enlightenment, in the same manner as everywhere, but in a different and rather peculiar political situation. Polish poets of the late eighteenth century did not, on the whole, react too strongly to the disastrous partition of their country. The next generation had a much deeper patriotic consciousness, having gone through the bitter experiences of a nation under alien domination, all the hopes of Napoleonic wars, and new disaster. The poets of that time came

close to the nation, to the native songs and feelings. They redis-
covered the current of history. To the uprising of 1830 they reacted
with enthusiasm, to its defeat with boundless despair. Yet they
never neglected the very idea of ultimate liberation. Byron, by his
outspoken writings, and by his personal example, showed them a
definite way to defend the individual and the national identity.

His sense of historical reality we can trace even today in many of
his poems, as for example in these lines of *The Age of Bronze*:

> Lone, lost, abandon'd in their utmost need
> By Christians, unto whom they gave their creed,
> The desolated lands, the ravaged isle,
> The foster'd feud encouraged to beguile,
> The aid evaded, and the cold delay,
> Prolong'd but in the hope to make a prey; –
> These, these, shall tell the tale, and Greece can show
> The false friend worse than the infuriate foe,
> But this is well: Greeks only should free Greece,
> Not the barbarian, with his mask of peace.
> How should the autocrat of bondage be
> The king of serfs, and set the nations free?
> Better still serve the haughty Mussulman,
> Than swell the Cossaque's prowling caravan;
> Better still toil for masters, than await,
> The slave of slaves, before a Russian gate, –
> Number'd by hordes, a human capital,
> A live estate, existing but for thrall,
> Lotted by thousands, as a meet reward
> For the first courtier in the Czar's regard;
> While their immediate owner never tastes
> His sleep, *sans* dreaming of Siberia's wastes;
> Better succumb even to their own despair,
> And drive the camel than purvey the bear.

Or in these lines:

> Resplendent sight! Behold the coxcomb Czar,
> The autocrat of waltzes and of war!
> As eager for a plaudit as a realm,
> And just as fit for flirting as a helm;
> A Calmuck beauty with a Cossack wit,

And generous spirit, when 'tis not frost-bit;
Now half dissolving to a liberal thaw,
But harden'd back whene'er the morning's raw;
With no objections to true liberty,
Except that it would make the nations free.
How well the imperial dandy prates of peace!
How fain, if Greeks would be his slaves, free Greece!
How nobly gave he back the Poles their diet,
Then told pugnacious Poland to be quiet!
How kindly would he send the mild Ukraine,
With all her pleasant pulks, to lecture Spain!

The Polish readers must have responded with applause, at that
time, to such a political onslaught, being already well conversant
with the serious and uncompromising personal stand of the
author. Stanislaw Windakiewicz, once a prominent professor of
Polish literature at Cracow University, wrote in his book on Byron,
in 1914: "Byron has attracted Poles with the logic and consistency
of his character and with the consistency of his opposition. . . . In a
way this has perhaps been the cause of the consistent character of
Polish opposition. . . ."

It would be too much to suppose that Byron's poetry, or
example, inspired the Polish insurrection of 1830. There were
other, obvious enough, reasons. But certainly his spirit accompanied the warriors. In the situation of the Polish patriots who
understood the significance of the events, and in view of their
current, practical problems, the direct political aims of Byron's
poetry, and the reality and consistency of his actions, must have
been taken by them and kept in mind with especially warm
concern.

After all, among his first and even subsequent translators there
was no lack of former Polish officers of Napoleon's army (as
General Franciszek Dzierzykraj Morawski, and others) – the very
same Napoelon whom Byron so much adored as the breaker of old
tyrannies. And after all, the fate of Poland did not seem to be wholly
hopeless yet, although after the Congress of Vienna it was in fact
sealed. And, after all, while disappointed with the abortive uprising in Italy, Byron, with a faith in the unbending vitality of the
Polish nation, many a time recalled Kosciuszko, commander-in-
chief of the first Polish insurrection. A practical and direct – not just
idealistic – attitude towards the political events in his poetical

polemics, and a rebellious pattern of personality in his dramas and tales – all this must have evoked a vivid response among the generation of Poles who were not pleased with their world, who after outliving so many a stormy change did not cease to believe in its new possibilities, and who still tried to look for some practical and effective means of rescue. For Polish Romanticism in its first decades was truly "Byronic" – that is to say, it was politically militant and alert, conscious of the definite national problems, sober in the face of reality, in a word: realistic.

And, again, all this could be verified by quoting Adam Mickiewicz, who in December 1842 said in one of his Sorbonne lectures:

> Byron begins an era of new poetry. He was the first to show the people that poetry is not a futile pastime, that it does not end in desires, that one should live up to one's writings. . . . This strongly felt need to make his life poetic, to bring the ideal near to the reality, is all the poetic value of Byron. . . . His poetical power was so great that it could be felt in a few words, that those few words had been able to wake and shock the souls, and to disclose to them what they were. . . . He was known to see through any political problems with his sharp eye, and to reach to the source of the chief mystery of human history. . . . Everything that tormented the minds of men, that had found response in the souls of the young people of our generation was faithfully given expression in Byron's writings and in his life. In the works of Slavic poets we may detect like feelings and like tendencies.

Polish Romantic poets believed – quite rightly – that a writer who does not express the general feelings, who does not speak for others, for the oppressed, is not a writer at all.

So, finally, Byron found his way to Poland, and stayed there quite a long time after his death in Greece. His spiritual influence abated when Polish political orientation – after the failure of the third insurrection in 1863 – began to steer towards calmer waters of the so-called "organic work", gathering up the economic and educational strength of a nation under alien rule. But during nearly half a century he was fully alive in Polish literature. Professor Windakiewicz in his book on Byron puts it this way: "Byron's poetical works have found such a precise reflection in Polish romantic poetry that we could almost study him on the basis of Polish literature. If Byron's works were lost, one could recreate them again roughly from the echoes of his poetry."

This certainly refers not only to the large library of translations, but above all to his deep and evident influence on original poetry itself. Adam Mickiewicz – who died of cholera in 1885 in Turkey where he was busy organising a Polish Legion against Russia – wrote in his unfinished essay on Byron: "As the minstrels in the Middle Ages, singing in the spirit of their times, had been well understood by their contemporaies, so the songs of Byron appealed to the broad European masses and created a host of followers. Just so a string of a harp when plucked, makes other, silent, but similarly tempered strings resound."

I recall these words of the great Polish poet and thinker to commemorate Byron 150 years after his death, when the spirit of the Congress of Vienna he hated still prevails, and the sober romanticism he represented is not yet altogether dead.

8   Byron and Portugal

The Progress of an Offending Pilgrim

F. de MELLO MOSER

When Byron died for the cause of Greek freedom in 1824, the rise of Liberalism was under way in Portugal, despite a few serious set-backs and a civil war to come in the thirties, that would end in the surrender of the last absolute monarch and his supporters in 1834, leaving the constitutional monarchy to last until 1910. The early decades of the nineteenth century, here as elsewhere, were a time of great political upheaval, going back through various roads to the French Revolution, and encompassing a series of major events and momentous factors: the Peninsular War (1807–10), the prolonged absence of the Royal Family in Brazil (1807–21), the assimilation of new ideas by the political emigrés at different stages, the loss of Brazil (1822), the early Liberal plots, the 1820 Revolution and the counter-revolutions, all of these connected with changes in the trading, economic and social situation.

Inevitably, as it seems to us, there were many contradictory features in the process as regards ideological foundations, allegiances, interests at stake and foreign support. But, all things considered, one cannot help thinking what an inspiring symbol Byron could easily have become among the Liberal party in general but for the fact that he had aroused the resentment of many Portuguese patriots against him through what he had written in the all too closely autobiographical poem *Childe Harold's Pilgrimage*.

Leaving aside, for the moment, the strictly literary influence, the story of Byron's reputation in Portugal until the later nineteenth century is, to a great extent, the story of a grievance, stressed by those on one side who repeatedly showed that Byron had grossly exaggerated and had, in fact, been prejudiced in his remarks concerning the Portuguese people, and attenuated by those on the other side who tried, not too successfully, to justify Byron's ways to

132

their compatriots.

Much of what follows will illustrate the foregoing. However, while Byron thus did not – indeed, could not – exert any deep political influence in Portugal, in the strict sense, it is a fact that he was present in the thoughts of a few Portuguese poets and writers who were politically active, or at least politically-minded, and who found in the man and in his work both relevance and inspiration.

By any standards, and granting Byron's style and aggressiveness, all his references to the Portuguese people in *Childe Harold*, Canto I, are surprisingly harsh, unmitigated, and even stressed by explicit contrast with the landscape. There is, in fact, an interplay of the two themes – wonderful Nature and the despised Portuguese – throughout XV to XVIII :

> Oh, Christ! it is a goodly sight to see
> What Heaven hath done for this delicious land;
> What fruits of fragrance blush on every tree!
> What goodly prospects o'er the hills expand!
> But man would mar them with an impious hand:
> And when the Almighty lifts his fiercest scourge
> 'Gainst those who most transgress his high command,
> With treble vengeance will his hot shafts urge
> Gaul's locust host, and earth from fellest foeman purge.
>
> What beauties doth Lisboa first unfold!
> Her image floating on that noble tide,
> Which poets vainly pave with sands of gold,
> But now whereon a thousand keels did ride
> Of mighty strength, since Albion was allied,
> And to the Lusians did her aid afford:
> A nation swoln with ignorance and pride,
> Who lick yet loathe the hand that waves the sword
> To save them from the wrath of Gaul's unsparing lord.
>
> But whoso entereth within this town,
> That, sheening far, celestial seems to be,
> Disconsolate will wander up and down,
> 'Mid many things unsightly to strange ee;
> For hut and palace show like filthily:
> The dingy denizens are reared in dirt;
> No personage of high or mean degree
> Doth care for cleanness of surtout or shirt;

> Though shent with Egypt's plague, unkempt, unwash'd,
> unhurt.

> Poor, paltry slaves! yet born 'midst noblest scenes –
> Why, Nature, waste thy wonders on such men?
> Lo! Cintra's glorious Eden intervenes
> In variegated maze of mount and glen.
> Ah me! what hand can pencil guide, or pen,
> To follow half on which the eye dilates
> Through views more dazzling unto mortal ken
> Than those whereof such things the Bard relates,
> Who to the awe-struck world unlock'd Elysium's gates?

The whole attitude is summed up in the last lines of stanza
XXXIII, which is like a final thrust:

> Well doth the Spanish hind the difference know
> 'Twixt him and Lusian slave, the lowest of the low.

Curiously enough, though in his letters to Francis Hodgson
(from Lisbon, 16 July 1809), to John Hanson (from Gibraltar, 7
August 1809) and to his mother (from Gibraltar, 11 August 1809)
Byron expressed similar admiration for Cintra, disappointment
with Lisbon and one sweeping statement concerning the Portuguese, he does so without the intensity – one is tempted to add, the
loathing – that the poem expresses. The statement occurs in the
letter to John Hanson: "Cadiz is the prettiest town in Europe,
Seville a large and fine city, Gibraltar the dirtiest most detestable
spot in existence, Lisbon nearly as bad, the Spaniards are far superior to the Portuguese, and the English abroad are very different
from their countrymen." However, the letters were not then available to the general reader, but only the poem and the notes, two of
which perhaps should be mentioned at this time. Let us take them
in reverse order, both as to composition and text referred to, for
reasons that will subsequently become clear.
    In 1812 Byron wrote the following note to the last lines of *Childe
Harold* I, XXXIII, quoted earlier, which, admittedly, cancels the
apology it had only begun to formulate:

> As I found the Portuguese, so I have characterised them. That
> they are since improved, at least in courage, is evident. The late

exploits of Lord Wellington have effaced the follies of Cintra. He has, indeed, done wonders; he has, perhaps, changed the character of a nation, reconciled rival superstitions, and baffled an enemy who never retreated before his predecessors.

In all fairness it should be noted that the text includes plenty of criticism of the English and expresses Byron's unsuppressed admiration for Napoleon. But it could hardly be found endearing by the Portuguese.

In order to justify the line "Throughout this purple land, where law secures not life", Byron wrote:

It is a well-known fact that in the year 1809, the assassinations in the streets of Lisbon and its vicinity were not confined by the Portuguese to their countrymen; but that Englishmen were daily butchered: and so far from redress being obtained, we were requested not to interfere if we perceived any compatriot defending himself against his allies. I was once stopped in the way to the theatre at eight o'clock in the evening, when the streets were not more empty than they generally are at that hour, opposite to an open shop, and in a carriage with a friend: had we not fortunately been armed, I have not the least doubt that we should have "adorned a tale" instead of telling one.

Byron's friend Hobhouse confirms this in an entry in his diary for 19 July 1809: "Attacked in street by four men." However, neither of the travellers offered any explanation, whereas in Portugal authors unfriendly to Byron would later spread a version in which they laughed at Byron's expense, as in some well-known lines by Jõao de Lemos, that may be rendered thus:

> Of our manner and wits you complained
> Because husbands were on the look-out
> So that virtue was safe and not stained,
> Whereas you were beaten about.[1]

In 1812, shortly after the publication of the second edition of *Childe Harold*, in the monthly *O Investigador Português* – a periodical of Portuguese political emigrés in London, first issued in 1811 – there appeared an anonymous letter containing the earliest Portuguese version and review of the stanzas devoted to Portugal. The author of this letter confesses that the poem excited his ill-humour – "and it could not be otherwise, considering that I am a Portuguese patriot" – but he is accurate and objective in his remarks, and is even prepared to offer a few suggestions of his own as to things deserving criticism in Portugal. This interesting document, the text of which is now available in both Portuguese and English,[2] does not, however, mention the alleged married lady behind the street attack, which proves nothing either way. But what should be noted is the fact that the patriotic emigrés, many of whom were later to return and take part in the political process of their country, could not help resenting greatly Byron's comments, all the more as the latter came when these patriots were painfully homesick and aware of the heroic struggle which was being waged by their fellow countrymen.

Thus, it is easy to see why Byron could not become very popular for quite some time: for the nationalist politicians of the Romantic–Liberal period, he had offended the country; to the more conservative, not to say puritan-minded, he was of too scandalous a reputation to be accepted. The notable exceptions, as might be guessed, are all writers and poets, and their reference to him and their vindication or even their imitation of him is usually connected with an impatient desire for reform of some sort: they sympathised with his outburst and with all that was or could be seen as protest against conventions and institutions. Nor was it indifferent that there was, in liberal and radical circles, a good deal of ostensible anti-clericalism, though not always necessarily meaning atheism or an irreligious attitude, but usually connected with the changes in regime and establishment (the monasteries were closed by government decree in 1834), and with the assertion of the concept of free-thinking, which, incidentally, was to remain for a long time a peculiarly male concept.

While we are discussing the cultural background there is one further point that should be noted. In all likelihood, most of the people who discussed, and many of those who admired Byron in Portugal, never actually read his text in English, but used the famous French translation by Benjamin de la Roche which was completed in 1837.[3] Portuguese translations of separate works and fragments began to appear in the thirties, irregularly and at long intervals, by different authors,[4] thus leaving de la Roche holding the field. This is not altogether surprising, in view of the prevailing hegemony of the French language in this country, then as later, and all exceptions granted.

A final assessment of Byron's reputation must, of course, await a painstaking examination of data to be collected from letters and journals of the period which might offer additional evidence as to the varieties of feeling aroused by his name in polite circles – though one can make a pretty good guess. In any case, such a task is, for the time being at least, impossible to carry out.

The one really important figure as regards Byron and Portugal and the interplay of poetry and politics is Almeida Garrett, with whose poem *Camões*, published in Paris in 1825, Romanticism officially begins in Portuguese literature. We now turn our attention to him in some detail.

An outline of his biography will be sufficient to show his position and significance. Between his birth in 1799 and his death in 1854, his was a singularly active, intense life, to a certain extent typical in kind, though greatly excelling in degree when compared with his contemporaries. As a child, he had to seek shelter in the Azores at the time of Napoleon's second invasion, commanded by General Soult; having studied Law in Coimbra, he soon took an active interest in both theatre and politics, which were to attract him all his life; a voluntary exile after the 1823 counter-revolution, he spent some time in Birmingham and London, Le Havre, and finally Paris, where he eventually published his two first definitely romantic poems, *Camões* and *Dona Branca*; he returned to Portugal, only to leave again in 1833, during the temporary triumph of the young absolutist king, Dom Miguel; in England again, he collected and published his earlier poetry; he joined the Liberal army that was to invade Portugal, was sent to England on a diplomatic mission, and finally came back to take an active part in political events, and to devote most of his energy to the renewal of the stage, founding the National School of Dramatic Art, and the National Theatre, and writing a number of plays that earned him the second highest place in the history of Portuguese drama.

Though far from complete, the above outline clearly shows the intimate connection between Garrett and the political events of his time. Yet many interesting traits remain to be mentioned, not the least being the peculiar relationship of the man and writer to the concept of Romanticism. For though Garrett and his friend Alexandre Herculano were both practising romanticists in one sense of the word, they both protested that they were not "romantic" in the then currently accepted and already decadent sense of that much

misused word. It is also true that they both stand within and
beyond Romanticism at the same time, towering above their contemporaries and standing out, each one of them in his uniqueness,
in the cultural history of Portugal.

In Garrett we find yet another prominent feature which is connected with Byron: his deliberate dandyism, a facet in which he
offers a striking contrast to his austere friend Herculano. Garrett
was, indeed,

> a man of many faces . . . a poet and a politician, a folklorist and
> an orator, a novelist and a pedagogue, a lawyer and a diplomat, a
> man of the world and a devoted father – in all things striving for
> the balance that made him reject being described as a "romanti-
> cist" and to seek supreme elegance in the reconciliation of oppos-
> ites. . . . In few men was the *persona*, or mask of the man in
> society, so different from the truer reality of the inner *anima*.[5]

Garrett, the patriot and political émigré experiencing that
peculiar kind of longing homesickness for which the Portuguese
have the word *saudade*, found in the figure of Camoens, the great
poet whose epic *The Lusiads* was the very national poem of Portugal
and who had died almost at the same time as Portugal came under
the rule of the Spanish kings for sixty years, the ideal central image
through which to focus his own feelings, in a work where narrative
alternates with lyrical, epic and melodramatic passages. Byron is
present in the poem in more ways than one, as we shall now see.

In a letter written to a friend in 1824 concerning the poem to be
published, Garrett reveals that "generally speaking the style is
moulded on that of Byron and Scott (neither known nor used in
Portugal as yet), but not servilely nor *apishly*, because *above all*, I
wanted to achieve a national work".[6] And in his preface to the first
edition, after stating that the poem lies outside the established
rules and models, he writes:

> Nor did I write it to imitate the style of Byron, which the French,
> here, so ridiculously *ape* right and left nowadays, without taking
> heed of the fact that to indulge in Byron's liberties, and to
> commit his feats of daring with impunity it is necessary to
> possess such ingenuity and talent that with but one flash of its
> light, it may dim the faults and prevent the marvelled sight from
> noticing any imperfection.[7]

It is not intended to recall, here, all the real or possible indebtedness of Garrett to Byron, nor even to list all quotations and references to the author of *Don Juan*, but only to offer a significant selection. Thus, in *Camões*, while at first sight it might appear that we are in the presence of purely literary relations, on second scrutiny it becomes obvious that there are, broadly speaking, underlying political implications. In addition to passages expressly inspired by *Childe Harold's Pilgrimage*, the poem contains both an apology for Byron's unpleasant comments, and lines dedicated to Byron and his then still recent death at Missolonghi.

Thus, in stanza VIII of Canto One, there occurs a description of the arrival of the poet at the Tagus, and the author has supplied the following note, as from the first edition:

The description of the arrival in Lisbon, etc., in Byron's splendid poem *Childe Harold* is worth looking up. The Portuguese reader will find there something not very flattering to our national self-respect: but bear it patiently, for the injustice of the noble lord is not, after all, so very great.[8]

Coming from one who was later to play an important part in changing English official policy and public opinion in favour of the Portuguese liberals,[9] these words read like something of an appeal towards national awakening, however indirectly – which is, at best, what other politically-minded writers were to do with Byron in the future.

In stanza XIII of Canto Five Byron is recalled in connection with the beauties of Cintra, which he had praised, and there follow some lines of dirge in imitation of Thomas Moore, as we are told in a note to the first edition: "At the time when this was being written, this great poet, the greatest of the present century, had just died in Greece, where his noble feelings had taken him."[10] The lines in question may be rendered thus, beginning after the name of Cintra:

> Carried beyond the stream of passing ages
> In the eternal song of that mysterious bard
> Whose harp sublime now sadly muted hangs
> From the Pamisian laurels – where a sigh
> Of death broke off at last the finest chord
> That divine Eleutheria herself had tuned –

The importance of Byron as a formative influence on Garrett has been included recently in a scholarly study of the poet's early years and his development.[11] Garrett was not only the first but also the greatest of the Portuguese that Byron influenced. Also, he was among those – comparatively few, I believe – who read Byron in English and, partly on that account possibly, does not seem to have misunderstood him.

Alexandre Herculano, the other major figure in Portuguese Romanticism, being an altogether different person from Garrett, was quite hostile to Byron, whom he seems to have looked upon as the very Devil incarnate. He is, in fact, one of the authors who set down the story of Byron's attempted affair with a married woman as the cause for the beating he was given on the way to the São Carlos Theatre.[12] Herculano's sometime patroness, whom he aptly called the Portuguese Madame de Staël, the Marquesa de Alorna, wrote an Epistle to Lord Byron which is included in her posthumous works.[13]

Byron's influence has been clearly detected in writers and poets who at present enjoy little or no popularity at all, some of them being barely named – perhaps unjustly – in general surveys of the period. Among the poets mention may be made of Luís Augusto Palmeirim, a follower of Garrett, whose *Poems* (1851) pay tribute to the author of *Childe Harold* and *Don Juan*. The book was prefaced by António Pedro Lopes de Mendonça, who wrote that Byron was the greatest modern poet. He had already published (in 1849, aged 23) , a novel called *Memoirs of a Madman*, the hero of which is truly Byronic in many ways.[14] Among novelists, the powerful and prolific writer Camilo Castelo Branco is the major figure to have been influenced by Byron's demonic heroes, but only for a while (c. 1848–50).[15]

Two politically-minded writers who greatly admired Byron in the second Romantic generation were Bulhão Pato (1829–1912) and Luis Augusto Rebelo da Silva (1822–71). The former was a poet whose relevance lies more in the manner in which he reflects trends of his times than in his actual literary or artistic merit. The latter, who was a historian, novelist and remarkable orator among other things, was probably the first to find affinities between Byron and the earlier Portuguese poet Bocage (1765–1805).

The latter half of the nineteenth century witnessed the rise of republicanism, branching out from the earlier liberalism. By 1870 the republican ideas were being spread by periodicals and gaining ground all the time. Immobility and inadequate management at home, difficulties overseas and in foreign policy and an intensely active ideological propaganda were accelerating the process. The ineffectual reaction of the government, leading up to and after the English ultimatum of 1890, cleverly exploited by the opposition as shock treatment for the nation, the last resort dictatorship of Prime Minister João Franco, offering a pretext for the assassination of the king, Carlos I, and the heir to the Throne, Luis Filipe, leaving on the throne the younger brother for a brief period of two years, are some of the facts and aspects in the final chapter of the Portuguese monarchy.

One of the poets who, starting in the more radical sector of the liberal tradition would become, as a satirist, an intensely active promoter of the republican cause was Guerra Junqueiro (1850–1923). To a certain extent he may even be said to have contributed a fair share to the hostile atmosphere against the monarchy that was to prevail in given circles. Late in life he was to undergo a conversion which silenced the satirist and blasphemer, even the political poet, who now turned to his often naive, sometimes vaguely mystical poetry. In 1874 he published *The Death of Don Juan*, which, it is generally agreed, owes much more to Hugo than to Byron, whatever the author's intentions may have been. In fact, it has been suggested that it arose from a misunderstanding of Byron's poem, through lack of direct knowledge. Thus, *The Death of Don Juan* is a somewhat dubious piece of evidence concerning Byron's reputation. For the author tried to express through the hero all the vices of bourgeois degeneracy, which clearly places him apart from the "lascivious wanderer of the sensual poem of the great English lord", as well as from many other Don Juans written in a more tragic vein.

There remains to be mentioned a work intended to rehabilitate Byron's reputation published in 1895 by a poet, scholar, and, later, twice President of the Portuguese Republic: Teófilo Braga (1843–1924). In a long narrative poem entitled *Harold's Weariness*, which he included in the second edition of *Vision of the Times* (the title of which immediately evokes Hugo's *Légende des Siècles*), Teófilo Braga praises Byron's moral dignity and generosity, thrusts a few blows against England (this was, after all, pretty soon after the British ultimatum of 1890), and drawing on the possible analogy between the period when Portugal was under Beresford and his own times, he concludes that "like man, there are nations that are slaves", thereby giving a clever turn to what Byron had written in 1809.[16]

We have, thus, run our course. Starting from the moment when Byron the "pilgrim" offended Portuguese national feeling through his remarks in *Childe Harold*, we have accompanied the progress of his reputation and influence in what we have called politically-minded authors, to the end of the nineteenth century. We can conclude that, though seriously hampered by the hurt feelings of many Portuguese, Byron's influence was nonetheless important, an inspiring force to men actively concerned with the future of their country and the need to awaken its latent moral energies.

NOTES

1. João de Lemos, *Cancioneiro*, vol. 2, p. 253.
2. J. Almeida Flor, "A Portuguese review of *Childe Harold's Pilgrimage*" in *Byron/Portugal 1977* (A symposium volume published by the Portuguese National Committee of The Byron Society), pp. 59ff.
3. Witness the copy of the 7th ed. (1851), now in the possession of Dr Alves de Azevedo, which was once owned by Camilo Castelo Branco, who annotated it.
4. See C. Estorninho, "Portuguese Byroniana", in *Byron/Portugal 1977*, pp. 81ff.
5. Translated from the article by João Mendes on Garrett in *Verbo, Enciclopédia Luso Brasileira de Cultura*, vol. 9, p. 209.
6. Letter to Duarte Lessa, dated 27 July 1824, in Almeida Garrett, *Obras Completas*, Grande Edição Popular (Lisbon, 1904) vol. 2, p. 779.
7. Dated from Paris, 22 February 1825.
8. Note *k* to Canto One.
9. Edgar Prestage, *The Brother Luis de Sousa of Viscount de Almeida Garrett* (English translation, London, 1909, Introduction, p. 17.)
10. Note *d* to Canto Five.
11. Ofélia Milheiro Caldas Paiva Monteiro, *A Formaçãe de Almeida Garrett: Experiência e Criação* (published doctoral dissertation), 2 vols. (Coimbra, 1971) (see Index under Byron).
12. In *O Pároco de Aldeia* (1825), Chapter IV; also in the periodical *O Panorama* (Lisbon, 1844) p. 119.
13. *Poesias e Inéditos*, edited by H. Cidade (Lisbon, 1941).
14. The hero's name is Maurício. Lopes de Mendonça himself became insane, perhaps from overwork, shortly after becoming a teacher in the Curso Superior de Letras in 1860, and never recovered.
15. See Note 3 above.
16. My attention was drawn to this poem by Dr Luis de Sousa Rebelo, Lecturer in Portuguese, King's College, London, in an unpublished paper on Byron which I was graciously allowed to read.

9 Byron and Russia

Byron and Nineteenth-Century Russian Literature

NINA DIAKONOVA
and
VADIM VACURO

Among the numerous paradoxes characteristic of Byron's personality, of his work and posthumous reputation, scholars have long pointed out the conspicuous difference between his significance in England and his stature in other European countries as well as in America. Britain's attitude was, after a few years of extravagant admiration, generally hostile, to be succeeded only at the close of the century by serious study which, however, resulted in only a very moderate appreciation of his poetic gift. Continental Europe and America were far more constant in their high regard for the poet.

In Russia Byron won almost universal recognition and gratitude. Just how far these went, he was never to know, but certain rumours of his Russian admirers seem to have reached him.

> ... And now rhymes wander
> Almost as far as Petersburgh, and lend
> A dreadful impulse to each loud meander
> Of murmuring Liberty's wide waves, which blend
> Their roar even with the Baltic's.
> *(Don Juan,* VI, 93)

Before Byron wrote these lines he had met some of his Russian readers. As early as 1814 he had talked to Prince P. B. Kozlovsky, a diplomat and man of letters, a friend of Prince P. A. Vyazemsky and later Pushkin; then in 1816 he had received Admiral Čičagov and, between 1818 and 1820, Count A. G. Stroganov.[1]

The first reference to Byron by a Russian man of letters dates from 1814. In a letter to V. A. Žukovsky dated 20 December 1814 S. S. Uvarov says: "I have found some likeness between your poetry and Byron's, but he is actuated by the spirit of evil, and you by the spirit of good."[2]

In 1815 Byron is first mentioned in the Russian press. In the journal *Rossiyskiy Muzeum* V. V. Izmaylov, a highly educated follower of Karamzin, abreast of European thought and letters, reviews *The Corsair* and writes about the growing fame of Byron and Walter Scott. A year later V. I. Kozlov, another journalist, also belonging to the Moscow group of Karamzin's adepts, speaks about Byron in his review of English literature. He says that Scott voluntarily yielded his poetic laurels to Byron (*Russkiy invalid*, 1816). Kozlov, who possessed good knowledge of English and of English literature, also referred to Coleridge's *Kubla Khan* and Wilson's *City of the Plague* (*Russkiy invalid*, 1817).[3]

Beginning with 1818 the anti-Karamzinist journal *Vestnik Evropy* (published by M. T. Kačenovsky) starts a continuous publication of papers on Byron's work, derived mainly from French, but also partly from German, magazines. In the period 1818–24 there are notices of new Byron editions, of *Marino Faliero* (prior to publication) and two detailed articles on Byron in *European Criticism* (1821, no. 23, pp. 199–213).

Although the tone of these references is generally sympathetic and sometimes even enthusiastic, a marked difference in views of Byron's art is nevertheless to be discerned. Late sentimentalists stressed his "sensitiveness ever tender and vivid"; The *Vestnik Evropy* emphasised the "bleak colouring" and the "rebellious passions" of the heroes. Both views proved to be important for the interpretation of Byron's work and personality in Russian poetry. In D. P. Glebov's epistle *To V. L. Pushkin who Sent the Author Some Works by Byron* (1822), in Glebov's and V. L. Pushkin's translations from Byron, the latter emerges as a melancholy and elegiac poet. This view coloured Batyuskov's well-known translation from *Childe Harold* ("There is a pleasure in the pathless woods" – IV, 178–9) in 1819 – the first poetic version of Byron in Russian. It grew to be an important part of Russian poetry, no less than Žukovsky's *Song* – a free version of *Stanzas for Music* ("There's not a joy the world can give").

In Žukovsky's circle Byron was read in the original, and his new works arrived straight from London by means of D. N. Bludov. In 1819 *Childe Harold, The Bride of Abydos* and *Mazeppa* were eagerly read; these readings are often mentioned in the letters of A. I. Turgenev, and in the diary of I. I. Kozlov, Byron's future translator. According to Turgenev, Žukovsky was "crazy" about Byron and planned many translations. These plans were only partially realised: Žukovsky admired Byron but not his rebellious fierceness. Later, in 1848, he was to refer to the English poet as a "Spirit lofty and powerful but one of Negation, Pride and Scorn" (*Slova poeta – dela poeta*).[4]

Nevertheless, in 1822 Žukovsky achieved the best nineteenth-century Russian translation of Byron in *The Prisoner of Chillon*, which was to exercise a powerful influence on Russian literature, particularly upon the technique of rendering English romantic poetry into Russian by using four feet iambic verse and masculine rhyme throughout – a technique firmly established in Russian poetry by Lermontov (*Mcyri*).

The duality of Žukovsky's attitude to Byron can partly be accounted for by the political and literary discussions that centred upon his name at the beginning of the 1820s. Reactionaries were united in rejecting him. Thus, in a letter to D. P. Runič (1820) Byron is an "atheist poet" and a prophet of destructive ideas. "Byron's poetry . . . breeds the Sands and the Louvels."[5] Literary conservatives denounce him as one of the upholders of literary anarchy. In his poem *Dva Veka* (1822) A. Rodzianka says: "the noble lord sings about the convulsive cries of victims, the wails of hellish hordes and the shouts of executioners."[6]

In the 1820s arguments about Byron are frequent in Russia's largest literary society, *Vol'noe obšiestvo lyubiteley rossiyskoy slovesnosti* (The Free Society of Admirers of Russian Letters) and its journal *Sorevnovatel' prosveščeniya i blagotvoreniya* (The Competitor in Enlightenment and Beneficence). Romantic critics and their allies P. A. Pletnev, O. M. Somov see Byron as a genius who has wantonly broken all literary conventions and a powerful personality of stormy passions and tragic fate. Thus the romantic interpretation of Byron differed from the earlier sentimental version.

A specific variant of the former was the concept of Byron in the poetry and thought of the Decembrists and their immediate surroundings. The brothers Bestužev, I. D. Yakuškin, N. M. Muravyev, W. Küchelbäcker, K. F. Ryleev – all of them outstanding ideologists and leaders of the Decembrists – and the great dramatist Griboedov whose affinities with them were very obvious, were devout readers of Byron. Never was love of him so great as in the period of universal disappointment with the policy of Alexander I and the rise of secret societies in Russia. The poet who had so openly stood up against the victory of reaction in Europe, who had sung the liberation movement in Spain, Italy and Greece, who had participated in the struggle put up by the *carbonari* and in the Greek revolution, meant more to the Decembrists than any other European writer.

P. A. Vyazemsky, who in those years was very close to literary liberalism, stated that Byron spoke a language which appealed to the sons of the nineteenth century and created characters that the hearts of those who had taken part in the recent staggering upheavals longed for. Vyazemsky reproached his friend Žukovsky for political indifference and strongly advised him to study Byron: "The mind that witnesses the present events and watches the scaffolds piled up to murder the peoples and liberty cannot and must not abandon itself to the idealities of Arcady.... Byron who soared in heaven comes down to earth to denounce the oppressors, and his romanticism assumes a political colouring."[7]

The voice of political opposition makes itself heard in the elegy *Byron in Prison* (1822), written by the poet and essayist P. A. Gabbe under the direct influence of Vyazemsky.[8]

It is in this tense social atmosphere that Pushkin turned to Byron. The first poem he wrote after his exile to the South was the elegy *The orb of day is gone* (*Pogaslo dnevnoe svetilo*), 1820. The central motif of voluntary exile was inspired by *Childe Harold*. Byron's influence is still more to be felt in the so-called "Southern poems" – *The Prisoner of the Caucasus*, 1821, *The Robber Brothers*, 1822, *The Fountain of Bakhčisarai*, 1823 and *The Gypsies*, 1824. In these, problems and stylistic devices similar to those of *Childe Harold* and the Oriental tales can be traced, though at the time Pushkin knew Byron mainly in French translations.

The Byronic romantic individualist, banished by society and in his turn rejecting its laws, first appears in *The Prisoner of the Caucasus* (*Kavkazskiy plennik*). But the hero, a Petersburgh officer, is different from Byron's early heroes with their vague romantic setting and would probably have been distasteful to the English poet in his early period. Pushkin's Prisoner possessed the definite biographical, social and psychological features of the author's young Russian contemporaries. Both readers and critics felt his kinship with actual representatives of Russian liberalism. P. A. Vyazemsky whose personal and literary tastes were akin to Pushkin's, specially emphasised this social aspect of his friend's poems. It was in connection with the *Prisoner of the Caucasus* and Žukovsky's *Prisoner of Chillon* that he wrote about symptoms of literary reform to be followed – he hinted – by political reform. *The Robber Brothers* (*Brat'ya razboyniki*) also lent themselves to a political interpretation, as a glorification of freedom in the wider sense of the word. Unfortunately, only a fragment of the poem as conceived by Pushkin has come down to us, and we know too little to judge.

The most "Byronic" of Pushkin's poems is *The Fountain of Bakhčisaray* (*Bakhčisaraysky fontan*), 1823. Like the *Prisoner of the Caucasus* it is a lyrical poem with a conventional oriental setting whose structure rests only on loosely bound and highly dramatic scenes, intentionally and deliberately fragmentary, with many episodes sketchy and vague and whose purpose is deliberate destruction of the received notion of the epic. In this poem Pushkin came closer than anywhere to imitating Byron. But very soon he learned to laugh at the Byronic exaggerations in the way the passions of his own characters are drawn.

The Gypsies (Cygany) too are listed among Pushkin's Byronic poems, and indeed, the exotic Gypsy background, the hero himself, with his mysterious and evil past rooted in the vices of city civilisation, are certainly derived from Byron. But the central concept and the plot of the poem are largely polemical as far as Byron is concerned (cf. the old man's speech to Aleco: "You want freedom for no one but yourself. . . . Leave us, O proud man."). After that, Pushkin also stood indebted to Byron for certain details in his further work, but the debt was not more important than his debt to European culture at large. *The Gypsies* were a good-bye to Byron, who had captivated him for about three years.

Upon breaking loose from the spell of Byron, Pushkin also gave up the structural principles of the Byronic poem. The lyrical element is dominated by the epic; the hero no longer reigns supreme; the problem of character and milieu gradually emerges. Pushkin's principles of realism assert themselves in the first chapter of *Eugeniy Onegin*. Characteristically, it was coldly received by adherents of "political romanticism", who had hoped that the new poem would follow Byron's *Don Juan* in becoming a satire upon contemporary society. But in discussing the subject with Ryleev and Bestužev, Pushkin gave them to understand that in his new work he had different purposes. The more salient points of similarity between *Onegin* and *Don Juan* can be observed in the first and last chapters of the former and the final "English" cantos of the latter. Yet up to 1826 at the very least Pushkin had read (in French translation) only the opening five cantos of Byron's epic, radically different from his own. As we well know, he always carefully planned his work, and the plan of *Onegin* was certainly laid as early as 1823. Therefore the likeness is typological and is not due to mere imitation.

Pushkin's exile came to an end just when the news of Byron's death reached him. In his lyric "To the Sea" (1824) he speaks about the poet as "lord of the minds" of a whole generation, as one who was shaped by the "spirit" of the sea and was just "as powerful, as deep, gloomy and indomitable". This appreciation exercised a considerable influence upon the succeeding poetic presentation of Byron in Russia. And yet Pushkin never wrote a special poem on Byron's death in spite of the repeated requests of Vyazemsky, D. V. Daškov (a writer and partisan of the freedom of Greece) and others. In his poem *André Chenier* (1825) he rather pointedly contrasted Byron and the French poet who lost his life during the Jacobin terror. To the shrewder of Pushkin's contemporary critics (e.g. I. V. Kireevsky) it was quite obvious that by 1824 the short Byronic period of the poet's life was well over.[9]

A poetic summary of the Russian attitude towards Byron was drawn in the numerous poems dedicated to his untimely death. Nearly all of them are eloquent of the authors' political opinions. To these authors Byron is first and foremost a fighter for the independence of Greece, as a symbol of the hellenophile sympathies so common in advanced Russian society. Even in I. Kozlov's politically neutral poem giving a romantically high-flown history of the poet's life, notes of true enthusiasm ring out when he comes to speak of Byron's final deed. The poet, Kozlov writes, "was the first to hurry to the clash of the swords of freedom, bringing along harp, soldiers, and gold . . . In the fatal struggle his great soul supported the great cause – the sacred liberation of Hellas." (*Byron*, 1824).

In the poem *The Death of Byron* (1824) V. Küchelbäcker stressed the greatness of the deceased, his share in the salvation of Hellas, and the wreath of glory and martyrdom, of suffering, and fame, of blood and light, he had assumed for her sake. He was also quick to realise that Byron's poetry, though rejected by his country, belonged to the Universe.

M. A. Bestužev devoted a long poem to the honour of the British muse, in which Byron apostrophises the Greek insurgents (*The*

Dying Byron, 1826).

Both the philosophical and political aspects of Byron's art and activity are treated in P. A. Vyazemsky's poem *Byron* (1827): "In his marvellous sounding song the freedom-loving poet has blended the poetry of his soul with the poetry of Nature, the harmony of Earth and the harmony of Heaven." This poem was written after the defeat of the Decembrists' uprising in 1825. It made part of the propaganda of Byron's poetry that Vyazemsky persistently waged in the *Moskovskiy Telegraf*. His articles met with disapproval on the part of the government; D. N. Bludov was voicing the official opinion when he wrote to Vyazemsky that Byron "had long been an outspoken enemy of all established laws of society, of morality and religion; apology of his work, accordingly, was a proof of the journal's political unreliability".[10]

Byron's sacrifice to the holy cause of the Greeks' war against their oppressors is the subject of an unfinished prologue by D. Venevitinov entitled *The Death of Byron* (1825). But it was Ryleev whose tribute to the poet most emphatically characterised the latter's daring and revolutionary spirit. Like Küchelbäcker, he appeals to England:

> Oh proud Queen of the seas! Do not pride thyself on thy gigantic strength, but on thy civic fame and the valour of thy children! Byron, thy son, friend and poet, the great spirit and luminary of the age, has expired at his prime in the holy war for the freedom of the Greeks.

However different the views and talents of the numerous authors of these poems, they all have one thing in common: in keeping with the Russian tradition, there is no borderland between literature and politics, ethics and aesthetics, between the individual and the public, personality and work.

The poems on Byron's death mainly reflect the influence on Russian society of the poet's personality; his poetry left an imprint upon the so-called Russian Byronic poem. In his well-known book, *Byron and Pushkin*, V. M. Žirmunsky demonstrated that this genre, represented in Russian literature by scores of various samples and specimens, developed on lines traced by Pushkin rather than on those traced by Byron himself, the authors drawing inspiration from Pushkin's interpretation of Byron's oriental tales. It was in the earlier 1820s that the more important of the Russian Byronic poems came into being: K. F. Ryleev's *Voynarovsky* (1824), I. I. Kozlov's *Černets*; E. A. Baratynsky, a far greater poet, contributed to the Byronic tradition in his long poems *Eda* (1825) and *The Ball* (1828).

In *Voynarovsky* Ryleev, a leading figure among the Decembrists, endeavoured to create a heroic and national variant of the Byronic poem.[11] He had introduced Byronic situations before in his *Meditations* (Dumy), as, for instance in the scene where Khmelnicky is set free in a way definitely not unlike the one described in *The Corsair* etc. Byron's influence upon *Voynarovsky* was noticed by many of his contemporary readers. It is clearly traced in the plot and structure of the poem, in the characteristic use of confession (a nephew of the hetman Mazepa, Voynarovsky tells his interlocutor the story of his life after the same fashion the Giaour had confessed his to the monk) no less than in such borrowings from *Parisina* and *Mazeppa* as in Ryleev's respective descriptions of the execution and the mad ride, and particularly in the typological identity of the central characters. Ryleev endows Voynarevsky with features very similar to those of the Giaour and the Corsair. He has the same "restless and gloomy look, the lineaments of his face are harsh and melancholy". He says: "Nothing brings me joy, love and friendship are alien to me, sadness oppresses my soul like lead, and there is nothing my heart cares for."

The characterisation of Mazeppa and of the robber in the fragment of the poem *Gaydamak* (1825) runs much on the same lines. Like the characters of Byron, those of the Russian poet rise superior to the crowd, being remarkable for unconquerable pride and scorn of the cruel fate dooming them to exile and solitude.

And yet, Ryleev never is a mere imitator. The political and civic elements are even more strongly marked in his works than in Byron's. The famous confession of Nalivayko, for example (*Nalivayko*, 1824–25) is certainly pretty close to the confession of Byron's Hugo and the Giaour, but it rings not so much with individualistic revolt as with selfless patriotic feeling:

> I know that death awaits the one who first rises against the oppressors of the people. I know I am doomed, but tell me: was ever freedom bought without sacrifice? I will die for my land, I feel it and, holy father, I gladly bless my fate.

A similar reinterpretation could be pointed out in the way

Ryleev deals with the episode in Byron's *Mazeppa* describing the hero who, on recovering consciousness, suddenly sees a youthful Cossac-woman. In *Voynarovsky* the girl is as sympathetic in her care of the dying man as her predecessor, the young Cossac woman in *Mazeppa*, but Ryleev endows her with exemplary firmness and noble patriotism. "How passionately her lofty soul loved her native land!... She could and knew how to be a citizen and a spouse...." This selfless and heroic female character lived on in the Russian Byronic poem under Ryleev's direct influence, for example in I. I. Kozlov's as Princess Nathalie Dolgoruki (*Knyaginya Natalya Borisovna Dolgorukaya*, 1827).

The defeat of the revolutions in South Europe and the subsequent crushing of the Decembrists' uprising, at the end of 1825, resulted in profound social and psychological changes in Russian society. A tragic note clearly made itself heard. Thence the wide popularity of eschatological motifs. These had already been cultivated by the Decembrists. Many of them had followed up the tradition of eighteenth century Russian poetry in leaning heavily on the Old Testament and giving poetic versions of the Psalms (F. N. Glinka, V. K. Küchelbäcker and others). This had obvious social connotations, being a way to expose public vices and prophesy future cataclysms that were to bring about the triumph of social justice. Biblical symbolism coloured some of the most constant themes of the Russian poetry of the period (e.g. the theme of the poet–prophet). In the years immediately succeeding the rout of the Decembrists' revolt, the tragic lamentations of the prisoners by the Rivers of Babylon assumed the nature of a rather pointed allusion.

Byron's lyrics were interpreted in the light of the national tradition. It is certainly not an accident that his *Hebrew Melodies* had the greatest popularity. Interest for them increased throughout the 1820s. They were translated by authors who adopted the views of the Decembrists: N. I. Gnedič (*David's Harp–Arfa Davida–* 1821; *A Melody*, 1824), V. N. Grigor'yev (*The Complaints of the Israelites – Zaloby izrailtyan–* 1824; *The Lament–Setovanie–* 1827), A. G. Rotčev (*The Defeat of Sennacherib – Razbitie Sennakherima –* 1826; *A Melody*, 1826), A. I. Poležaev (*The Vision of Belshazzar – Videnie Valtasara –* 1829).

To Russian readers and poets the *Hebrew Melodies* held social and political implications. Yet this was not the sole source of their appeal: they were also a source of numerous love lyrics and translations (by I. I. Kozlov, N. A. Markevič and others).[12]

The eschatological motifs of Byron's *Darkness* became firmly rooted in Russian poetry. In the 1820s alone it was translated at least five times (by O. Somov, F. Glinka, D. Glebov, M. Vrončenko, A. Rotčev); in the years to follow it attracted Lermontov (1830) and I. S. Turgenev (1846).

In the 1830s the number of translations from Byron does not directly testify to the depth of his influence. Lermontov, for one thing, though he wrote an exact prose translation of *Darkness*, made very free with Byron's text in his poetic version – so much so that in his three *Nights* – I, II, III (*Noc'* I, II, III) Byron's poem does not so much serve as a source but as a poetic impulse.

The same is true of the meditative lyrics of E. A. Baratynsky, wherein the connection with Byron's is only that of genre and subject (see *The Skull* – *Čerep* – 1824, *The Last Death* – *Poslednyaya smert'* – 1827). This phenomenon may be looked upon as typical and implies a new period of the assimilation of Byron in Russian poetry after the change the latter suffered along with the changes in the spirit of the age.

The Russian Romanticism of the post-Decembrists' period is not only characterised by increasingly tragic intonations but also by a deeper philosophical significance, by a break with rationalism and, accordingly, a growing cult of lyrical emotion. The Russian romantics of this period care preferably for the aspect of Byron's work that lends itself best to a philosophical interpretation. Besides *Darkness* there is a growing interest in the Goethean *Manfred*. It was first translated by M. P. Vrončenko in 1828; a fragment of the drama was translated by D. A. Obleukhov and two special papers on the subject were written by S. P. Ševyrev and I. V. Kireevsky in *Moskovsky vestnik*, the organ of Moscow Schellingians. The motifs of *Manfred* and later of *Cain*, along with eschatological subjects, find their way into the Russian mysteries widely popular in the 1830s.

In the same period there is a change in the Russian Byronic poem. Its lyrical intensity increases. In the leading character the features of Byron's criminal heroes stand much more clearly revealed. In the 1820s these features had not yet been very obvious. An important step towards the interpretation of the Byronic hero as a man of evil was made in I. I. Kozlov's poem *The Monk* (*Černec*, 1826): the story of the monk whose confession takes up the greater part of the poem is the story of a crime. True, Kozlov who was a follower of Žukovsky, laid a heavy stress on the hero's repentance. In the poems of the 1830s this motif is considerably reduced or non-existent, but the melodramatic element gains in intensity (see, e.g. *Borsky* (1828) and *The Beggar – Nisčiy* – 1830, by A. I. Podolinsky). All this came to matter a great deal to Lermontov.

His poetry was the fullest and deepest expression of the Russian Byronism. At the initial stages of his artistic development (1828–9) the boy Lermontov got to know Byron in translation and through the Byronic poems of Žukovsky and Kozlov. Yet it was Pushkin who became the principal intermediary between Byron and Lermontov. However as early as the 1830s Byron's influence upon his poetry became more direct and obvious, as in the poems *Giulio, Litvinka,* and *The Confession (Ispoved').*

Byron's protest against social and political oppression, his flaming rhetoric, was just the right answer to Lermontov's innermost problems. In his translations from Byron (*Fare Well – Proščay; A Ballad – Ballada; Lines Written in an Album – V al'bom*) Lermontov emulates Byron's declamatory style, his predilection for hyperboles, absolutes, antitheses and aphoristic *pointes*. Nevertheless, in the mid-thirties there already appears a certain originality in the plot of his poem, a greater local and historical preciseness (*Khadži–Abrek*, 1833–4, *Boyarin Orša*, 1835–6, and even earlier in *Izmail Bey*, 1832). Byron's influence is practically at an end in *Mcyri*, where details of manners are far more concrete than in Byron's oriental tales, and where the main subject-matter was specifically linked with Russian problems, with the tragedy of unfulfilled political expectations.

There is no doubt that the young Lermontov saw Byron in the light of the Russian literary tradition. His own variant of the Byronic poem bears all the lyric and dramatic intensity characteristic of the poetic style of the Russian 1830s. The gloomy, suffering and demonic individualist, at war with society and sometimes burdened with crime had links with both Byron's evil heroes and their Russian equivalents. At the same time Lermontov's interpretation of Byron was influenced by the new philosophic trends of Russian thought. Through the *Moskovsky Vestnik* Lermontov got to know Schelling, and thus a post-Byron and a post-Enlightenment stage of philosophical thought, of moral and aesthetic culture. The Byron tradition becomes blended with the tradition of Russian philosophical poetry.

This means that Lermontov's Byronism was a highly complex and original phenomenon. The very fact that Lermontov adhered

to Byron revealed the stand he was taking in the literary battles of
his time. Just then a revaluation of Byron had started in Russian
criticism. In the 1830s even N. A. Polevoy, editor of the *Moskovsky
Telegraf*, who had always highly appreciated Byron as an eloquent
spokesman of his time and had always popularised his art, started
finding fault with him as a dramatist, and placed him below Dante
and Shakespeare on the ground that he was a lyric, while they were
epic poets.[13] For the *lyubomudry*, the philosophic editors of the *Moskovsky Vestnik*, Goethe decidedly ousted Byron from the fore to the
background; the leading spirits of the rising slavophile movement
(e.g. S. P. Ševyrev) were soon to adopt an inimical attitude towards
the Russian Byronists as well. The most consistent of Byron's
detractors of the 1830s was N. I. Nadeždin, editor of the *Teleskop*
who in those years did not differ in this respect from the editorial
staff of the *Moskovsky Vestnik*: he looked upon Byron as the forerunner of the Satanic poetry, as a bearer of gloom, despair and pride,
hostile to religion and morality (*On the Origin of Nature and Fate of
Poetry, Called Romantic – O proiskhoždenii, prirode i sud' bakh poezii, nazy-
vaemoy romantičeskoy* – 1830).

Under these conditions Lermontov deliberately set out not only
to study Byron's work but to correlate his own personality to
Byron's, as if he were thinking of the English poet as his model (To
xxx: "Do not think I deserve regret," – K xxx: *Ne dumay, čtob ya byl
dostoin sožalenya*); ("No, I am not Byron, I am different," – *Net ya ne
Byron, ya drugoy*, 1832). Byron's influence on Lermontov's artistic
personality was greater than that of any other single European
author, even including Shakespeare. There are numerous verbal
coincidences between the poetry of Byron and that of young Lermontov, but they can be seen in proper perspective only when considered in the general context of the latter's evolution, his links with
the Russian literary tradition and with European romanticism at
large. Even if the heroes of Lermontov's early dramas resemble
those of Byron, they are at the same time born of his observations of
Russian social life.

Though Lermontov's Byronic period ended with his early
youth, yet even in the brief period of his maturity his connection
with the English poet's work was not broken. His long poems *Saška*
1835–6) and *Childrens' Fairytale* (*Skazka dlya detey*, 1840) owe something to the satire of *Beppo* and *Don Juan*. Like Byron and Pushkin,
Lermontov blends elements political and lyrical, pathetic and
comic, and rises from the extremes of subjectivity to objectivity,

from heroic individualism to a sane evaluation of the relation between man and society. His novel *A Hero of Our Times* (*Geroy našego vremeni*, 1839–41) is in many ways the successor of French early nineteenth-century novels and also (a thing not noticed before) of Byron's *Letters and Journals* published by Thomas Moore in 1830 (Lermontov refers to this edition three times in his autobiographical notes).

Byron's correspondence no less than his diary reveal a complex personality whose passions are inseparable from rationalistic analysis and self-analysis. Such a personality could not fail to impress highly Lermontov, who was long before fascinated by the author's poetry, and imposed itself upon the treatment of Pečorin, particularly of Pečorin as the writer of a journal called, like Byron's, a "journal" and not a "diary" ("*žurnal*" not "*dnevnik*"). The philosophical tone of Byron's prose writings, the numerous aphorisms and maxims he introduces, the prosaic details, the humorous sallies directed against common poetic clichés, the alternation of subjective lyric narration with ironic and objective comment are just as characteristic of Lermontov's prose style as of Byron's. But the difference between them is more important than the points of likeness. In Byron's *Letters and Journals* the hero is the author himself while Pečorin as the author of the Journal is a character of Lermontov's and a fictional character at that. His is not just another personal confession. It is a generalised experience of a whole generation, and he rises to be the hero of a realistic psychological novel who is viewed objectively by the author.[14]

Lermontov is still more of an innovator in his late lyrics (1836–41). Though we again find him translating Byron – and now his translations are more exact than before (*My Soul is Dark – Duša moya mračna*, 1836, etc.) – and though in his original verse Byronic reminiscences still occur, as in the *Contract* (Dogovor, 1841), Lermontov is now obviously not an imitator but a successor of Byron, and his poetry belongs to a later aesthetic system. It is more carefully individualised and psychologically motivated by concrete and definitely specified emotional situations; it is more historically determined and in delineating relations of man and woman he is free from such social and moral prejudices as Byron could never quite reject.

Lermontov quietly and coldly discusses his joyless and illegitimate union with a woman branded by public scorn – and scorns that scorn (*To a Lovely – Prelestnice*, 1830; *A Contract – Dogover*, 1841);

Byron sides with the public in regretting the "light fame" of his love whose "vows are all broken", and shares in her shame (*When We Two Parted*). Though neither poet could abide the cant of the age and defied public opinion, Byron never made a prostitute the heroine of his poem as did Lermontov in Saška (her very name – Thyrza – is rife with polemics against Byron, who had dedicated to an unknown Thyrza a number of his best lyrics).

In contrast to Byron's, the language of Lermontov's poetry is free from the influence of classicism and nineteenth century philosophic rationalism. It is simpler, more succinct, closer to the speech of everyday life. Whereas the emotions of the Byronic lyrical hero stand associated with things poetical and tragical, and are, accordingly, rendered by means of lofty phraseology and elaborate syntax, with Lermontov both feelings and language are more prosaic and colloquial, which only emphasises the tragic inner world of the poet. In making common soldiers and officers his dramatis personae (*Borodino*, 1837; *Valerik*, 1840; *A Testament – Zaveščanie*, 1840) Lermontov displays a simplicity and objectivity, a disdain of poetic conventions Byron was never to equal. At the same time, in new and different historical and national conditions Lermontov expressed that protest, skepticism and despair, the embodiment of which had drawn universal attention to Byron in the first decades of the century.

Lermontov's art was the culminating point of Russian Byronism. It implied a debt to it, a triumph over it and a ridicule of the parody to which it was finally degraded.

Like any outstanding social and literary phenomenon, Russian Byronism, we now know, was complex. It was both a powerful political influence which stimulated the most advanced men of Russia, and particularly Russian writers who, in their turn, stimulated Russian readers and public opinion, and also a passing literary and psychological fashion which, in due time, fell into disrepute as most fashions do as soon as they are carried to violent extremes. Both these aspects of Byronism found their way into Russian literature.

On the one hand, Byron was the embodiment of the ideal of civic and intellectual liberty, of contempt for political, moral and aesthetic authorities. In their search for truthful and courageous art, Russian writers found inspiration in him who recognised no limitations to his mind and will. On the other hand, there arose a different and quite superficial interpretation of the English poet as the bard of mystery and woe, a man disappointed and blasé, entirely dominated by selfish passions. That sort of interpretation was not impossible, because Byron's work was only very imperfectly known: there was the language-barrier – few read him in the original, and it was only *Childe Harold* (the greater part, but not the whole of it), the Oriental tales and a good many of the lyrics which reached Russian readers; *Don Juan* and other satirical poems were known only in excerpts, so that the concept of Byron could hardly be other than one-sided. More important still, that sort of idea seemed to suit the mentality of certain sections of aristocratic Russian society who suffered from vague dissatisfaction with the established order of things and pined for some sort of ideal that would bring some poetry into the prose of their lives.

Byronic heroes seemed to grow like mushrooms, and in due time became objects of parody and disdain. Among the characters in whom elements of these can be detected Onegin was one of the first, and Grušnicky (in *The Hero of Our Time*) one of the last.

In the 1840s Russian Byronism ceased to exist as a social and cultural fact. I. S. Turgenev, A. A. Foeth and A. A. Frigor'yev went through a short period of infatuation with Byron, but with them it was not to grow into a lasting and fruitful interest. Nonetheless, for the elder generation of "the men of the 1840s" Byron remained a living presence. To V. G. Belinsky Byron was a symbol of negation. This was also the view of his friend B. P. Botkin who saw negation and struggle as the poet's leading features, and realised their historical and social background (see Botkin's letter to Belinsky, 22 March 1842). Belinsky also laid special stress on the fact that Byron's negation and pessimism were a peculiar expression of a positive ideal. The Russian critic's concept of Byron was an integral part not only of Belinsky's social and philosophical system but also of his polemics against reactionary critics of the Nadeždin type.[15]

At the same time in the 1840s the readers' and writers' attitude towards Byron considerably lost the interest of actuality. Debates no longer centred on the poet himself, for his reputation had become fixed, but on problems of Russian Byronism, particularly in connection with Lermontov. Belinsky and his "Westerniser" disciples tended to emphasise the importance of the "negative" Byronic element in Lermontov, which the slavophile critics preferred to see as alien to Russian life and literature. While Russian Byronism gradually exhausted itself, breeding only belated epigones of Lermontov such as M. V. Avdeev, its historical role palpably decreased; discussions on the subject of the "superfluous men" (*lišnie lyudi*) of the 1860s (i.e. on the historical significance of the 1840s generation) were indirectly also discussions of Russian Byronism.

In 1877 E. M. Dostoevsky spoke about the importance for European and Russian society of Byron as an answer to those young people who in the heat of polemics were disposed to look down on formerday Byronists. His words are all the more remarkable as Dostoevsky's attitude towards the influence of Byronism was at that time negative. While he was writing these words, papers and articles were appearing in Russian journals not only criticising Russian Byronism but starting the first scholarly studies of its problems.

Referring to the heyday of Russian Byronism, Doestoevsky declared: "At the time when men were the prey of profound melancholy, of disappointment, almost of despair . . . a great and powerful genius, a passionate poet appeared . . . in whose voice . . . the grief of men sounded . . . No great mind and generous heart could then avoid Byronism."

NOTES

1. M. P. Alekseyev, "*Avtografy Bayrona v SSRR*", *Literaturnoe Nasledstvo* (Moscow, 1952) vol. 58, pp. 975–6. This study also includes information that Russian interest in Byron lasted well up to the middle of the nineteenth century, when the poet's manuscripts were collected by his admirers. Some of Byron's autographs derived from Russian collections (a rough copy of the *Hebrew Melody* "A Spirit Stood Before Me", a letter addressed to Mr Trevannion dated Milan, 15 October 1816) were here published for the first time. The authenticity of these autographs was questioned in the English press (*The Times*, 15 July 1955, and 8, 9, 19 May 1958) but then established beyond the shadow of a doubt. Byron's letter to Trevannion was reproduced by Sir Gavin de Beer (*The Times Literary Supplement*, 16 May 1958), who used the autograph preserved by the Public Library of Leningrad but unfortunately did not refer to its previous publication by Professor Alekseyev.
2. *Russkiy arhiv*, 1871, no. 2, p. 0163.
3. Yu. D. Levin, "*Prižiznennaya slava Valtera Skotta v Rossii*", *Epoha romantizma*, Leningrad, 1975, p. 8.
4. A. N. Veselovsky, *V. A. Žukovsky, Poesiya čuvstva i "serdečnogo voobraženiya"* (Petrograd, 1918) pp. 297–303; V. I. Maslov, *Načal'ny period bayronizma v Rossii* (Kiev, 1915) pp. 4–5, 21–5.
5. *Russkaya starina*, 1896, no. 10, pp. 135–38. Cf. Yu. G. Oksman, "*Bor'ba s Bayron-*

om v aleksandrovskuyu epohu" in *Načala*, 1922, no. 2, pp. 256–63.

6. *Poety, 1820–1830*, Leningrad, 1972, p. 164.
7. *Ostafievsky arhiv* (Petersburg, 1899) vol. 2, pp. 170–1.
8. *Poety, 1790–1810* (Leningrad, 1971) pp. 737–41.
9. N. P. Daškevič, *Stat' i po novoy russkoy literature* (Petrograd, 1914) pp. 330–97; N. K. Kozmin, *Pushkin o Bayrone – Puškin v mirovoy literature* (Leningrad, 1926) pp. 99–112.
10. M. I. Gillelson, *P. A. Vyazemsky: Žizn' i tvorčestvo* (Life and Work) (Leningrad, 1969) pp. 43–6, 158–64.
11. See V. I. Maslov, *Literaturnaya deyatel'nost' K. F. Ryleeva* (Kiev, 1912).
12. E. A. Bobrov, *O bayronizme A. I. Poležaeva* (Varšava, 1906); I. Eyges, *K perevodam I. Kozlova iz Bayrona* – "Zven'ya", Book 5 (Moscow and Leningrad, 1935) pp. 744–8.
13. *Moskovsky Telegraf*, 1828, no. 20, p. 461; N. Polevoy, *Očerki russkoy literatury* (Moscow, 1839) no. 1, p. 175.
14. N. Diakonova, "Iz nablyudeniy nad žurnalom Pečorina", *Russkaya literatura*, 1969, no. 4, pp. 115–16.
15. N. Brodsky, "Bayron v russkoy literature", *Literaturny kritik*, 1938, no. 4, pp. 134–6.

10   Byron and Spain

Byron's Poetic Vision of Spain

ESTABAN PUJALS

Lord Byron's poetry is a mixture of imagination and romantic fantasy, overwhelming passion and impressionistic realism, and in his poetic vision of Spain, these characteristics stand out. There are three of Byron's poems in which Spain appears, in some aspect or another, as an important theme: *Childe Harold* Canto I, *Don Juan* Canto I and part of II, and *The Age of Bronze*. In essence these constitute, respectively, a poetic narrative of Byron's trip from Lisbon to Andalusia at the beginning of the Peninsular War; a humoristic fantasy of the social morals and customs of Spain during the eighteenth century; and a severe political criticism in support of the liberty of the Spaniards during the reign of Ferdinand VII (1822).

Childe Harold is a lively poem, of diverse quality and content, written in the rhythm of the personal adventures of the poet, which attracted the romantic public because of its subjective feeling, its tone of confession and its expressive and direct language. The first two cantos, which include his trips through the Iberian Peninsula and the Eastern Mediterranean countries, surprised the English people of that time because of the originality of the text and the authenticity of its presentation. After an introductory section in which Byron gives some romantic reasons for his disdainful hero's leaving England, the contents of Canto I are devoted almost exclusively to his travels through Portugal and Spain and practically constitute a description of and poetic comment on Spain during the Peninsular War.

Byron entered Spain by way of Badajoz and was greatly surprised at finding but one insignificant "silver current" separating both countries. Nonetheless, if there did not exist a geographic difference between Spain and Portugal, Byron states that there definitely was a great difference between the people of these two

countries. He crosses the frontier and, once in Spain, the river Gua-
diana flows before him.

> Dark Guadiana rolls his power along
> In sullen billows, murmuring and vast . . .

The presence of the memorable river stirs the imagination of the
poet to think about the story of Don Roderigo, the last of the Goths,
the encounters between the Christians and the Moslems, whose
blood was mixed in the waters of the current, and the connection
between the feats of the past and the present. He exclaims:

> Oh, lovely Spain! renowned, romantic land!
> . . . .
> Where are those bloody banners which of yore
> Waved o'er thy sons? victorious to the gale,
> And drove at last the spoilers to their shore?
>
> Awake, ye sons of Spain! awake! advance!
> Lo! Chivalry, your ancient goddess cries,
> But wields not, as of old, her thirsty lance,
> Nor shakes her crimson plumage in the skies:
> Now on the smoke of blazing bolts she flies,
> And speaks in thunder through yon engine's roar:
> In every peal she calls – "Awake! arise!"
> Say, is her voice more feeble than of yore?
> When her war song was heard on Andalusia's shore?

In spite of the Spanish victory at Bailén and the advance of Wellington from Portugal, which was soon to materialise in the favourable action of Talavera, the presentiments that Byron had of the
contest were not optimistic. The French army was extraordinarily
powerful and the Spanish–English military alliance lacked the
necessary cohesion. The poet realised that Spain was facing at the
moment the problem of national life or death, and as an Englishman, he regarded the French invasion as an affront. He feared the
triumph of Napoleon's army.

> . . . heard you not those hoofs of dreadful note?
> Sounds not the clang of conflict on the heath?

His fierce disdain made him consider the paradox of war – colourful and spectacular; were not friends and brothers fighting? War's hot breath pushed the warlike hounds beyond the chase so that everyone joined in the hunt, though few participated in the triumph. The tomb would claim the major part.

> Three hosts combine to offer sacrifice:
> Three tongues prefer strange orisons on high;
> Three gaudy standards flaunt the pale blue skies;
> The shouts are France, Spain, Albion, Victory!
> The Foe, the Victim, and the fond ally
> That fights for all, but ever fights in vain,
> Are met – as if at home they could not die –
> To feed the crow on Talavera's plain,
> And fertilize the field that each pretends to gain.

The idea of Byron is that man is merely an instrument (the dead being the broken instruments) which the tyrants use by the millions to achieve their ends. And meditating on this, he supposes that the traveller is crossing Albuera and foresees the battle:

> Oh, Albuera! glorious field of grief!
> As o'er thy plain the Pilgrim pricked his steed,
> Who could foresee thee, in a space so brief,
> A scene where mingling foes should boast and bleed!

Byron moves on to Andalusia. Each fold of the Sierra Morena hides a battery and the pyramids of shells are piled on the side of the road to stop the advance of the French troops to Seville. This they would besiege and take easily at the end of January 1810.

> Full swiftly Harold wends his lonely way
> Where proud Sevilla triumphs unsubdued:
> Yet is she free? the Spoiler's wished-for prey!
> Soon, soon shall Conquest's fiery foot intrude.

Nevertheless, unconscious of the menace, Seville continues to kill time in diversions, presenting all types of amenities to these Spaniards who do not seem to hear the trumpets of war nor suffer the wounds of their country, lured by the incentives of love or the attractions of vice which any city can provide. But this is not true,

Byron believes, of the Andalusian farmers who are sad and fright-
ened by the idea that their vineyards may be parched by the "dun,
hot breath of war".

> Ah, Monarchs! could ye taste the mirth ye mar,
> Not in the toils of Glory would ye fret;
> The hoarse dull drum would sleep, and Man be happy yet!

The traveller continues to Seville and listens to the songs that the
muleteer intones to shorten the journey. He asks if the songs are
ballads of love, devotion, or adventure. He soon discovers that they
are patriotic songs "many of which are very beautiful".

> And must they fall? the young, the proud, the brave,
> To swell one bloated Chief's unwholesome reign?
> No step between submission and a grave?
> The rise of Rapine and the fall of Spain?

In this section of the poem, where the traveller tells of his
impressions and thoughts, there are praises of the Spanish women:
their feminine elegance, their attractiveness, their entrancing
shyness. No, the Spanish women definitely do not belong to the
race of Amazons. Rather they were created

> for all the witching arts of love:
> . . . .
> In softness as in firmness far above
> Remoter females.

> The seal Love's dimpling finger hath impress'd
> Denotes how soft that chin which bears his touch:
> Her lips, whose kisses pout to leave their nest,
> Bid man be valiant ere he merit such:
> Her glance how wildly beautiful!

However, in spite of the generous poetic eulogy which Byron
makes of the Spanish women, he does not want it to be understood
that their attractiveness and femininity prevent them from co-
operation in the national cause. Agustina of Aragón [The Maid of
Saragoza] is an obvious symbol of the responsibility that the
Spanish women felt during the Peninsular War; and the poet lauds

the girls who substitute for their lovers in the war, those who cling to the guns their husbands leave when they die, or with a kiss or a look encourage their men to battle.

Once in Greece, Byron's fantasy transports him back to Spain to the city of Cadiz, surrounded by the sea, one Sunday morning when the church bells call the faithful. Later on, we are taken to the bullfights. There is a description of the bullfight Byron saw in the Port of Santa Maria in which he gives us an impression of the brilliance, the danger, the gracefulness and the violence of the entertainment. The poet leaves Cadiz with a nostalgic goodbye:

> Adieu, fair Cadiz! yea, a long adieu!
> Who may forget how well thy walls have stood?
> When all were changing, thou alone wert true,
> First to be free, and last to be subdued. . . .

Byron refers to the fruitless siege of Marshal Soult during the summer of 1812, and contemptuous of the lack of harmony between the Spanish ruling class and the people, he adds:

> Here all were noble, save Nobility!
> None hugged a Conqueror's chain, save fallen Chivalry!

His imagination as a poet, his appreciation of the qualities of the Spanish women, his romantic evocation of the bygone days of grandeur do not hinder his observations of the realistic tragedy in Spain; and in a fragment which I feel should be famous for the Spaniards, he writes:

> Such be the sons of Spain, and strange her Fate!
> They fight for Freedom who were never free,
> A Kingless people for a nerveless state;
> Her vassals combat when their chieftains flee,
> True to the veriest slaves of Treachery:
> Fond of a land which gave them nought but life,
> Pride points the path that leads to Liberty.

The penetration, clearness and sincerity with which Byron witnesses the instinct which directed a country that had no guidance, whose aristocracy was corrupt or loose and whose defense was just as heroic as it was unco-ordinated, is absolutely impressive. The poet, apparently feeling incapable of describing with the necessary vigour the Spanish reality of those days, invites those who want to comprehend it to read of the horrors that were written about "the most bloody of wars" in which the sickle, the knife or the most rustic of tools were transformed into weapons. The sympathy of Byron for the brave Spanish attitude becomes, by contrast, ruthless when he refers to the invader. France is still rich in men to fulfil the ambitious frenzy of her Emperor, and the Spanish defence, however firm and obstinate, is undisciplined:

> Nor yet, alas! the dreadful work is done;
> Fresh legions pour adown the Pyrenees:
> It deepens still, the work is scarce begun,
> Nor mortal eye the distant end foresees.
> Fall'n nations gaze on Spain; if freed, she frees
> More than her fell Pizarros once enchained.

The war continued and neither Byron nor anyone else – except the stubborn and fiercely independent instinct of the Spaniards and the unwearied tenacity of the British – could see signs of hope for a definite victory. The traveller has to confess, still at the beginning of 1812, the time in which Byron prepared the first two Cantos of *Childe Harold* for publication, that:

> Not all the blood at Talavera shed,
> Not all the marvels of Barossa's fight,
> Not Albuera lavish of the dead,
> Have won for Spain her well asserted right.
> When shall her Olive-Branch be free from blight?
> When shall she breathe her from the blushing toil?
> How many a doubtful day shall sink in night,
> Ere the Frank robber turn him from his spoil,
> And Freedom's stranger-tree grow native of the soil!

But what Byron definitely perceived with abundant evidence was the constant and heroic sacrifice of the Spaniards in this interminable fight, and the fact that it signified much more than the independence of Spain in the European conflict launched by Napoleon. This is the central theme of the first two Cantos of *Childe Harold*.

Between the first two Cantos of *Childe Harold* and Cantos I and II of *Don Juan* there is a great difference in style, quality and in basic intention. Canto I of *Childe Harold* constitutes a poem which is predominantly epic in mood and argument about Spain in 1809–11. It is a work of youth, written when the poet was about 22 years old. It is a good example of Byron's narrative capacity, but it lacks flexibility and manifests his passionate trend of mind and his rhetorical attitude. It shows Byron's grasp of reality and his faculty to transform it into poetry. It manifests his intellectual agility; but it presents a certain rudeness of rhythm and defects in composition. It is not compact, it is somewhat repetitive, and his phrasing is usually conventional.

Canto I of *Don Juan*, on the other hand, is a humoristic fantasy located in Seville, the traditional fatherland of the folk figure of Don Juan. Byron's *Don Juan* is considered his best work, and, as Shelley understood it in his day, it is a vigorous and original poem which offers both a realistic and a romantic vision. In its projection, it is a picture on a large scale of many of the defects and qualities of humanity and a criticism of the fame, the folly and the limitations of life.

Don Juan Canto I, and the initial stanzas of Canto II, are located in Spain; but it is well to note that as a work of humour and irony, whose principle motive is not an exact approach to truth and reality but a burlesque vision of Andalusia, the characterisation of its personages is intentionally vague and superficial. The hero as well as his parents and his lover and the other Spanish characters who appear in this part of the poem are rapidly sketched, they do not need more psychological penetration than that which is required by the argument, and their distinctiveness consists in the fact that they are Andalusians and are surrounded by some elementary Spanish characteristics to serve as a poetic framework. The strokes with which Spain and the Spaniards are drawn from the beginning are very general and they only provide the necessary local colour for the argument and situations of the poem.

The hero of *Don Juan* was very fortunate in being born in the pleasant city of Seville, "famous for oranges and women":

> Who has not seen it will be much to pity,
> So says the proverb – and I quite agree;
> Of all the Spanish towns is none more pretty,
> Cadiz, perhaps – but that you soon may see;
> Don Juan's parents lived beside the river,
> A noble stream, and called the Guadalquiver.

Byron describes Don José, the father of Don Juan, as a true gentleman, free from the slightest stain of Moorish or Jewish blood, whose ancestry he could trace back to the Goths of the best origin. He was rather careless and free; he had his weaknesses, and was not very interested in learning nor in those who were learned. In the character of Don José Byron may have been intending to portray the typical upperclass Andalusian man, and at the same time represent the traits of the typical English gentleman. As a direct descendant of Eve, Don José knew how to gather the fruits of life without asking permission of his wife.

Don Juan's mother, Doña Inéz, was very different. She was a curious mixture of strange devotion, hypocrisy, false moral rectitude, a pedantic varnish of culture of which she was most proud and the absolute conviction that she was the epitome of virtue and the living example of perfection (definitely a caricature of Lady Byron).

> His mother was a learned lady, famed
> For every branch of every science known –
> In every Christian language ever named;
> With virtues equalled by her wit alone.
> . . . .
>
> Her memory was a mine: she knew by heart
> All Calderon and greater part of Lopé,
> So, that if any actor miss'd his part,
> She could have served him for the prompter's copy;
> . . . .

She knew how to recite the Lord's Prayer in Latin and she could also read the alphabet in Greek. Her philological intuition inspired her to like English for its similarity to Hebrew, and her favourite science was mathematics (Byron called his wife the "Princess of Parallelograms"). She was perfect, beyond comparison. But as, according to Byron, perfection unfortunately is "insipid in this naughty world of ours", the conclusion can not be more evident and the lack of adjustment between the scrupulous Doña Inéz and her engaging and disorganised husband is entirely understandable.

> Don José and Donna Inez led
> For some time an unhappy sort of life,
> Wishing each other, not divorced, but dead.

Their friends tried to reconcile them; but this charitable intent, as can well be imagined, made the situation worse. Their lawyers recommended divorce; but before any fee was paid, Don José died, solving their matrimonial problems.

Don Juan, their only son and heir, being still so young, remained under the care and custody of his mother, who intended to bring him up the perfect gentleman. So, she called in tutors of recognised puritanical morality, to teach him the most recondite sciences, that is to say, the most useless:

> Arts, sciences – no branch was made a mystery
> To Juan's eyes, excepting natural history.

> The languages, especially the dead,
> The sciences, and most of all the abstruse,
> The arts, at least all such as could be said
> To be the most remote from common use.

The missal, sermons, lectures, lives of the saints, formed part of his curriculum; but Saint Augustine's *Confessions* were excluded. The same was true of many lessons of classic literature, mythology, and so on, because they presented serious breaches of strict morality.

As Doña Inéz was a very wise mother, she took enormous care to choose her maids who should be either old or extremely ugly. Nevertheless the instinct of the lad showed enough decision to break all dikes built up by the maternal foresight. Byron narrates with swiftness the ten years of Don Juan's story from when he was six until he was sixteen. It happened that as soon as he had reached the latter age, this healthy and handsome young man was confronted by love in the person of Julia, precisely a close friend of his mother, a married lady only a few years older than Don Juan:

> Amongst her numerous acquaintances, all
> Selected for discretion and devotion,
> There was the Donna Julia, whom to call
> Pretty were but to give a feeble notion
> Of many charms in her. . . .

> The darkness of her Oriental eye
> Accorded with her Moorish origin;
> (Her blood was not all Spanish; by the by,
> In Spain, you know, this is a sort of sin;)
> . . . .
> . . . . of Donna Julia's kin
> Some went to Africa, some stayed in Spain –
> Her great great grandmamma chose to remain.

Byron describes with graceful complaisance the accomplishments of Doña Julia and her unlucky matrimony with Don Alfonso, who more than doubled her in age.

> Her eye (I'm very fond of handsome eyes)
> Was large and dark, suppressing half its fire
> Until she spoke, then through its soft disguise
> Flashed an expression more of pride than ire,
> And love than either.

Julia had been several years married to Don Alfonso, without loving or hating him. They lived together, like many other couples, compelled by custom and social convention. Although Byron's opinion is that, in cases like Julia's, instead of a husband of over fifty,

> 'Twere better to have two of five-and twenty,
> Especially in countries near the sun.

Julia had known Juan well since he was a boy and was used to caressing him when he was thirteen and she no more than twenty. But this interval of three years caused a great turmoil in their hearts and relationship, and something inevitable came to pass. Juan didn't know what was happening to him and Julia didn't want that which she most desired to happen. Poor Julia's heart was full of anguish and she resolved to make a great effort for the sake of honour, pride, religion and virtue.

> She prayed the Virgin Mary for her grace,
> As being the best judge of a lady's case.

But little could the Virgin do to help her when she desired the opposite thing. Juan was bewildered: silent, thoughtful, weary. He used to leave his house and walk in the woods; sometimes he read Boscán and Garcilaso; but all these things availed nothing and only showed Julia the truth of what was happening to herself.

Don Juan is a fundamentally humorous poem and in Juan's and Julia's love affair, Byron wants to present a burlesque version of the romantic conventions and a comical social satire. This is why he insists on showing a caricature of the situations and the environment.

> It was upon a day, a summer's day; –
> Summer's indeed a very dangerous season;
> And so is spring about the end of May;
> The sun, no doubt, is the prevailing reason.

It was the 26th of July, "Towards half past six in the evening – perhaps nearer seven," Byron says, when Juan and Julia were sitting together in the most enchanting bower that you can imagine. Both felt something that was more powerful than themselves. They took each other's hands, definitely by mistake, and by mistake further caresses followed:

> The sun set, and up rose the yellow moon:
> The Devil's in the moon for mischief; they
> Who called her chaste, methinks, began too soon
> Their nomenclature. . . . .
>
> There is a dangerous silence in that hour,
> A stillness, which leaves room for the full soul
> To open all itself, without the power
> Of calling wholly back its self-control;
> . . . .

Julia and Juan lost their voices, their sense of responsibility, and even their heads:

> A little still she strove, and much repented,
> And whispering, 'I will ne'er consent' – consented.

They surrendered to the fascinating temptation of love; and after this, they could only want more freedom to strengthen the ties fostered by their passion.

One November night an unhappy incident took place which was the scandal of Seville. Don Alfonso, being suspicious of his wife, arrived home when he was not expected with the idea of surprising Doña Julia with her possible lover. Although her maid Antonia was very quick to warn the couple, Don Alfonso reached the spot accompanied by an army of husbands afraid of becoming victims of the same transgression. He entered Doña Julia's bedroom with an earnest purpose and his escort of witnesses. Byron tells us very cautiously that:

> Examples of this kind are so contagious,
> Were one not punished, all would be outrageous.

Don Juan was very lucky at the beginning and managed to hide himself under the bedclothes. Antonia pretended to be Julia's bed-fellow to keep her company and protect her during her husband's absence. The two ladies looked like innocence in person in their bed. Shielded by the situation, Julia began to attack her husband with vigour, defending herself with a tirade of accusations:

> Is it for this I have disdained to hold
> The common privilege of my sex?
> That I have chosen a confessor so old
> And deaf, that any other it would vex,
> And never once he has had cause to scold,
> But found my very innocence perplex
> So much, he always doubted I was married –
> . . . .
>
> Was it for this that no Cortejo e'er
> I yet have chosen from out the youth of Seville?
> Is it for this I scarce went anywhere,
> Except to bull-fights, mass, play, rout, and revel?
> . . . .

At this point Byron reinforces the farcical note as Julia gives a disconcerting relation of her suitors:

> Have I not had two bishops at my feet?
> The Duke of Ichar, and Don Fernan Nunez;

And is it thus a faithful wife you treat?
I wonder in what quarter now the moon is?

When Alfonso, defeated by Julia's Chaucerian loquacity, tried to excuse himself and began to feel ashamed of his rash attitude, he stumbled upon a pair of man's shoes forgotten under the bed. This was proof conclusive enough. He became furious, began searching the room, and found Don Juan now in the closet. The two men came to grips, Antonia had a fit of hysteria, and Julia fainted. Don Juan made his escape naked through the streets of Seville, in emulation of the chaste biblical Joseph.

As for Juan's mother:

> . . . . to divert the train
> Of one of the most circulating scandals
> That had for centuries been known in Spain,
> At least since the retirement of the Vandals,
> First vowed (and never had she vowed in vain)
> To Virgin Mary several pounds of candles;
> And then, by the advice of some old ladies;
> She sent her son to be shipped off from Cadiz.

Pressed by this most awkward circumstance, Doña Inéz decided that her son should visit all the countries of Europe, specially France and Italy, in the hope that Don Juan's conduct and morals would be straightened and purified. Of course, Byron here makes fun of the "grand tour", taking advantage of the English traditional attitude towards French and Italian moral freedom. Doña Inéz to occupy her time and find justification for her life, opened a Sunday School to teach the catechism. Dona Julia, on the other hand, retired to a convent to mitigate her sorrow, from where she wrote her beautiful love-letter to Don Juan as soon as she learned of his departure.

Canto II of *Don Juan* begins with humorous advice to all the tutors of the European nations – Holland, France, England, Germany and Spain – not to lose the opportunity to whack the boys if they want to raise their moral level. The neglect of this efficient method showed that the best-intentioned mother and the most calculated system of education spelled disaster for Don Juan's modesty. If he had been sent away to a school in Northern Europe, its discipline would probably have curbed Don Juan's overwhelming fantasy. But why would Doña Inéz have thought of sending her only son to an English public school? For her, Spanish education was definitely better. Byron seems not to be exactly of the same opinion, and adds ironically:

> Spain may prove an exception to the rule,
> But then exceptions always prove its worth –
> A lad of sixteen causing a divorce
> Puzzled his tutors very much, of course.

Don Juan sailed from Cadiz on board a Spanish ship as if this "ship were Noah's Ark" taking him on his way to salvation. At least this is what Doña Inéz thought when she sent her son to sea to separate him from the perversions of the land. Byron remembers here his own many voyages, thinks of the rough sea of the Bay of Cadiz wetting his face with spray, and writes:

> And there he stood to take, and take again,
> His first – perhaps his last – farewell of Spain.

> "Farewell, my Spain! a long farewell!" he cried,
> Perhaps I may revisit thee no more,
> But die, as many an exiled heart hath died,
> Of its own thirst to see again thy shore."

Juan says farewell to his land, his mother, his Julia, and his Seville, and on board the Ship *Trinidad* he crosses the Mediterranean towards Leghorn, expecting to be met there by a respectable Spanish family. Many will be Don Juan's travels and even more his amorous and social adventures as the poetic figure of this gallant Spaniard begins his long and amusing itinerary throughout Europe.

The "Spanish Cantos" of *Don Juan*, written in royal octaves as they are called in Spanish metrics, represent Byron's extraordinarily supple, agile, and attractive style in which he pours out a loose and engaging argument full of humorous wisdom and satirical entertainment.

Byron's *Age of Bronze* includes a savage attack on the Congress of Verona and severe political criticism in support of the liberty of the Spaniards during the reign of Ferdinand VII (1822). It is a satirical poem of great interest in its reflection of Byron's position with respect to the major events in Europe after Napoleon. In this poem Byron refers to several incidents of the last phase of Napoleon's career, gives a selective account of the most important political and military events from the Battle of Marengo to Waterloo, and reaches the definitive ethical conclusion that honesty is the best policy, even when empires and thrones may be imperiled by it.

The Age of Bronze was written between December 1822 and January 1823. The motive was the celebration of the Congress of Verona (November 1822) when, under the instigation of Alexander I of Russia, an armed intervention was proposed to be carried on against the liberal government of Spain (whose leader was General Riego), with the aim of re-establishing the absolute power of King Ferdinand VII. France considered that a constitutional Spain was a menace and she decided to intervene. The Duke of Wellington, as a representative of George IV, refused to sign, because England believed that the internal problems of Spain should be solved by the Spaniards themselves. Wellington knew too well the political problems of Spain and the Spanish character.

Byron is, as usual, sceptical about the human ability to promote what is good for the community. In the last period of his life he had lost confidence in the capacity of sacrifice and goodwill to establish liberty and justice. Thus, on writing the very first lines of *The Age of Bronze*, he says with contempt:

> The "good old times" – all times when old are good –
> Are gone; the present might be if they would;
> Great things have been, and are, and greater still
> Want little of mere mortals but their will:
> A wider space, a greener field, is given
> To those who play their "tricks before high heaven."
> I know not if the angels weep, but men
> Have wept enough – for what? – to weep again!

But, consistent with his liberal ideals, in this political satire Byron accuses the Holy Alliance and its projects and attacks with great efficacy the decision of the Russian Emperor to intervene. His sympathy for a liberal Spain gives inspiration to the poet who, after relating several important events of Spanish history, makes use of the classical figure of Diogenes to tell the Czar Alexander boldly that the Greek philosopher still shines his lantern on the faces of European monarchs, trying to discover among them an honest man.

Afterwards, Byron attacks France and especially England for supporting the Holy Alliance; and he severely criticises Wellington, Chateaubriand, Metternich and other important representatives of the Alliance. Even Marie Louise, Napoleon's wife, he blames for contenting herself with a mini-realm when her proper throne was awaiting her on her husband's tomb on St Helena.

The Age of Bronze is a most interesting work from the Spanish point of view, since Byron was well-informed on the subject; he adopts a sympathetic attitude towards a liberal Spain and represents the Spanish problem in the complicated frame of Europe of that epoch. Some of his verses are reminiscent of *Childe Harold*:

> The dawn revives: renowned, romantic Spain
> Holds back the invader from her soil again.
> Not now the Roman tribe nor Punic horde
> Demands her fields as lists to prove the sword.

And, after offering a poetic description of some aspects of Spanish history, Byron comes to the present, uses symbols and allusions of the past with a new significance and develops his narrative in a compact blend of implications, many of which need further explanation for readers unacquainted with that period.

> The stern or feeble sovereign, one or both,
> By turns; the haughtiness whose pride was sloth;
> The long degenerate noble; the debased
> Hidalgo, and the peasant less disgraced,
> But more degraded; the unpeopled realm;
> The once proud navy that forgot the helm;
> The once impervious phalanx disarrayed;
> The idle forge that formed Toledo's blade.

Where is that Spain that has filled up with exploits the history of the world? This time the invaders are not Romans or Vandals or Visigoths. Rather, again the French, pretending to imitate the campaigns of Napoleon. Byron calls Spain to arms and appeals to the indomitable spirit of her sons:

> Mount, chivalrous Hidalgo! not in vain
> Revive the cry – 'Iago! and close Spain!'
> . . . .

The knife of Arragon, Toledo's steel;
The famous lance of chivalrous Castile;

The unerring rifle of the Catalan;
The Andalusian courser in the van;
The torch to make a Moscow of Madrid;
And in each heart the spirit of the Cid: –
Such have been, such shall be, such are. Advance,
And win – not Spain! but thine own freedom, France!

Byron's liberty of expression, his independence of mind and his detachment in judging the monarchs who attended the Congress of Verona – the King of Prussia and the Emperors of Russia and Austria – are extraordinary:

                                    Who renew
This consecrated name, till now assign'd
To councils held to benefit mankind?
Who now assemble at the holy call?
The blest Alliance, which says three are all!
An earthly Trinity! which wears the shape
Of Heaven's as man is mimicked by the ape.
A pious Unity! in purpose one –
To melt three fools to a Napoleon.

After a quick description of Verona and some of its historical events and important monuments, Byron again launches his attack against the three "holy" persons gathered there to save the political situation in Spain, making the world forget the Capulets, Catullus, Dante and the art and archaeology of the city.

Thrice blest Verona! since the holy three
With their imperial presence shine on thee!

Then he addresses himself particularly to Alexander of Russia:

Resplendent sight! Behold the coxcomb Czar,
The Autocrat of waltzes and of war!
. . . .
How kindly would he send the mild Ukraine,
With all her pleasant Pulks, to lecture Spain!

How royally show off in proud Madrid
His goodly person, from the South long hid!
. . . .
Spain, too, hath rocks, and rivers, and defiles –
The Bear may rush into the Lion's toils.
Fatal to Goths are Xeres' sunny fields;
Think'st thou to thee Napoleon's victor yields?

The interest of the Czar to show himself off in an easy invasion of
Spain is evident, according to Byron, and the poet attacks the
Russian Emperor with directness and efficacy. The poem was
published before Spain was invaded in 1823 by the "One Hundred
Thousand Sons of St. Louis", a theatrical imitation of Napoleon's
invasion. France was responsible for this. It was a political
arrangement that, due to circumstances different from those of the
Peninsular War, did not stir the roots of the Spanish national spirit
and, in consequence, the Spaniards remained unconcerned.

Lord Byron continues his diatribe against the Czar:

Spain wants no manure:
Her soil is fertile, but she feeds no foe:
Her vultures, too, were gorged not long ago;
And wouldst thou furnish them with fresher prey?
Alas! thou wilt not conquer, but purvey.
. . . .
But were I not Diogenes, I'd wander
Rather a worm than *such* an Alexander!
Be slaves who will, the cynic shall be free;
His tub has tougher walls than Sinopè:
Still will he hold his lantern up to scan
The face of monarchs for an 'honest man.'

After the necessary conferences and the inevitable entertain-
ments, the Congress of Verona ended leaving to France the decision of intervening if she thought best. Louis XVIII was tempted
to put in practice that travesty of the Napoleonic invasion and he
sent to Spain the Duke of Angoulême at the head of an impressive
army of 100,000 to restore Ferdinand VII to his throne. But Spain
was politically bewildered, emotionally unaffected and remained
indifferent.

The Age of Bronze, published 1 April 1823, is an attempt to raise the Spaniards' courage in defence of a constitutional and representative government. As Byron had written the poem before the intervention of the Duke of Angoulême, he could not foresee what was going to happen in Spain. But he does his best to encourage the Spanish people and warns the possible invader against the obstacles to be encountered. The difficulties and defeats that Napoleon suffered in Spain were still in everybody's mind. Byron's poem is a courageous and energetic satire in which the poet, outraged by the selfish intrigues of the three great monarchs of the Congress of Verona, confronts them openly on their own level with the efficacious weapon of his pen and defends the liberty of nations, especially the political liberty of Spain, against the authoritarian control of the Holy Alliance.

These three aspects of Lord Byron's poetical vision of Spain, which I have sketched, correspond to the beginning, the middle and the end of his literary career. From the aesthetic point of view the best is Canto I of *Don Juan*, although it is the most fantastic and least Spanish; the things that happen in *Don Juan* are so general that they might happen anywhere. But it is Canto I of *Childe Harold* and *The Age of Bronze* which reveal Byron, the liberal aristocrat, with his amazing grasp of political realities. He is passionate and concrete in the first; he is a lofty and disdainful accuser in the second; but in both poems he reveals himself as an accurate and objective observer of Spain, her people, her history and her contemporary circumstances. Aristocratic and liberal, Byron is always faithful to the basic principles of human dignity and the independence of nations.

Throughout his entire career Lord Byron was ever the champion of the oppressed. He defended the claims of the English Catholics. He raised his voice against the French in the Napoleonic Wars. He accused the monarchs who intended to overthrow the Spanish constitution in 1822. And he died at Missolonghi in the cause of Greek liberty from the Turks.

Lord Byron would gladly have fought in Spain against Napoleon. He aided the Italians in their struggle against Austria. And he gave his life for the Greeks, pointing them to the path to freedom, and at the same time, by his death, warning England of her responsibilities towards Hellenic independence. He was indeed one of the most influential figures of his era – a dauntless champion of political freedom and the liberty of nations.

11 Byron and Switzerland

Byron's Political Dimension

ERNEST GIDDEY

Byron was first brought into direct contact with Switzerland in 1816 when he spent several months at the Villa Diodati near Geneva; from Geneva he started on a tour of Lake Leman with Shelley, visited the castle of Chillon and wrote *The Prisoner of Chillon* at Ouchy. A few weeks later, with Hobhouse, he made an excursion to the Bernese Alps which provided him with the setting of *Manfred*.

Swiss public opinion did not know much about Byron when he settled at the Villa Diodati. He was just a name. The *Gazette de Lausanne* mentioned his arrival, which is all the more remarkable as Switzerland was then swarming with British tourists. Byron is presented as living on the outskirts of Geneva; he is one of the most distinguished poets of England; years before, he travelled in the East; his works are full of imagination and good taste, but their general colouring is often dark.[1] Shelley's presence (he also was staying at Geneva) passed unnoticed.

Byron's four months' stay in Switzerland did not contribute to a better knowledge and understanding of his personality and his poetry on the part of the Swiss. Byron preferred Shelley's company to the social life of Geneva. He was invited to a soirée at the house of Mme Eynard-Châtelain, who was related to Jean-Gabriel Eynard, a banker who was soon to be one of the prominent Swiss philhellenes. He met Marc-Auguste Pictet, one of the editors of the *Bibliothèque universelle* and Pellegrino Rossi, the Italian economist who had fled Italy and was now a citizen of Geneva. He spoke with Victor von Bonstetten, an old gentleman who had known Rousseau and Voltaire and had been Thomas Gray's friend. He visited Mme de Staël at Coppet and was introduced to some of the members of the European intelligentsia that surrounded the famous French writer. But his social contacts with Swiss people

179

remained superficial. He put into practice a piece of advice Mme de Staël's second husband, Rocca, had given him when he had spent an evening at Coppet: "Try to avoid meeting people from Geneva; believe me, Mylord, do not enter that cave of honest people."[2] Byron took more pleasure in the visit of two young Greeks who were passing through Geneva in September 1816, the brothers Nicolas and Francis Karvellas, than in the Swiss gossips of the time. Byron, however, was interested in the Swiss political system. Later, when he was in Greece, he envisaged the introduction of a non-standing army on the Swiss model. But he could not bear the artificiality of the social life of a provincial town. The true nature of his feelings is clearly indicated in a letter he wrote to Thomas Moore five years later, at a time when he was asking himself whether he would move to Switzerland or remain in Italy: "Switzerland is a curst selfish, swinish country of brutes, placed in the most romantic region of the world. I never could bear the inhabitants, and still less their English visitors...."[3]

In the meantime, the Swiss "brutes" had realised that Byron's works were worth reading. Their knowledge of his poetry had been almost non-existent so far. The editors of the *Bibliothèque universelle*, a periodical published at Geneva, decided that educated readers, even in Switzerland, should be more familiar with Byron and Byronism. In October 1816 they published an article entitled "Coup d'oeil sur la littérature anglaise", in which "two men of genius", Walter Scott and Byron, were briefly presented. Byron, they declared, wrote poems remarkable for their sombre colouring; when visiting Greece, he sang the natural beauties of the country and stigmatised the cruel despotism of its rulers; in men he uncovers the primitive greatness and the tempestuous passions of tormented souls; he is both a thinker and a poet and his verse is a happy mixture of harmony and deep meaning. And the Swiss reviewers insisted on Byron's originality, his energy and the gloomy sadness pervading his poetry.

In the following issues of the *Bibliothèque universelle*,[4] from 1817 to 1819, twelve articles were devoted to Byron's major works: the four cantos of *Childe Harold*, *The Giaour*, *The Corsair*, *Lara*, *The Siege of Corinth*, *The Prisoner of Chillon*, *The Lament of Tasso*. The twelve articles cover more than 200 pages. Apparently, Byron was the favourite writer of the editors. Only Walter Scott enjoyed a comparable popularity. And far behind we find Thomas Moore, whereas Shelley and Keats are totally ignored.

The notices on Byron's poems are a combination of long quotations and general comments on the poet's literary tendencies. Quotations are given in French, sometimes with the English text in footnotes; the translation (adaptation would be a more appropriate term) is true to eighteenth century standards and is often free to the point of being but vaguely evocative of the English original. The critical passages are both eulogistic and superficial: *The Corsair* is "one of the best works written by Lord Byron, revealing with strength the true nature of his talent",[5] a statement which does not carry much conviction; *The Giaour* contains remarkable beauties, but these beauties are neither defined nor described; true poetry appears everywhere in *The Prisoner of Chillon*, but we are not told what true poetry is. When discussing *Childe Harold*, the reviewer tries to be more explicit about the nature of Byron's poetic gifts. That Byron is a real poet is an unquestionable fact. What deserves special notice is his audacious contempt, his lucid self-portrayal, his superb indifference to common feelings, and above all his predilection for dark subjects, his "gift for evoking shadows".[6] Though highly conventional, Swiss criticism has a certain convincing force: Harold envies the very creatures he openly despises; he wallows in pleasures succeeded by moments of utter disgust; under various names, he offers the same features, revealing his weakness and his generosity.

The distinction between Byron the man and the Byronic hero is not always clear in the reviewer's mind. He regards *Childe Harold* as a confessional poem and does not question the autobiographical value of Byron's poetry. He simply identifies Harold with Byron and discovers a disquieting figure, "a phenomenon one cannot observe without an admiration bordering upon terror."[7] The main trait of character is a total intellectual independence and a genuine love of freedom. Who but Byron could have described, in *The Prisoner of Chillon*, "the miseries of a painful captivity"?[8]

Swiss critics apparently felt that Byron's private life was no concern of theirs. They say only that Byron began to write poetry when he was a very young man, that his first productions were not received favourably, that he wrote satires to be revenged on his enemies, and finally left England, full of resentment against the literary circles of his own country. No allusion to Byron's love affairs and his unfortunate marriage is made.

In 1816 Lady Caroline Lamb had published *Glenarvon*. The novel was reviewed by the *Bibliothèque universelle* in 1817. But not a single word of the notice showed that the reviewer suspected that Byron was personally involved in the plot imagined by Caroline Lamb. The first paragraph merely said that the central character was a famous writer.

So, at the end of the second decade of the nineteenth century, public opinion in Switzerland had generally identified Byron with Harold, the hero who had made him famous. The places which had been visited by the pilgrim in 1816 were gradually becoming objects of pilgrimage, the more so as thousands of English travellers were now touring Europe, a consequence of Napoleon's fall. Even though they disapproved of his morals, the Englishmen who went roaming about the Continent were fascinated by the noble wanderer who had rejected his country and was looking for happiness under foreign skies. Then, in 1823, came the news of Byron's second (and last) journey to Greece.

Without repeating what competent scholars have written on the outburst of the Greek rebellion and the rise of philhellenic movements in Europe,[9] one should remember one minor point: philhellenism developed early in Switzerland. Swiss professors of classics or theology imitated their German colleagues and warmly supported the cause of Greek independence. And Swiss young men responded to their appeal. We find several Swiss names among the volunteers who, from November 1821 to August 1822, left Marseilles for Greece.

Public opinion was favourable to Greece. Newspapers regularly printed letters from Corfu, Zante or Hydra in which Greek determination was warmly praised. Periodicals dealt with various subjects associated with ancient Greece or insisted on the necessity of a Greek regeneration. In 1816–17 the *Bibliothèque universelle* gave extensive extracts from Henry Holland's *Travels in the Ionian Islands*, a book issued in London in 1815 and advocating the possibility of a Greek revolution. A few years later, the same journal initiated its readers into the beauties of Greek popular songs. Notices on various political or historical studies about Greece and Turkey by German or French scholars were also published.[10] In this way the interest in philhellenism was aroused and maintained.

Gradually, however, what had first been the generous impulse of enthusiastic youths or the intellectual dream of liberal pamphleteers assumed a more coherent form. Greek societies were founded in Geneva, Lausanne, Bern, Basel, Zurich, Saint Gall, Glaris, etc. It soon became obvious that their efforts would be in vain if each committee had its own plan and consciously ignored the actions promoted by similar groups in the country or abroad. If money were to be collected without disappointing public generosity, a certain amount of co-ordination was indispensable; if soldiers were to be recruited in South Germany or in Switzerland, assurances had to be given as to the seriousness of the Swiss help to the victims of Turkish tyranny.

The man who soon became the leading figure of Helvetic Phil-hellenism was the Geneva banker Jean-Gabriel Eynard. He was a friend of Capodistrias, whom he had met at the Congress of Vienna. A dynamic personality, he often travelled from Geneva to Paris and corresponded with the most important representatives of European philhellenism. He managed to establish a commission controlling the funds collected by French, German and Swiss societies. Eynard was not the only Swiss philhellene deserving notice. Others should also be mentioned: Dr Louis-André Gosse, Amenaus Emmanuel Hahn,[11] Johann Jakob Meyer, Albert Müller, etc.

Byron had now found a tragic stage on which he could display the richness of his personality. The poet whose name had been as-sociated with the idea of melancholy suddenly appeared in a new light. He had been considered the victim of disillusionment and despair; he was now a politician facing the realities of an inter-national conflict. In 1816, the word liberty, though sung with con-viction and strength, was in his mouth a purely literary theme; in 1823, it inspired the behaviour of a leader who seemed to put more emphasis on actions than on words. The man had acquired a new, unsuspected dimension.

In his new capacity, Byron appeared in a Swiss newspaper as early as June 1823. *L'Ami de la Vérité*, which was printed at Laus-anne, announced that Byron had informed the Greek Committee of London that he would soon sail to Greece and was willing to spend all his income on the cause of Greek independence; he urgently asked for his countrymen's help; Greece needed a park of light artillery, gunpowder and medical supplies. Obviously the in-formation given by the Swiss paper was based upon the letter sent by Byron to John Bowring on 12 May 1823.

When Byron reached Greece a few months later, information about his movements and actions became more regular: news-papers insisted on Byron's generosity, his selling possessions in England (the sale of Rochdale) in order to get liquid assets with which to pay soldiers or buy supplies, his enrolling, equipping, and training foreign volunteers forming a special brigade, his intention to lead forces against Lepanto, his being granted Greek citizenship; Byron is "the soul of Greek affairs"; he had been recognised as "Proedros or President of the foreigners"; he is very popular with the Greek clergy and will be beheaded by the Turks if they succeed in taking him prisoner. His poems are fervently read by his Greek admirers.[12]

Byron, Swiss papers added, constantly tries to co-ordinate the efforts of the various Greek factions. He believes in a possible collaboration with Theodore Kolokotrones; and in order to ensure complete reconciliation among Greek leaders, he will go to Tripolitza in February 1824, an erroneous piece of information, as we know that Byron did not leave Missolonghi.

A new Byron was being born in public opinion at a moment when the poet's health was declining. The Swiss reception of the reports on Byron's fatal illness, his last days, his death, and funeral has been analysed elsewhere.[13] Suffice it to say that the information given out by Swiss newspapers (the *Gazette de Lausanne*, the *Journal de Genève*, *L'Ami de la Vérité*, the *Nouvelliste vaudois*, etc.) was neither original nor accurate; Swiss journalists simply copied what they could find in the French press (the *Moniteur universel*, for instance) or reproduced information second-hand from London or Constantinople. The interest of the articles published in the first months of 1824 lies in their general tone. Byron's "dark genius", his powerful thoughts, his misanthropic disposition, the strong passions and great crimes of his heroes are occasionally alluded to. Stress, however, is laid on his political influence. His death – the disappearance of a star of the first magnitude – is a severe blow to the cause of philhellenism. If the muses grieve over the end of the poet, Hellas will mourn the loss of a hero.

So strong were philhellenic feelings that Swiss journalists, in various issues of local papers, made use of Byron's death and its consequences to promote principles or ideas which, they knew, would be popular with Swiss readers: some aspects of Byron's political action in Greece were analysed; fragments of letters sent by Byron to Yussuf Pasha, to the provisional Government of Greece, and to Prince Mavrocordato were quoted; the last moments of the poet were vividly described and his last words recorded for the benefit of posterity; the atmosphere at Missolonghi in the days that followed the fatal 19th of April was briefly recalled; a short passage of Spiridion Trikoupi's funeral oration was reproduced; allusions were made to other religious services, and to Edward Blaquiere's efforts to secure the arrival and impartial distribution of the famous Greek loan.

Swiss newspapers were so intent on fostering thoughts and feelings favourable to Greece that they embellished the circumstances of Byron's death. The readers of the *Gazette de Lausanne* were told that Byron died in Mavrocordato's arms, an alteration of truth underlining the political significance of the event. Byron's last words (one knows that the poet was delirious with short intervals of lucidity, that he muttered disconnected words, and that his last coherent sentence before sinking into coma was "I want to sleep now") were turned into a sort of political oration in favour of Greek independence: "I die happy, with the sweet hope that Greece will soon be free from her barbarous oppressors and that the sovereigns of Christendom will consider it a sacred duty to proclaim her independence. And you, good people, persevere in your glorious enterprise, crush the tyrants, and do not forget your motto: to liberate Greece or die."[14]

Consciously or unconsciously, Swiss journalists adopted a version serving the cause of Greek independence. Propaganda was taking possession of Byron's death. Byron was no longer a poet shuffling off his mortal coil, but a hero, a demigod in the modern pantheon of Greece. Speaking in Mavrocordato's arms just before shutting his eyes, he was becoming a symbol of Greek revolution: Europe helping Hellas and dying for a noble cause.

So two Byrons shared Swiss sympathy in 1824: on the one hand, the disenchanted pilgrim who had visited Bonivard's dungeon and was soon to fascinate Delacroix and haunt young Flaubert's imagination;[15] on the other hand, the political idealist who had tried to practise the literary philhellenism of "The Isles of Greece". How could these two Byrons be brought into harmony with one another?

In fact they coexisted in public opinion. In the years that immediately followed the death of the poet, the second aspect of Byron's personality was predominant. A few weeks after that fatal 19 April, 1824, two local poets wrote elegies on Byron's death. They were both published in the *Nouvelliste vaudois*, anonymously, on 28 May and 4 June, and probably appeared in other local periodicals. The unknown authors drew their inspiration from the same feeling of Byron's love of liberty. The two elegies have little literary value but are not worse than most of the pieces of poetry which French poetasters lavishly produced in the weeks that followed Byron's death. They do not reveal any knowledge of Byron's poetry. They also show that their authors were not familiar with Byron's mental frame. The phraseology (Byron is compared with an old man in the second piece) is not in tune with Byron's character and poetic originality. The interest of the two poems is purely political or historical. They bear evidence of the strength of Swiss Philhellenism and show that the name of Byron was intimately associated with the defence of Greek independence.

Greek independence is the cause supported by *Le Courrier du Léman*, a paper which had an ephemeral existence in 1826–27. Byron is mentioned several times. His name (if pronounced with the French "on" nasal sound) is made to rhyme with "Parthenon"; the poet's lute, now resting against his coffin, is a symbol instilling courage in Admiral Cochrane's mind and making him persevere in his plan to relieve the Greeks besieged in the Acropolis.[16]

Byron in Switzerland as well as in the rest of Europe, had focused public attention on a small place almost unknown before his death: Missolonghi. In the newspapers published at Geneva and Lausanne (the *Gazette de Lausanne, Le Nouvelliste vaudois*, the *Journal de Genève*), Missolonghi became a magnet attracting public sympathy; it was often considered the bulwark of Christendom. Letters from Missolonghi were published at regular intervals. Some of them were written by special correspondents. History remembers the name of a man who by his articles modestly contributed to the fame of Missolonghi in the months that followed Byron's death: the Swiss chemist Johann Jakob Meyer, who became editor of Stanhope's *Greek Chronicle* and perished among the ruins of the town when it was taken by the Turks.

News from Missolonghi was received with hope and anxiety. For Missolonghi was now the symbol of the Greek war of independence. When in the first weeks of 1826 the situation of the town became desperate, the name of Missolonghi appeared in almost each issue of the Swiss periodicals. And when Missolonghi fell, in April 1826, the Swiss papers gave vent to feelings of utter consternation. The "irreparable loss of Missolonghi" was even related in popular almanacs, with engravings illustrating the cruelty of the Turkish soldiers.[17] In creative power, local artists could not compete with Delacroix painting "Greece expiring on the ruins of Missolonghi"; but their drawings had a sort of naive sincerity with a real emotional appeal.

Byron was no longer there; his great figure however seemed to be looming in the desolation. His spirit could still inspire all those who believed in Greek independence. We shall do our best, they wrote in a letter to the editor of the *Nouvelliste vaudois*, to avenge the overthrown tomb "of the generous Englishman who gave his songs, his love, and his life".[18]

Was Byron's sacrifice to be useless? "The Greeks are in danger," the *Journal de Genève* wrote at the end of April 1826. "Death and slavery will be their fate."[19] The Greek committees of Switzerland redoubled their efforts. In a few months they gathered large sums of money. They realised that starvation was the worst enemy of Greece and that the most useful form of philhellenism was to relieve suffering. And money was collected in different ways: concerts and theatrical performances were given in favour of Greece; Swiss citizens were asked to contribute three "sous" per week to the Hellenic cause; various articles were sold for the benefit of Greek refugees. In 1826 a newspaper recommended an "*Ode sur la chute glorieuse de Missolonghi*", written by Adrien Michaux, a gentleman from Lyon; as a piece of poetry, it did not rank very high, but its price was the equivalent of fifty cents only and the cause it defended was a noble one.

Byron's death had another political consequence. Before 1824, Swiss philhellenes had taken their lead from Germany. After Byron's death, they transferred their support to the British committee. Eynard and his friends realised that only a European power such as Great Britain could bring the decisive help in the struggle for independence.

The idea that Byron's last pilgrimage was a glorious chapter in the history of modern Greece and that the name of Missolonghi was now indissolubly linked with the fame of the English poet became commonplace. It appeared in history textbooks used in schools. Lamartine's *Dernier chant du pèlerinage d'Harold* contributed to its becoming a myth accepted by public opinion. Interest in Byron's political behaviour was renewed in 1858 when the *Bibliothèque universelle* reviewed Trelawny's *Recollections of the Last Days of Shelley and Byron*.[20]

Months and years, however, were passing. Byron's Greek dream was slowly losing its vividness and dissolving in the mist of political history. The other Byron, whose popularity had been overshadowed by the renown of the hero of Missolonghi, resumed his rights in the imagination of Swiss readers. He could provide them with the emotional Romanticism they needed and secretly longed for; as they had already won their political independence, the brilliant colours of Byron's Greek apotheosis did not appeal to them as they did to the Italian patriots fighting against Austrian tyranny.

The Byron who was now accepted and admired by the majority of readers in French-speaking Switzerland was not the Byron who, to quote Professor Trueblood, "with unflinching resolve ... turned from poetry to politics".[21] He was the pale young man who in 1816 had come to Chillon, had meditated on the victims of tyranny and, a few days later, in the yellow light of a cloudy day with moments of sunshine, had written at Ouchy the stanzas on the captivity of Bonivard. Swiss public opinion also remained faithful to the poet who, a few weeks later, had ascended the Col de Jaman and imagined *Manfred* in the majestic solitude of the Alps. If Switzerland refused to forget the politician and the warrior who had tried to be the leader of the Greek rebels, she did not suspect the depth of Byron's political thought.

Even intellectuals familiar with the intricacies of political history and more interested in the development of public affairs than in literary achievements considered Byron a poet and a poet only. Henry Druey, who was one of the greatest statesmen of nineteenth century Switzerland (he became Federal Councillor in 1848) did not understand Byron's political realism. In his correspondence he mentioned Byron several times; but in him he saw only the desperate Byronic hero who gave up hope and found nothing in passions but his justification "for hating human nature".[22]

Imitations of Byron, translations from his poems, notices on his literary life continued to be published in Swiss periodicals and newspapers.[23] But Swiss readers lost remembrance of the glory of Missolonghi; Missolonghi was just a name coupled with the memory of the poet who had carved his name on one of the pillars of Bonivard's dungeon.

With a sense of realities that is one of their cardinal virtues, Swiss innkeepers did not forget that the author of *The Prisoner of Chillon* had incited thousands of travellers to stop in their country on their way to Italy. He deserved the tablet that in 1909 the local authorities fixed to the wall of the Hôtel d'Angleterre (formerly the Hôtel de l'Ancre) at Ouchy-Lausanne where he had written his famous poem.

That Byron was a two-dimensional character was evident from the celebrations that marked the centenary of his death in 1924. Solemn festivities took place in Geneva and at Chillon. Several newspapers, some of them mere local periodicals, devoted a few lines or a few pages to the man who had moved and shaken Europe in the first decades of the nineteenth century.[24]

The majority of Swiss journalists were but vaguely familiar with Byron's poetry. It is his poetic gifts, however, that they described, using the stereotyped images which have so frequently appeared in nineteenth century criticism: gloomy wanderer, nostalgic sadness, passionate turmoil, etc. Some of the best journalists, however, reminded their readers of the circumstances of the poet's death: Byron's best work, Henri de Ziegler wrote in the *Journal de Genève*, was his life; when he went to Greece for the second time, Byron, who had acquired all the advantages given by literary genius, reached the "summit of sublimity". Jean Nicollier, in the *Gazette de Lausanne*, also insisted on Byron's political influence; his duty compelled him to die for Greece.[25]

Childe Harold and Mavrocordato's friend, the man of letters and the political figure.... In Switzerland rare were those who were able to gain a comprehensive view of so rich and complex a personality. In the meantime hordes of tourists were visiting Chillon, looking for the poet's name on one of the big pillars of the dungeon; they tried to imagine Byron's thrill of horror as he was pacing the dark room; and they were so fascinated by Byron's romantic halo that they were likely to forget that Byron had also written his name in the book of history, where signatures are preserved even when cities are plundered and castles or monuments reduced to ashes.

NOTES

1. *Gazette de Lausanne*, 25 June 1816, p. 3.
2. H. W. Häusermann, *The Genevese Background* (London, 1952) p. 57.
3. *Byron, A Self-Portrait*, Peter Quennell (ed.), (London, 1967) vol. 2, p. 669.
4. *Bibl. univ. (Litt.)*, 1817, vol. 5, p. 72–100 (*Childe Harold*, III); 1817, vol. 5, pp. 286–302 (*The Prisoner of Chillon*); 1817, vol. 6, pp. 179–98 (*The Corsair*); 1817, vol. 6, pp. 289–307 (*Lara*); 1817, vol. 6, pp. 392–406 (*The Giaour*); 1817, vol. 7, pp. 85–93 (*The Lament of Tasso*); 1817, vol. 7, pp. 173–85, 273–81 (*The Siege of Corinth*); 1818, vol. 9, pp. 286–308, 390–414 (*Childe Harold*, IV); 1819, vol. 11,

pp. 163–90 (*Childe Harold,* I); 1819, vol. 11, pp. 220–43 (*Childe Harold,* II).

5. Ibid., 1817, 6, p. 197.
6. Ibid., 1818, 9, p. 286.
7. Ibid., 1818, 9, p. 287.
8. Ibid., 1817, 5, p. 286.
9. See William St. Clair, *That Greece Might Still Be Free* (London, Oxford University Press, 1972); Douglas Dakin, *The Greek Struggle for Independence, 1821–1833* (London, Batsford, 1973).
10. *Bibl. univ.*, 1824, vol. 26, pp. 35–59; 1824, vol. 27, pp. 233–48; 1825, vol. 28, pp. 25–49, 145–63; 1825, vol. 29, pp. 228–48, 313–38; 1826, vol. 32, pp. 34–52, 149–69, 249–59; 1827, vol. 34, pp. 267–85; 1827, vol. 35, pp. 36–57; 1828, vol. 39, pp. 348–78.
11. See "Gen. Lieut. Hahn's Memoiren über seine Betheiligung am griechischen Freiheitskampfe aus den Jahren 1825–28" in *Berner Taschenbuch, 1870* (Bern, 1870) pp. 1–89.
12. *Gazette de Lausanne*, 30 January 1824, and 9, 12, 16 March 1824; *L'Ami de la Vérité*, 14 June 1823; *Nouv. vaud.* 2 January 1824, 27 February 1824, 2, 9, 12, 23 March 1824.
13. Ernest Giddey, "The Influence of Byron's Death on French-speaking Switzerland" in *The Byron Journal*, 1977, pp. 80–93.
14. *Gazette de Lausanne*, 2 July 1824.
15. See Ernest Giddey, "Les Trahison du byronisme" in *Etudes de Lettre*, Lausanne, 1970, série III, tome 3, pp. 89–109.
16. *Le Courrier du Léman*, 17 March 1827, 7 April 1827.
17. *Le Véritable Messager Boiteux de Verne et Vevey*, 1827, 1828.
18. *Nouv. vaud.* 13 June 1826.
19. *Journal de Genève*, 27 April 1826.
20. *Bibl. univ.*, 1858, 1, p. 638; 3, pp. 146–7.
21. Paul G. Trueblood, "Byron's Political Realism" in *The Byron Journal*, 1973, p. 56.
22. Henry Druey, *Correspondence* (Lausanne, Michel Steiner and André Lasserre, 1974), vol. 1, p. 60.
23. *Almanach genevois*, 1825, pp. 129–31 ("La Tempête, imitation de Lord Byron" by M. Durand), pp. 133–6 ("Sur le lac Léman, imitation de Lord Byron" by the same); *Le Courrier du Léman*, 30 September 1826, 4 and 14 October 1826; *Revue Suisse*, 1845, 8, pp. 684–94, 1847, p. 500 (translations of *The Prisoner of Chillon*).
24. *Gazette de Lausanne*, 16, 20, 24 April 1924, 28 May 1924; *Journal de Genève*, 14, 18, 22, 30 April 1924, 1 May 1924; *Journal de Nyon et Feuille d'Avis de Coppet*, 19 March 1924, 28 May 1924; *Feuille d'Avis de Lausanne*, 19 April 1924; *L'Effort* (Le Locle), 28 April 1924, etc.
25. *Journal de Genève*, 14 April 1924; *Gazette de Lausanne*, 16 and 24 April 1924.

12 Conclusion: Byron and Europe

PAUL GRAHAM TRUEBLOOD

Professor Douglas Dakin, in his brilliant "Historical Back-ground", a comprehensive yet succinct account of the revolution-ary and counter-revolutionary ideas and movements in Europe from 1788 to 1848, provides an excellent introduction for the several national accounts of Byron's political and cultural rel-evance to the European countries surveyed in this symposium. Dakin's profound scholarship and prestige, as a leading authority on the diplomatic history of nineteenth century Europe, make his historical introduction invaluable and indispensable to the purpose of the symposium: a survey and assessment of the political and cultural relevance and influence of Lord Byron in nineteenth century Europe.

The primary problem that all participants in the symposium have had to face is the problem of balance between the claims of literature and the claims of history in order to avoid the inherent danger of over-magnifying Byron's actual influence on the course of history as opposed to his pervasive influence on the climate of thought. This problem has been, I believe, faced squarely by each contributor and resolved with admirable objectivity. Each essay seems to bear out Professor Dakin's shrewd and just observation that "great literary works are not so much the generating power of the ideas they contain as the evidence for the widespread existence of those ideas. It is nevertheless probably true", he continues, "that, in preaching to the converted, a writer (and this must cer-tainly be true of Byron) increases the number of his admirers, strengthens their admiration, and makes that admiration more fervent and more likely to lead to political action."

Although most of the symposium contributors deal with the time-framework 1812–48, all the essays can be better understood and appreciated against the extended historical background Professor Dakin has provided. Dakin captures and delineates the two salient influences of the French Revolution: nationalism and democracy, the former outstripping the latter as a political force in the nineteenth century. With regard to Napoleon's purpose to achieve French hegemony in Europe, Dakin sees, as one of the many causes for Napoleon's decline and fall, the fact that he sowed the seeds of his own destruction by planting ideas of nationhood among the Germans, Italians and other Europeans.

Dakin develops the very important concept that there were many French revolutions (social, economic, political, middle class, liberal, etc.) and not just a single French Revolution. This is also true to a degree, he shows, of the numerous counter-revolutions inside and outside of France. Likewise, he pays some attention to two other powerful revolutionary movements of the past two hundred years: the Agricultural and Industrial Revolutions, both instrumental in effecting the breakdown of the Old Order.

Against this panoramic historical background let us review the manifestations of Byron's political and cultural influence in nineteenth century Europe, taking the several countries in the alphabetical order of their treatment in the symposium, and observing the respects in which the participants concur or diverge in their assessment of the dominant trends in European Byronism. The essay on Byron and England is considered last because of the marked difference between British and Continental Byronism.

Professor Robert Escarpit in his study of Byron and France, "Byron As A Political Figure", tells us that the death of Lord Byron at Missolonghi in 1824 brought about an irruption of Byronism in the ideological environment of Young Europe between 1825 and 1848, a fact corroborated by all the participants in the present symposium. Byron's death, he declares, set a militant and irrefutable example which acted as a catalyst for the resolve of youthful liberals throughout Europe. His fight in Greece was not for the Greeks alone but for the independence of the peoples everywhere.

Although in France Byron fell victim to the contradictions of the mid-nineteenth century intellectuals, nevertheless the "underground and often unconscious influence of Byron", writes Escarpit, has endured for generations in French minds. Byronism symbolised the yet unorganised drive of the peoples toward freedom and independence. And although it took Byron his whole life to find his appointed place in the "first skirmishes" of that long struggle, Escarpit concludes, "We now know that place was not the one he deserved, and only now can we appreciate the full significance of Byron as a political figure."

Turning to Dr Cedric Hentschel's study of Byron and Germany, "The Shadow of Euphorion", we learn that no other British writer except Shakespeare has appealed so much to the German imagination, nor been so lavishly praised and avidly imitated, as Byron. Dr Hentschel tells us that Byronism in Germany differed conspicuously from Byronism elsewhere in Europe, largely because of the fact that in the post-Napoleonic era, with the failure of the 1830 and 1848 revolutions, the would-be social reformers, lacking foreign oppressors to inveigh against and prevented from attacking their domestic ones, remained largely apathetic and ineffective, with a few exceptions.

The conservative nature of German internal politics throughout the nineteenth century blunted the edge of Byron's social criticism, and his other role as champion of nationalism could "evoke little resonance" in the German Reich under Prussian hegemony. Thus, on the German political front, Byron was chiefly remembered as "the saviour of Greece", and generations were to pass before his dual role as a "champion of democracy" was to be recognised.

German Byronic literature, Hentschel concludes, in spite of its frustrating and dichotomised political background, is no mean achievement, for its influence on German life and literature is "wide in compass and varied in treatment". German Byronism focussed mainly on the Manfred aspect of Byronism, prompted by the fact that Byron's hero was perceived as "a link in a dynasty of titans stretching from Goethe's Faust to Nietzsche's Superman". Unfortunately, the aspects of Byron we celebrate and appreciate today – the Don Juanesque qualities of wit, zest for living, and sheer fun – were either not known or not adequately appreciated.

The central importance of Greece in our symposium enterprise of assessing Byron's relation to Europe goes without saying. Byron, on his first visit to Greece in 1809, writes Professor E. G. Protopsaltis, deeply admired the ancient temples and ruins of antiquity, but the noble poet was outraged by the plundering of the classic works of art by northern Europeans, and especially by his own compatriot, Lord Elgin.

But of far greater importance, Protopsaltis reminds us, was Lord Byron's deep distress in finding the beautiful land, in which the miracle of Greek civilisation and democracy had flourished, occupied by a race of poor, oppressed slaves of barbarian overlords. Byron, however, did not scorn these degraded descendants of the ancient Greeks but rather challenged them to become worthy of their glorious past. The Greeks were fighting for the ideals and rights that Byron himself worshipped. With unflagging faith in the ability of the modern Greeks to cast off the yoke of the Ottoman Empire, Byron felt that he had no alternative but to lend his help to a cause which eventually enveloped him entirely.

Byron's efforts at Missolonghi were fruitful and creative, Protopsaltis testifies, both financially and militarily. Byron's death in the Greek cause, when people all over Europe were fighting for liberty, gave new status to the ideal of freedom for all people everywhere. "That is why", Protopsaltis concludes, "liberals from all over the world regard Byron as a pioneer in the democratic restoration of the social and political independence of all people, regardless of geographic boundaries."

Byron's political involvement in Italy is well-known, but his cultural influence preceded his political influence, as Professor Giorgio Melchiori tells us in his study of Byron as "Catalyst of the Risorgimento". However, Byron's importance in "defining and disseminating in Italy some of the principles of the new liberal ideology of England should not be underestimated", writes Melchiori. Byron's involvement in the *carbonari* movement in 1821 fitted the Italian pattern of blending philosophical, cultural and political issues.

Much of Byron's real influence in Italy, Melchiori informs us, dates from his death in the cause of Greek freedom. His death in Greece served an extremely useful purpose for Italian patriots, mirroring as it did their own feelings about Italian liberation and unification. "By 1826", writes Melchiori, "the association of Byron with the fight for Italian freedom was well established." Mazzini hailed Byron as, both man and poet, the champion of the oppressed peoples of post-Napoleonic Europe, whether Greek, Italian, or otherwise.

Long before the achievement of Italian unification in 1870, Byron's greatness was acknowledged as beyond doubt, regardless of political differences of opinion. It can safely be said, Melchiori concludes, "that the complex and at times contradictory human and poetic personality of Lord Byron acted as a catalysing factor for the Italians at the crucial moment of their national history" – the beginning of the *Risorgimento*.

In Poland, as in Italy, Byron's influence was first cultural, but soon became political as well. Juliusz Zulawski, in "Byron and the Polish Romantic Revolt", describes and explains the "unbelievably great influence" Byron exerted on Poland's Romantic poets of the first half of the nineteenth century on both their poetical mood and their patriotic attitude. Byron's polemical poetry aimed at social ills appealed strongly to the Poles, especially his direct attack upon those ills nurtured by the Congress of Vienna and the Holy Alliance. Particularly appreciated by Polish readers was Byron's *Age of Bronze* reflecting, by virtue of his keen sense of historical reality, the plight of partitioned Poland. Both Byron's polemical writing and personal example, writes Zulawski, showed Polish patriots "a definite way to defend the individual and national identity".

The influence of Byron on Polish literature grew apace, Zulawski tells us, after Byron's death, not only in a flood of published translations but as "a real, measurable influence penetrating deeply into the imagination of Polish poets of the first and most eruptive period of Polish Romanticism". And Byron's influence remained fully alive throughout the remainder of the nineteenth century.

Zulawski concludes his assessment of Byron and Poland with the eloquently ironic understatement that 150 years after Byron's death "the spirit of the Congress of Vienna he hated still prevails, and the sober romanticism he represented is not yet altogether dead".

Turning from Poland to Portugal, we find Byronism of quite a different nature as presented in Professor Fernando de Mello Moser's "The Progress of an Offending Pilgrim". The rise of Liberalism was under way in Portugal when Byron died in 1824 for Greek freedom. And Byron could easily have inspired the Portuguese Liberals if he had not earlier offended many of them by his animadversions on Portugal and the Portuguese in *Childe Harold's Pilgrimage*. Portuguese political emigrés in England, who later returned to help in the political liberation of their country, deeply resented Byron's hostile attitude as expressed in *Childe Harold*. Byron had succeeded in offending the nationalist politicians of the Romantic–Liberal period in Portugal; as for the more conservative

Portuguese, he was beneath contempt for his moral laxity. Thus, Byron had to wait for some time, Moser tells us, to acquire any popularity in Portugal.

The one truly important figure with regard to Byron and "the interplay of poetry and politics" in Portugal, Moser informs us, was Almeida Garrett whose poem *Camões*, published in Paris in 1825, represents the official beginning of Romanticism in Portuguese literature. Garrett's defence of Byron seems to have represented, according to Moser, an appeal toward a "national awakening, however indirectly, which is, at best, what other politically-minded writers were to do with Byron in the future".

In assessment, Moser makes clear that although Byron did not, indeed, could not, "exert any deep political influence in Portugal", he was, in fact, both as poet and man, an inspiration to certain important politically-minded Portuguese poets and writers. Byron's influence in Portugal, he concludes, though seriously undermined by his harsh criticisms of the Portuguese, was nevertheless an important "inspiring force to men actively concerned with the future of their country and the need to awåken its latent moral energies".

"In Russia Byron won almost universal recognition and gratitude", we learn from Professor Nina Diakonova and Dr Vadim Vacuro. By the 1820s a dual attitude toward Byron, political and cultural, was conspicuous in Russia. Literary conservatives rejected him as "an atheist poet" and an upholder of "literary anarchy". Romantic critics saw Byron as a genius who had broken all literary conventions and who celebrated "stormy passions and tragic fate".

In the 1820s Byron was devoutly read by the outstanding ideologists and leaders of the Decembrists, Diakonova and Vacuro tell us. Love of Byron reached its height in the period of "universal disappointment with the policy of Alexander I and the rise of secret societies in Russia". The poet who had so openly and bravely opposed and denounced reaction in Europe, celebrated the liberation movement in Spain, Italy and Greece, and participated in the struggle in Italy and Greece, "meant more to the Decembrists than any other European writer".

In this tense social atmosphere, we are told, Pushkin, Russia's most famous poet, turned to Byron. Russian Byronism was a complex social and literary phenomenon, not only a powerful political influence that stimulated Russian writers, but also a temporary literary and psychological fashion. In Russia, as in

Switzerland, as we learned from Professor Giddey's study, Byron was on the one hand the embodiment of intellectual liberty and contempt for authority, and, on the other hand, the poet of mystery and woe, of the "Byronic Hero".

Lermontov's Byronism was a highly complex and original phenomenon, revealing the stand Lermontov was taking in the literary conflict of his time when the rising slavophile movement was adopting a hostile attitude toward Byron and Russian Byronists. In the face of this opposition, Lermontov deliberately set out to take Byron as his model. "Byron's significance for the shaping of Lermontov's artistic personality", according to Diakonova and Vacuro, "was greater than that of any single European author, Shakespeare himself not excepted."

In the 1840s Russian Byronism ceased to exist socially and culturally, we are told, yet for the elder generation of the time Byron "remained a living presence". In 1877 Dostoevsky defended the importance of Byron for European and Russian society in response to younger people who were inclined to disparage earlier Byronists. "No great mind and generous heart", he declared, "could then avoid Byronism."

Professor Estaban Pujals, in his "Byron's Poetic Vision of Spain", makes a somewhat different approach in his assessment of Byron's relationship to the symposium topic. Confining his discussion to *Childe Harold*, Canto I, *Don Juan*, Cantos I and II, and *The Age of Bronze*, he delineates Byron's "poetic vision of Spain" as a mixture of romantic imagination, passionate feeling and political realism.

After examining *Don Juan* as a humorous treatment of Spanish culture, Pujals finds in Canto I of *Childe Harold* Byron's fierce disdain for French aggression in Spain and Byron's perception that the heroic and sacrificial struggle of the Spaniards represents more than a fight for national independence but an integral part of the general European struggle for political freedom. But it is *The Age of Bronze* (1822–3), Pujals believes, which best reflects Byron's position with respect to the major political events in Europe after Napoleon. Inspired by his strong sympathies for a liberal Spain, Byron recalls Spain's past and appeals to the indomitable spirit of the sons of Spain to resist the French now trying to imitate Napoleon's conquests.

Thus, Pujals concludes, Byron in *Childe Harold* and *The Age of Bronze* "reveals himself as an accurate and objective observer of

Spain, her people, her history, and her contemporary circumstances".

In Switzerland, as in Russia, Byron's role ultimately came to be regarded as two-dimensional: the poet of mystery and woe, the creator of the "Byronic Hero"; and the champion of political freedom who put his libertarian principles into action. From Professor Ernest Giddey we learn that Byron was initially known in Switzerland in the first of these dimensions. It was not until 1823 that the English poet came to be known in what Giddey calls "Byron's Political Dimension" and to be associated in Swiss minds with politics, Greece and philhellenism in particular.

When in 1823 came the news of Lord Byron's "last journey to Greece", Greek societies sprang up all over Switzerland. Byron, the poet whose name had been associated exclusively with his misanthropic Byronic Hero, now became a politician. As he had celebrated liberty as a purely literary theme in his *Prisoner of Chillon*, he now became known as a champion of liberty in action. Byron, the man, had acquired a new "political dimension".

Byron's death in Greece in 1824 was regarded in Switzerland as a severe blow to philhellenism. Undaunted, the Swiss re-doubled their efforts in the philhellenic cause, transferring their support from the German to the British Greek Committee. However, Giddey informs us, as the decades passed, the earlier Byron of *Chillon* and *Manfred* returned to overshadow the "renown of the hero of Missolonghi". Switzerland never forgot Byron's "political dimension", writes Giddey, but "she did not suspect the depth of Byron's political thought". In Switzerland, Giddey concludes, rare were those who comprehended the rich complexity of Byron's life as man and poet and understood and appreciated his "political dimension".

Professor William Ruddick's treatment of Byron and England, "The Persistence of Byron's Political and Social Criticism", I have chosen to consider last in this survey because its scope extends from Byron's day to the time of Shaw, Orwell and Auden, and because British Byronism differed markedly from Byronism on the Continent. Although the direct influence of Byron's political poetry and heroic death was immediate and powerful outside England, at home his social and political animadversions were dismissed as irrelevant or insincere. Prior to 1832 Byron's liberal views on English policies and politics were largely ignored, in sharp contrast to his reputation on the Continent as a "prophet of liberation". The English were not in the mood for Byron's more radical warnings. The main tendency in English politics and society throughout the first half of the nineteenth century, Ruddick observes, was one of cautious social and political readjustments as the norm.

But as Byron's understanding of European politics deepened, his new mode of ironic and satiric analysis, though baffling to his readers generally, became, Ruddick declares, "one of his most enduring gifts to the English liberal–radical tradition". Though the British public was "slow to absorb the political message of Byron's late poetry", writes Ruddick, Byron's clarion call in defense of liberty overseas was not lost on them. From the Greek War onwards a new spirit became manifest in British political thinking of "sympathetic willingness to intervene in, or guarantee the survival of, moderate liberal movements for national self-determination".

And here Ruddick makes the point that is the crux of his essay on the persistence of Byron's political and social criticism: Byron, by linking the current movement for nationalism with the spirit of ancient liberty in all his political poetry, "helped effect a change of perspective" among thinking men of the period, and especially during the High Victorian Era. Ruddick credits Byron with playing a significant part in breaking down English conventions and establishing a polemic tradition in which "sceptical analysis fulfils a purifying role" in the service of society. "This", Ruddick asserts, "is perhaps Byron's most lasting benefaction to the English Liberal tradition." By the mid-nineteenth century, he writes, "Byron's Liberal and social reforming ideas ... were becoming directly relevant to the condition of English society ... relating to the current preoccupations of its most socially concerned writers."

From the belated discovery of Blake's social poetry, and on through the social thinking of Ruskin and Morris, the line of Byron's "social vision" is continued and expanded. "In the writing of Shaw it finds a voice whose capacity for truth-discerning wit and passionate commitment to justice are at last equal to Byron's own", Ruddick declares. "The full fruits of Byron's ideas and idealism were slow to reveal themselves", Ruddick acknowledges, but Byron's was "most markedly a humanising and liberating influence" in the heyday of British Liberalism, "helping men to find social and political truth beyond the confines of custom and accepted thought." And Ruddick concludes, "The degree to which Byron's poetry, born of an age of oppression, lived again as an inspiration to Auden and Orwell in another age in which progressive Liberal ideas were once again in peril affords further testimony to the still vital power of Byron's political poetry."

Plainly, all the participants in this symposium concur in acknowledging Byron's pervasive influence on the "climate of thought" in nineteenth-century Europe, both cultural and political. The cultural influence, especially on literature, was most pronounced in Italy, Germany, Russia and Poland. In Germany and Russia it was the *Manfred* rather than the *Don Juan* aspect of Byronism that predominated. Byronism in Germany was conspicuously different from Byronism elsewhere in Europe owing to the conservativism of German internal politics which blunted the edge of Byron's social criticism in that country.

In Russia and Switzerland a dual attitude toward Byron, both cultural and political, existed. Russian Byronism was a complex social and literary phenomenon: on the one hand, Byron was the exponent of intellectual liberty; on the other, the creator of the Byronic Hero. Many leading writers were influenced by one or the other aspect of Byron including, among others, Vyamensky, Ryleev, Pushkin, Lermontov and Dostoevsky. In Switzerland, likewise, there were two Byrons: initially the Byronic Hero Byron, and later the political Byron, especially as philhellene and inspirer of Philhellenism. In Switzerland the two-dimensional character of Byron ultimately came to be acknowledged, though the depth of his political thought was never suspected.

Byronism in Portugal was uniquely different because Byron had offended the Portuguese. Thus Byron had only a few, though politically influential, defenders in Portugal, notably Garrett and Braga. Eventually, however, Byron became an inspiration to many Portuguese politically-minded poets and writers. By contrast, in Poland Byron was regarded from the first as a romantic "realist", rather than an idealist, who exerted a great influence both culturally and politically, and whose political–social ideals are still relevant and viable in contemporary Poland.

All the symposium participants agree that Byron's death at Missolonghi in 1824 had a catalytic effect on the struggle for political liberty and nationalism throughout Europe, conspicuously in Italy and Greece, and in varying degrees in France, Germany, Poland, Russia and Spain. More than the writings of any other major Romantic poet Byron's political poetry, especially the later cantos of *Childe Harold* and *Don Juan* and *The Age of Bronze*, reflects the revolutionary upheaval of the peoples all over the Continent seeking political freedom and national identity.

By contrast, Byronism in England was markedly different from its counterpart on the Continent both in nature and influence. Whereas Byron's influence on the Continent, though significantly cultural, was predominantly political and acted as a catalyst of the general struggle for political liberty and national independence, in England Byron's social–political criticism was primarily a humanising and liberating influence. It helped effect a change in perspective toward a new liberal and progressive spirit in English social–political thinking, breaking down conventions and establishing a polemic tradition of "cleansing cynicism" reflected in the social thinking of writers from Carlyle, Ruskin, Morris, Dickens and Disraeli, to Shaw, Orwell and Auden.

In assessment, it seems evident that Lord Byron's poetry exerted a pervasive influence on the climate of social and political thought in nineteenth-century Europe and stimulated political action on behalf of freedom and nationalism. When *Childe Harold's Pilgrimage* appeared in 1812, bringing instant fame to the youthful poet and peer, Byron's fervent and eloquent advocacy of political freedom was unmistakable. From that event dates the beginning of Byron's eventual role on the Continent as the widely-acknowledged spokesman of political intransigence, enemy of tyranny, and catalyst of political insurgency. Byron's animadversions in *Childe Harold*, Cantos I and II, on the status of oppressed peoples on the Continent, were indeed timely and highly relevant to current political and military events in Europe.

Likewise, in his series of popular Eastern Tales Byron continued to exalt the spirit of revolt in his "Byronic Hero" protagonists and to encourage submerged peoples to rise against their oppressors. These tales, slender in literary merit but unmistakably anti-despotic, were much translated and widely circulated on the Continent and continued throughout the first half of the century to appeal to the emotions of the politically repressed and stimulate rebellion against established regimes of whatever variety. Thus, indirectly, Byron's role on the Continent was enhanced by his romantic Eastern Tales.

Self-exiled on the Continent in 1816, Byron continued his strong advocacy of political freedom. To Byron belongs much of the credit for the revival after Waterloo of the ideals of the French Revolution and the encouragement of insurgency among the oppressed peoples of Europe in spite of the efforts of the Holy Alliance and Metternich. Throughout the remaining eight years of his life, Byron's far-reaching and pervasive influence was felt wherever the spirit of liberty was at work in the hearts and minds of men.

In Switzerland in the summer of 1816 Byron celebrated the invincible spirit of political freedom in *The Prisoner of Chillon* and paid eloquent tribute to the spirit of Liberty in his *Sonnet on Chillon*. Byron now resumed *Childe Harold*, making the liberty of peoples one of the chief themes of Canto III, expressing some of his most deeply felt views on war and politics and condemning the Powers for re-forging old political chains after Waterloo.

In Italy in 1817 Byron continued *Childe Harold*, developing in Canto IV his earlier concern with tyranny and freedom in the post-Napoleonic era, especially his quickened awareness of the sharp contrast between Italy's past glory and her present ignominy under Austrian domination. Throughout his masterpiece, *Don Juan*, written in Italy, Byron consistently attacked tyranny and called for the freedom of peoples and nations. Involved in the *carbonari* effort in 1820 for Italian political freedom, Byron wrote in his Ravenna Journal, "... supposing that Italy should be liberated.... It is a grand object – the very *poetry* of politics." His faith in freedom never faltered and he flung the full force of his political poetry and pervasive influence and, finally, his dedicated action into the war against tyranny in Europe.

In *The Age of Bronze* Byron continued to champion the cause of renascent freedom with all the satiric force and eloquence at his command, celebrating derisively the Congress of Verona in 1822. As Professor Carl Woodring so succinctly puts it, "*Don Juan* points to the murderous instincts of despots: *The Age of Bronze* pulls their teeth."

When the cause of national independence was thwarted in Italy, Byron's chance to "war" in "deeds" as well as "words" came in Greece. The heroic–tragic story of Byron's last few months of life in Greece in 1824 needs no recounting here. The news of the noble poet's "last journey" electrified the minds and hearts of the friends of freedom everywhere. He became a tower of strength not only to the beleaguered Greeks but to the politically oppressed of the entire Continent. Sir Herbert Grierson's famous tribute to the power of Byron's political influence comes inevitably to mind:

"And Byron's voice rang through Europe. His every poem, his every action, was an historical event. When he went to Greece it was not only a man and an English peer who went but a Power in Europe."

And Byron's service to Liberty did not end with his death in April 1824. Rather, his pervasive influence on the climate of political and social thought continued to be felt in Europe throughout the nineteenth century. The imagination of European youth, writes Professor J. L. Talmon in his history of political Romanticism in Europe from 1815 to 1848, was fired by Byron as "the prophet and law-giver of revolutionary Romanticism on the Continent". Throughout the years following Waterloo, while renewed despotism lay heavily upon prostrate Europe, the spirit of independence and nationalism smouldered and sometimes burned fiercely. In spite of the "dull, stupid old system" of the Holy Alliance and Metternich, the oppressed peoples broke again and again into revolt. One after another, France, Spain, Italy, Greece, Poland and Germany struggled into open rebellion. And always, whether successful or thwarted, the rebellious peoples remained uncowed and intransigent. And everywhere throughout Europe the voice of Byron was the "Trumpet Voice of Liberty" as Byron became the veritable poet-laureate of political freedom.

In a fragment from his journal in Cephalonia, where he had come to aid the Greek cause, Byron "told all his heart":

> The dead have been awakened – shall I sleep?
> The World's at war with tyrants – shall I crouch?
> The harvest's ripe – and shall I pause to reap?
> I slumber not; the thorn is in my couch;
> Each day a trumpet soundeth in mine ear,
> It's echo in my heart –

The trumpet of Liberty would not let Byron sleep. Concern for the downtrodden was ever the "thorn" in his couch. His passionate spirit could find no rest except in struggle. His entire life was a warfare against all that obstructs human freedom.

With his strong voice – unmistakably articulate and fearlessly forthright – and his courageous action, Byron was ever the vigilant champion of insurgent freedom throughout nineteenth-century Europe. In his major poems Byron transformed the abstract and diffuse ideals of liberty of his time into tangible contemporary realities. He transmuted the vague romantic idealism of his era into pragmatic social and political realism and transmitted it powerfully and effectively to receptive minds and hearts throughout the length and breadth of Europe. His uncompromising independence of spirit, passion for freedom, persuasive eloquence and cleansing wit made Byron one of the most effective champions of political freedom and disseminators of progressive liberal thought in nineteenth-century Europe.

Index

(References contained in notes not indexed)